"Finally, a book that succinctly and accurately captures the social, political, and legal history of North American indigenous societies—societies that once reigned supreme in harmony with the lands and nature. The status quo can be tolerated no longer."

—THE HONORABLE GERRY ST. GERMAIN, FEDERAL CANADIAN SENATOR

"To overcome their history of entrenched dependency, Helin argues that Aboriginal nations must stop looking to colonizing nations to solve their problems. He effectively demonstrates that Aboriginal peoples can transform their current situation by relying on traditional values of self-reliance, self-discipline, complete interdependence, and moral leadership."

—B. THOMAS VIGIL, CHAIRMAN
AND MICHAEL E. ROBERTS, PRESIDENT
FIRST NATIONS DEVELOPMENT INSTITUTE

"Finally, a book that captures the true overall view of the economic model in Indian country. *Dances with Dependency* should be required reading for all tribal leaders throughout the continent. Aboriginal entrepreneurs will also find this exhilarating book helpful in understanding governmental economic mindsets while trying to attain their own vision in business. [A] truly inspirational book."

—JIM BOYD, INTERNATIONAL RECORDING ARTIST
FOUNDER, THUNDERWOLF PRODUCTIONS

"Gets at the core of economic issues facing indigenous communities around the globe. This book brings to light many important messages to help guide the decision making of indigenous leaders."

—LADONNA HARRIS
FOUNDER AND PRESIDENT, AMERICANS FOR INDIAN OPPORTUNITY

"Delicate, real, and profound. The ancestors had the right idea; they had the formulas to heal and foster self-reliance and true independence, formulas deeply rooted in traditional and cultural values. But somehow, somewhere, they were lost, stolen, or thrown away. Blessings, Mr. Helin, for being the warrior to open our eyes to that which has been lost."

— ROBERT MIRABAL, TAOS PUEBLO ARTIST AND MUSICIAN

"Like many of his contemporaries, Calvin Helin describes a long list of complex social, political, and economic problems facing indigenous people today. But unlike other scholars, he offers doable, solid solutions and masterfully describes great opportunities available to our people."

—LEE STANDING BEAR MOORE, MANATAKA AMERICAN INDIAN COUNCIL
EDITOR, *Smoke Signal News*

"An immensely readable manual for forging a pride-filled Aboriginal self-reliance from the rust of decades of social, economic, and chemical dependency. As practical as it is poetic and inspiring, *Dances with Dependency* could be the Bible for a new movement of tradition-inspired self-help among indigenous and nonindigenous peoples around the planet."

—HARVEY ARDEN, AUTHOR OF *Wisdomkeepers*

"An essential tool for understanding how to rebuild indigenous communities from within. Its lessons apply as much to U.S. indigenous and other ethnic communities as they do to Canada's Aboriginals."

—ALEJANDRO LÓPEZ
COFOUNDER AND COEDITOR, *Native Journal of Service Learning*

"At this time, in keeping with the prophecies of the Mayan calendar, Calvin Helin has come forward with the wisdom of the ancestors, holding the light high for all people. The time of separation is over. We will all benefit from the opportunities presented here."

—CYNTHIA WALKER, *aj'ik*, PRIESTESS OF THE MAYAN TRADITION
AND AUTHOR OF *The Radiance Practice Workbook*

DANCES *with* DEPENDENCY

OUT OF POVERTY THROUGH
SELF-RELIANCE

CALVIN HELIN

RAVENCREST PUBLISHING
WOODLAND HILLS, CALIFORNIA

PUBLISHED BY:

Ravencrest Publishing
A Division of Cubbie Blue Publishing
21900 Marylee Street, Suite 290
Woodland Hills, CA 91367

EDITOR: Candis McLean
BOOK DESIGN: Rosanna Hanser
COVER DESIGN: Angela Werneke
COVER ARTWORK: Four Clans Bright Spirit Sun Mask by Bill Helin

Printed and bound in Canada by Friesens

PUBLISHER'S CATALOGING-IN-PUBLICATION DATA

Helin, Calvin, 1959-
    Dances with dependency : out of poverty through self-
reliance / Calvin Helin. -- 1st US ed. -- Woodland Hills,
Calif. : Ravencrest Pub., 2008.
      p. ; cm.
      ISBN: 978-1-932824-07-0 (cloth); 978-1-932824-08-7
(paper)
      Originally published: Vancouver : Orca Spirit, c2006.
      Includes bibliographical references and index.

      1. Poverty. 2. Poor--Social conditions. 3. Poor--Services
for. 4. Self-reliance. 5. Civil rights. 6. Economic
development. 7. Indians of North America--Social
conditions. 8. Indians of North America--Economic
conditions. I. Title. II. Out of poverty through self-
reliance.

HC79 .P6 H45 2008   2007933952
362.57--dc22   0804

10 9 8 7 6 5 4 3 2 1

This book is dedicated to the four deceased chiefs in my family—

my grandmother, Sigyidm hana'a Nt'sit'hotk (Maude Helin) of the

Royal House of Gitchiis; my grandfather, Sm'ooygit Nees Nuugan Noos

(Henry Helin), Chief of the Royal House of Gitlan; my father, Sm'ooygit Nees

Nuugan Noos (Barry Helin) of the Royal House of Gitlan; and my uncle, Sm'ooygit

Hyemass (Art Helin) of the Royal House of Gitchiis—and my still-living mother,

Sigyidm hana'a Su Dalx (Verna Helin), matron of the Royal House of

Gitachn'geek. Without their vision, wisdom, guidance, encouragement,

and support, this book would not have been possible.

CONTENTS

LIST OF ARTWORKS

ACKNOWLEDGEMENTS

I would like to acknowledge the contributions of Tony Mayer whose ongoing comments, encouragement, advice, support, and assistance truly made this book a reality. I sincerely thank my cousin and internationally-renowned artist, Bill Helin, for graciously allowing me to use his beautiful, evocative paintings throughout the book. Also, I wish to acknowledge the very special contributions of editor, Candis McLean, and graphic artist, Rosanna Hanser, whose enduring dedication and hard work made the publication of this book possible. In addition, I would like to recognize former principal of the Grandview/?Uuquinak'uuh Elementary School in East Vancouver, Caroline Krause, for her general editorial contributions and her substantive comments and suggestions relating to Aboriginal educational issues. Thank you to my good friends Rob Hunt and Te Taru White for reviewing the manuscript and their valuable commentary. I would like to further acknowledge contributions, commentary, and ongoing support for this project from Chief Clarence Louie, Bernd Christmas, John and Inez Helin, Patrick Helin, Barrie Robbe, Stan Solberg, the late Chief Roy Mussell, and my good friends Dave Tuccaro, Chief Charles Kihega, and Billy Joe Takaro. Last, but by no means least, I would like to thank my dear wife Vernita, and my children, Georgina, Denise, Lewis, and wee grandson Lucius, for understanding and kindly giving up our shared time and attention together, thus allowing me to dedicate myself to this endeavor.

PREFACE

One who knows the enemy and knows himself will not be endangered
in a hundred engagements. One who does not know the enemy but knows
himself will sometimes meet with defeat. One who knows neither the enemy
nor himself will invariably be defeated in every engagement.

　　　　SUN-TZU, *The Art of War*

This revised edition of Dances with Dependency *universalizes the message
inherent in the original edition, which focused more exclusively on Canada's
indigenous people. While caution must be exercised in making comparisons, the
situation involving Canada's indigenous people can, in countless ways, serve as a
model for any impoverished population experiencing enforced dependency. As
such, it can inform policymakers and others around the world who are seeking
ways to sustain national prosperity levels while ensuring improvement in the lives
of the underprivileged by setting an attainable course away from crippling
dependency and towards the dignity that comes with self-reliance.*

In particular, this edition of Dances with Dependency *draws a parallel
between the demographic tsunami created by the Aboriginal population in
Canada and dilemmas now faced in the United States, where a massive tidal
wave is poised to swamp national finances. At a time when America's greying
baby boomers are relying increasingly on expensive social programs such as health
care for prolonged periods and a growing wave of ethnic minorities threatens to
deluge welfare coffers on an epidemic scale, viable turnaround solutions are
needed. This scenario is further exacerbated by massive annual national debt,
huge long-term budget shortfalls, an enormous burden of personal debt, and a
pension system in crisis.*

*In looking at solutions for reversing the descent of indigenous populations into
the chaos of poverty, it is hoped that the discussion in this book will provide
fodder for debate on tackling the much larger questions of social welfare policy,
reform of government entitlement programs, and the looming financial crisis facing America.*

The purpose of this book is to look at practical ways to move indigenous populations forward. Money has been liberally thrown at Indian problems with nominal impact. Neither mainstream nor indigenous politics has had lasting widespread impact on improving the lives of ordinary indigenous folk, no matter how many hyped political announcements and other solutions have been touted. It is time to look at the problems and issues at the broadest level in order to seek general solutions that might be tailored to the different circumstances of Tribes now.

This book will look at two areas critical to the long-term self-reliance of Aboriginal people: the views and attitudes of Aboriginal people themselves, and the question of effective economic integration. The indigenous populations appear to be at one of the most critical junctures in their modern evolution. The rapidly-growing populations and burgeoning wealth creation potential are set against a backdrop of archaic and largely unsuitable governance structures, a dependency mindset that has been entrenched by government policy, and a host of formidable social pathologies.

This book will examine how the respective demographic trends occurring in the mainstream and Aboriginal populations have direct and enormous fiscal implications to the fundamental health and future prosperity of Canada. Surely self-interest on both sides dictates a better understanding of the Aboriginal population and why constructive change is vital. It is also important to recognize that for the first time a "perfect storm" of circumstances is coming together to provide the opportunity to move Aboriginal people up the social and economic ladder in a manner that preserves the dignity of all concerned and benefits the entire nation.

While some folks have been successful at putting together pieces of the puzzle, the entire picture has not been painted in any meaningful way. The issue to date has confounded solution. In fact, it reminds many of Winston Churchill's description of Russia: "...a riddle, wrapped in a mystery, inside an enigma...." Although I am not very artistic, in writing this book I felt like an artist painting a picture, placing all the pieces of the puzzle in their proper place. I have endeavored to articulate honestly the indigenous condition as a starting point from which to move purposely forward. In doing so, I sincerely hope I have, in turn, provided some small honor to the many wolves, ravens and killer whales who have protected me and provided valuable life-long guidance.

In the most primal sense, an oath given to my father was an essential catalyst in my deciding to write this book. My father's English name is Barry Helin.

SM'OOYGIT NEES NUUGAN NOOS, Barry Helin, former Chief of the Gitlan Tribe of the Tsimshian Nation and father of author (taken in 1992). Bordered by his Wolf Crest, Chief Helin is the middle son of Tsimshian Chieftans, Maude and Henry Helin. Part of the legacy of Maude and Henry (grandparents to the author) was to encourage their children and grandchildren to work towards bettering the plight of indigenous people.

His Aboriginal name, as Chief of the Gitlan Tribe of the Tsimshian Nation, is Sm'ooygit Nees Nuugan Noos. His Tribe's primary crest or protector totem is the wolf (*Laxgibuu* in our language). In 1998 when he was dying, in the final stage of his gruesome stomach cancer he was taken by medivac air ambulance from our small village to the hospital in nearby Prince Rupert. In the village, people are accustomed to hearing the howl of wolves in the late evening or early morning, but never during the day. As the medical personnel were taking my father to the awaiting air ambulance helicopter (just past noon), a chorus of howling wolves erupted behind my father's house—as if to provide a final lament to honor the ancient connection between the Gitlan and the *Laxgibuu*, and to say goodbye to their Chief.

As the illness exacted its horrific toll, my father called my brothers and me to his bedside. He asked us to put our hands on the bed in which he lay and make a solemn pledge. In his heart of hearts, his dying wish was simply that, in whatever circumstances our family found itself after his death, we "stick together and always support each other." At the time, being consumed with the gloomy prospect of my Dad's impending demise, I did not have much opportunity to contemplate the deeper meaning of giving my word of honor in this way.

Upon later reflection, however, I thought about this oath and how it was the theme central to my father's existence. Sounds so simple—"sticking together," and sometimes can be so difficult, but in the end, is unquestionably of great value. I began to think how this principle, invoking self-reliance, loyalty and mutual support, was really the most crucial underlying element of tribal survival, and how utterly ruinous had been the government support that took its place. If you were to reformulate my father's wish in biblical language it might be: "What tribal bonds therefore Nature hath joined together, let no man put asunder." Yet when one looks at the unrelenting misery, pain, and massive confusion that is consuming indigenous people and developing populations around the globe, it is clear that colonial man has pulled apart these most precious bonds with wholly predictable results.

Extending my father's idea, I believe that there must be a return to the simple tribal and human values that spawned the complex and beautiful indigenous cultures in the first place—in effect, a contemporary reclamation of the lost tribal values and social DNA. Although it certainly might be helpful if more remnants of indigenous cultures were still in existence, we do not have to turn back the clock in order to find the still-pristine emotional legacy of our ancestors, stressing the importance of social interconnections and the necessary interdependence of families, Tribes, or Nations. Or to recognize the value of self-reliance, high moral conduct, loyalty, self-sacrifice, and leadership. This renewal must be done in a modern context in constructive partnership with the larger society.

This book divides the history of North America's indigenous population into four distinct waves of development. At the micro-level, there are relevant differences in the particular patterns of development of Aboriginal people in Canada and Native Americans in the U.S.. At the broadest level, however, such impacts arguably follow a sufficiently parallel track to make useful comparisons. Though this book focuses on the particulars of Canada, the same general analysis and suggested solutions, at least at the broadest level, may also be applied to Native Americans in the United States.

The first wave of development is by far the longest, involving the migration to, and occupation of, various parts of North America by indigenous groups. Some scholars contend this occurred no earlier than 10,000 BC. Others argue that particular physical evidence could push that date back as far as 400,000 years ago. More modest proposals suggest the actual date is 20,000 to 70,000 BC (with many agreeing that there was human occupation by at least 20,000 BC).[1] One writer has suggested that, if modern North American indigenous peoples can claim direct descent from the early people of 15,000 to 20,000 years ago, as some undoubtedly can, then the indigenous populations are by far the oldest known race on the earth.[2] Throughout this long period, indigenous societies flourished, developing intricate and sophisticated languages and cultures. The period of the first wave will be examined to determine how and what particular attributes contributed to the self-reliance and survival of indigenous people for millennia prior to contact with Europeans.

The second wave involved the supposed "discovery" of North America, and the subsequent colonisation of the North American indigenous populations by European imperial powers. This period precipitated the massive decline of the indigenous population due to disease introduced by Europeans to which there was no natural immunity. This second wave lasted until about 100 years ago.

The third wave, a period from about a century ago to the present, initially involved colonizing powers adopting specific strategies to assimilate indigenous populations. The third wave will be examined for how it developed the "welfare trap." It is this era that has resulted in destructive social and political pathologies that have created massive dysfunction and social chaos. The third wave has led to enormous dependency which has impacted not only social and economic conditions, but has created a dependency mindset and unrealistic expectations. These attitudes are neither sustainable nor do they hold any future answers to regaining the self-reliance that was once crucial to the indigenous world view from antiquity onward.

In recent times, indigenous people have become endangered and defeated in most engagements because, to paraphrase Sun-tzu, they no longer know themselves or their enemies. By comparing the strategies of the past (that ensured long-term survival) with the problems and internalized dependency conditions of the present, we should begin to relearn who we are and what our true historical legacy is—to start to "know ourselves" again in a collective sense. Certainly, our real legacy involves more than indigenous peoples being puppets controlled by strings of welfare and transfer payments on the stage of the federal government. To "know our enemy," there are the usual suspects of government, bureaucracy, and the "Indian Industry," but we also must acknowledge how the dependency mindset has been socialized internally into generations of the indigenous psyche. And how it is creating self-erected barriers to moving forward. In some respects, these destructive attitudes have resulted in indigenous people becoming their own worst enemies—defeating ourselves with our own caustic and pessimistic attitudes before we even engage the enemy.

The fourth wave, in Canada at least, coincides with the title of Part I of this book, "The Demographic Tsunami." The huge "greying" mainstream baby boom population (representing one-third of the population of Canada) may be combining with the rapidly-growing indigenous population in an immense demographic tsunami capable of swamping the finances of the country if corrective measures are not taken immediately. It is hardly an exaggeration to state that, in a fundamental manner, the very prosperity and competitiveness of the country is at stake. The fourth wave explores solutions that may instead turn this impending crisis into a colossal opportunity. In the United States, although Native Americans form a comparatively smaller percentage of the population than Aboriginals in Canada, the circumstances requiring innovative solutions are equally dire. Massive welfare dependency does not, and cannot work for any population.

Whether the fourth wave is a crisis or opportunity depends on the views we adopt and the action we take now. If we are prudent and thoughtful enough to adopt the right strategies now, indigenous people may not be, in Sun-tzu's words, "endangered in a hundred [future] engagements."

NOTE ON TERMINOLOGY

There are many terms used to describe the first peoples that occupied North America prior to contact with Europeans. The term in common usage in Canada is "Aboriginals." The terms used in the United States are "Native Americans" or "Indians." In Canada, the term "Indians" is only used for those persons defined in specific legislation (i.e., the Indian Act) as Indians. The word is not in popular usage in Canada because it is the expression that Europeans erroneously applied to the first peoples of North America as the result of Columbus' first voyage. Columbus believed that he circumnavigated the globe by going west and had landed in the East Indies. It turned out he actually landed in what is now called the West Indies in present day Puerto Rico. The name he mistakenly gave to the indigenous populations he met was "Indians." This later became the default term for how Europeans identified North American indigenous people. (The running joke is that we should be thankful he wasn't looking for Turkey.) In reference to the first peoples that occupied North America, I will simply use the word "indigenous" people. If I am speaking specifically about the populations in Canada, I will use the term "Aboriginal," and for the indigenous population in the United States I will use the term "Native Americans."

In the same vein, there are many terms used for the communities of indigenous peoples. In Canada the terms "Band" and "First Nation" are often used. In the United States the term "Tribe" is often used. I will adopt the usage of the term "Tribe" here to mean indigenous community or communities unless I am referring specifically to "Bands" or "First Nations" in Canada.

I also refer to current geo-political names rather than repeatedly stating, for example, "what is *now* called British Columbia."

NORTHERN MIRAGE

Wolves are referred to as *gyibaaw* in the Tsimshian language, Sm'algyax. The *gyibaaw* are singing their haunting songs near the village of Lax Kw'alaams (or Port Simpson) in northern BC. They are lounging beneath three totems. One of the totems is called "Mirage" and tells a story about three great chiefs with mystical powers. In the night sky the Creator is painting the celestial heavens with his supernatural paint brush representing the Northern Lights or *Aurora Borealis*. A limited edition of giclee method prints was made.

INTRODUCTION

I

Once upon a midnight dreary, while I pondered, weak and weary,
Over many a quaint and curious volume of forgotten lore—
While I nodded, nearly napping, suddenly there came a tapping
As of someone gently rapping, rapping at my chamber door.
"Tis some visitor," I muttered, "tapping at my chamber door—
Only this and nothing more."
   EDGAR ALLAN POE, excerpted from *The Raven*

BACKGROUND

I was brought up in a small coastal Indian village of Lax Kw'alaams on the northwest coast of British Columbia. My community was part of the Tsimshian Nation, a group known for its highly complex culture that developed in the mists of the mystical coastal temperate rain forest. For the last two centuries the rich culture, spirituality, and highly-evolved artistic traditions of the Tsimshian and other Northwest Coast Indian groups have captured the imagination of scholars. One eminent anthropologist has pointed out that, even though the coastal peoples were genetically and linguistically similar to the other tribes found across North America, in some ways they were different from all others.[3] These cultures have a pronounced oriental or Asiatic tinge which is thought to be evidence of a basic kinship, and long-continued contact, with the peoples around the north Pacific Rim.[4] Most of all, the cultures were distinguished by a local richness and originality, thought to be the product of vigorous and inventive people in a rich environment.[5]

When Captain Cook (in 1778) and other European explorers and fur traders first visited the coast, they encountered one of the highest densities of First Nations settlements found anywhere on the North American continent. Due to the bounty of a lush environment, fully one-third of the Aboriginal population in Canada lived in British Columbia. Between the Kodiak Archipelago of Alaska and San Francisco Bay, several hundred thousand people lived, speaking more than sixty distinct languages—a linguistic diversity far greater than that of the continental interior—attributed to the ecological complexity of the sustaining coastal lands and waters.[6] In only a few other places in the world did comparably-advanced societies arise on a foundation of natural abundance, rather than one of farming or herding.[7]

Although their patterns of land ownership and utilization did not accord with European legal notions, the coastal peoples were nonetheless quite sophisticated in this regard and had clearly-defined concepts, which were mutually-respected. For example, natural boundaries such as rivers and the ocean defined specific geographical areas where a tribe was recognized to have exclusive use and control of the natural resources contained within the boundaries of that area. If another group wanted to use those resources or conduct trade within that area they had to receive permission from the tribe and often had to pay what amounted to a tax for those privileges. They also proved to be shrewd business people who, the early fur traders soon learned, were formidable commercial competitors. Originally, tribal leaders of the coastal people exploited trade to develop their cultures further along their own distinctive lines. Had it not been for the ravages of several decades of introduced disease, alcohol and gunpowder, they would have been a greater force when settlers began to arrive.[8]

Throughout the nineteenth century, the Tsimshian were significantly involved in industrial production, manufacturing, mercantile enterprises, and wage labor.[9] The Tsimshian Chiefs were quick to expand their existing tribal trading privileges and monopolies to include the new European markets. "Through such [trading] monopolies, they could control a large amount of the trade, especially that of the land-based Hudson's Bay Company [the American and Russian fur traders, on the other hand, came in ships by sea], and to some degree could regulate the price of the furs (Fisher 1977: 30)."[10] The Tsimshian trade competitively expanded into the interior of British Columbia. By the time the Hudson's Bay Company (HBC) arrived from the east in 1826, the Tsimshians were already trading to the inland tribes European goods received from American traders on the coast. Upon their arrival, the Hudson's Bay Company traders were greatly surprised that they could not afford to match the prices for furs offered by the aggressive Tsimshians who already dominated those markets.[11] When diseases such as smallpox began to decimate the Aboriginal population, HBC traders had access to inoculations, but sometimes distributed these strategically to only those Tsimshians who were non-trade competitors.[12] Despite their purported "Christian" values, such decisions were tantamount to a death sentence for the most capable Tsimshian entrepreneurs of the time.

In 1834, the Hudson's Bay Company established its trading fort at what is now the site of the community of Lax Kw'alaams ("Island of Roses"). Nine tribes of the Tsimshian moved to Lax Kw'alaams soon after the establishment of the fort. The community is also known as Port Simpson, named after Amelius Simpson[13], superintendent of the marine department of the Hudson's Bay Company of the time. Lax Kw'alaams was soon to become headquarters of the fur trade on the Canadian side of the north coast.[14] One of the largest towns on the BC Coast at the time subsequently grew up around the fort at Lax Kw'alaams. In 1891, the first major hospital on the north coast was founded there by an Act of the provincial legislature.[15]

A FRONT ROW SEAT

Sadly, when I was a lad, the Tsimshian were but a pale shadow of their vigorous ancestors who prosecuted trade and commerce so enthusiastically throughout the Victorian era. Growing up on an Indian reserve, I witnessed first-hand the complex web of social and political pathologies resulting from a noveau culture based on welfare dependency and government transfer payments. My father was a commercial fisherman and a fine one. Though he had made a good life for our family, I was well aware that life in an Aboriginal Indian reserve had a very sinister side to it. Such a bad environment has persisted so long in most Aboriginal communities that many Aboriginal people have, over generations, been socialized into thinking that this widespread dysfunction is normal. Imagine a situation where tragically high youth suicide rates, gross unemployment figures, frequent banana republic-style corruption, and persistent abuse—both substance and physical—prevail, and you might begin to understand what life is like on many Aboriginal reserves.[16]

My grandmother, Maude Helin, was Chieftain of one of the largest of the nine tribes in our community. In the Tsimshian system it was not uncommon for women to be in high positions of power such as the role of Chieftain. Her Chief's name was Sigyidm hana'a Nt'sit'hotk ("Grandmother of the tribe"). Unlike the English system of assigning names, the Tsimshian system provided an example of a social structure built on the two themes of kinship and rank (which were much more important than to Europeans).[17] English people receive only one name, which usually reveals the sex of the individual and the father's line, while titles and honorifics can indicate marital status, educational attainment, occupation, or rank. Conversely, Aboriginals on the northern coast took a series of names of higher and higher rank as they aged. Such names usually revealed to the other members of the tribe the person's sex, age-group, lineage, rank, and sometimes role (such as successor Chief).[18] My Grandmother's Chief's name had been passed on from hereditary Chief to hereditary Chief in her tribe for thousands of years. Though it brought her great status, it also imposed many obligations that involved duties, responsibilities, and originally prescribed considerable formality and a code of conduct.

RESPONDING TO A CHALLENGE

> Kites rise highest against the wind... not with it.
> WINSTON CHURCHILL

In Tsimshian society, my grandmother was an aristocrat from the royal house of Gitchiis. No matter how blue her blood, however, she would have to endure first-hand the many humiliations of the legacy of colonial policy and law which ensured that Aboriginal people of her generation were treated like second-class citizens. Throughout most of her life, she could not vote in federal or provincial elections. Indians –along with Chinese and some other minorities—were forced to sit in separate areas from whites in movie theatres, could not go into bars, and were effectively barred from becoming doctors or lawyers. In many ways, her generation was subjected to grotesque racial indignities similar to those endured by African-Americans in the deep South, or South African Blacks under the apartheid regime.

Add to this a system where land and resources and the means to a livelihood were simply removed, and where Aboriginal culture and language were effectively outlawed. What was instituted to replace self-sufficient Aboriginal societies was an incompetent and patronizing bureaucracy whose prescription amounted to a heavy dose of welfare. In light of these circumstances, you might begin to understand what piqued my grandmother, raising her ire and indignation.

Along with my grandfather, Henry Helin[19], my grandmother worked tirelessly to improve the lot of Aboriginal people. Together they were instrumental in founding the Native Brotherhood of British Columbia, the organization that for almost 75 years has represented Aboriginal workers and fisherman in

GRAMPA AND GRANNY HELIN

Portrait of Henry and Maude Helin in traditional regalia. Tsimshian chieftains of two of the nine tribes of Lax Kw'alaams. Henry Helin's Chief's title was Sm'ooygit Nees Nuugan Noos and his tribe was the Gitlan. Maude Helin's Chief's name was Sigyidm hana'a Nt'sit'hotk which meant "Grandmother of the tribe." She was Chieftain of the Gitchiis tribe. Both were lifelong activists advocating for constructive action to make the lives of ordinary indigenous people better.

the fishing industry. Every chance she got, she would urge me to "Get an education and become a lawyer and fight for the rights of Indians."

In seeking to obtain an education, I was greatly handicapped by circumstances. As a child, I was stuck in an atrociously-run federal Indian Day School with very low academic standards and exceedingly low expectations from the federally-appointed administration. Since my family at the time were "non-status Indians" and quite poor, there was no money to obtain a better education elsewhere. I am indebted to the generosity and good graces of my grade 8 teacher, Greg Millbank and his family (particularly his father and mother, Bob and Betty Millbank), for providing an opportunity for me to attend school in the Lower Mainland of British Columbia. After finishing high school, I went into the fishing business where, thanks to 24 percent interest rates in the early 1980s, I earned my first PhD in business by going spectacularly broke. Failing miserably in the family business forced me to get around to earning a law degree.

Twenty years later, much observation and reflection has led me to conclusions I could never have imagined. I have learned that the Aboriginal population and its issues are not simply questions to be pondered at the leisure of do-gooders and altruistic liberals. I also realized the mainstream Canadian population has a very poor understanding as to why such a question is absolutely critical to the future well-being and vigorous development of Canada as a nation.

A contemporary translation of the question with which my grandmother challenged my generation is: "What can be done to make the lives of ordinary indigenous people better?" Sounds like a simple enough question, doesn't it? Nevertheless, after a century of high falutin' talk between the federal government and Indian politicians, ordinary Aboriginal folk are left to wonder: "What is the practical legacy?" Are Aboriginal people any further ahead? The truth is that for the vast amount of resources expended, most statistics indicate that the social and economic dividend has been nominal.

The crux of the problem is that parties have largely assumed that the whole solution to sorting out Aboriginal woes can be provided for, or solved by, the federal government. There is no question that its policies and programs are important. However, a search for a real solution must begin outside the current dependency mindset.

My grandmother's question has been pondered for the past 200 years, and most solutions proposed have had little effect. Government has put forward "solutions" that frequently have exacerbated already bad situations. Though the system was created through no fault of their own, a host of past Indian chiefs have made an industry of pointing fingers and assigning blame. Expensive Royal Commissions have come and gone with supposed answers. In the meantime, the stark reality of grassroots Aboriginal people in Canada has changed very little. Aboriginal children and youth see no hope at the end of the tunnel of despair and poverty. As shocking statistics reflect, Aboriginal youth continue to commit suicide and abuse substances at truly horrifying rates. Grassroots community members continue to be victims of an *Indian Act* system in which they are individually and personally disempowered and largely politically neutered. At the same time, Aboriginal folks have passed muster on the federal government-supported reserve system by voting with their feet. Today, approximately 50 percent of Aboriginal people in Canada live outside of reserve communities, primarily in urban areas where there are, quite simply, better employment, educational and economic opportunities, and higher incomes.[20]

The fact of the matter is that neither Aboriginal people nor the Canadian public can afford another lost generation of youth. The staggering human and economic costs are simply too great, particularly when the opportunity to take a giant leap forward is at hand.

The good news is that Aboriginals are likely in the best position ever to integrate economically with the mainstream, to partner with industry, and create wealth and opportunities for all. With reserve lands and only a handful of modern treaties concluded, Aboriginal people currently own, lock-stock-and-barrel, over 600,000 square kilometres of land—an area over eight times the size of Ireland, over twice the size of either New Zealand or England, and larger by a substantial margin than either France, Germany or Spain. And there are still many, many more settlements to come. Some estimates suggest Aboriginal people will eventually own or control one-third of the entire Canadian land mass—an area equivalent to a third of the total land area of Europe! Current settlements have resulted in approximately $2.5 billion to $5 billion in cash payments. Some estimate that there may be between $10 billion and $20 billion paid in future settlements.

With growing resource development in their traditional territories as the result of huge, unremitting commodities-demand in the world markets, and legal decisions requiring genuine consultation, Aboriginal Canadians for the first time have real leverage over a substantial area of the Canadian economy. This results in an unprecedented opportunity to forge a new era of self-reliance. There is real hope and a practical solution—albeit one that may not be popular with those parties benefiting under the current chaos, and whose interests are entrenched in maintaining the status quo.

1

Author's Grandpa (Henry) and Granny (Maude) Helin, both Tsimshian chieftains of the Gitlan and Gitchiis tribes, respectively

2

Totem pole raising in front of Chief Henry Helin's Lax Kw'alaams residence. Purpose was to commemorate his chief's position as *Sm'ooygit Nees Nuugan Noos* of the Gitlan Tribe (which name and title was passed down to his son Barry Helin on his death)

3 Author's Grannies, Georgina Scott, *Sa'gyep* "Seal coming out of the water" and Maude Helin, *Sigyidm hana'a Nt'sit'hotk* "Grandmother of the tribe"

7 Uncle Lawrence Helin, *Sm'ooygit Nees Nuugan Natt* (inherited position of Chief of the Gitchiis Tribe from mother, Maude). In traditional regalia with copper shield or *hyetsk* — symbol of great tribal wealth

4 Author's Mother and Father, Verna Helin (*Sigyidm hana'a Su Dalx*) and Barry Helin (*Sm'ooygit Nees Nuugan Noos*)

5 Helin Family Siblings
Bottom Row: Cindy (*sister*), Elaine (*sister*), Verna (*mother*), Crystal (*sister*), Barry (*father*).
Top Row: John (*brother*), Pat (*brother*), and Calvin

8 Uncle Arthur Helin, *Sm'ooygit Hyemass*. Chief's name held by great warriors of legend. A gifted athlete and basketball star, Art was recipient of the prestigious Tom Longboat Award

9 Chief Barry Helin, *Sm'ooygit Nees Nuugan Noos* in traditional blanket

6 Author's Family: daughters Denise & Georgina, wife Vernita, Calvin and son Lewis

10 Author's wife, Vernita Helin

11 Author's grandson, Lucius

12 Author with Cree elder Billy Joe Takaro.

13 + 14 Greg and Fong Millbank. Greg helped author out of small village to greater educational opportunities by welcoming him into his home. Long-time friend and mentor of author.

16 With Maori elder, Pihopa Kingi, in New Zealand, for the millennium celebration.

17 Receiving Canada's "Top 40 Under 40" with friend Dave Tuccaro (first two Aboriginals in Canada to receive this award).

15 Calvin, John, and Pat Helin with John & Pat's father-in-law, the venerable Chief Harold Dudoward (Sm'ooygit Sax sa'axt) of the Gitwilgyots Tribe. The photo was taken in Las Vegas marking the first reunion in sixty years with Chief Dudoward's sister. Upon his passing, Chief Dudoward was honored by having his name "buried with him." While it had been passed on for thousands of years, the name can never again be used by another Chief of that tribe.

18 Photo of Bill Helin, internationally renowned artist whose works grace the pages of this publication (also cousin to author and son of Arthur Helin), makes presentation to Maori leader, Te Taru White, at NITA Resource Expo 2004 Gala Dinner in Vancouver.

19 Sensei Toshiaki Nomada (4th degree black belt) and author (3rd degree black belt) pose in front of barn where their *dojo* (martial art practice gym) is located. Photo was taken for the *Province* newspaper in July of 2006.

THE RAVEN AND THE FIRST MEN

Bill Reid's famous cedar carving at UBC's Museum of Anthropology. Carved out of a giant block of laminated yellow cedar, this sculpture depicts the Raven coaxing the first men out of a giant clam shell he found on the beach.

It is one of the most beautiful compensations of this life that no man can sincerely try to help another without helping himself.

RALPH WALDO EMERSON

My own thinking about this question has been shaped by a number of influences. Such influences are partially summarized by a recent experience.

One night I had a tremendously powerful and frightening dream. I do not dream often (at least that I can remember), and this dream was so vivid that I awoke in a cold sweat. I dreamt that I was in a room in a building that was a cross between a traditional Tsimshian longhouse and a traditional house of a Chinese nobleman—a house built around a courtyard. I do not know how those two structures could be reconciled, but in the surrealistic nature of dreams, that is just the way it was. I was standing at the head of a room, talking to a group of anonymous people in a manner which was both condescending and arrogant (although I am not sure what I was talking about).

As I was talking, a gigantic raven flew into the house and landed at the end of the room. The raven was enormous. After I awoke, I realized it had been similar in size to the raven on the massive yellow cedar clamshell carving of the famous Haida artist, Bill Reid, located at the University of British Columbia's Museum of Anthropology. In my dream, however, this was not a stylized figure of Northwest coast art, but a *real* raven and a big one, with a wingspan of 15 feet. It flew right past my face. I could hear the distinctive and graceful swishing sound of its wings—swish, swish—a sound familiar to anyone who has heard the elegant rustle of a raven on the wing.

The giant raven landed at the end of the room. It said nothing but fixed upon me a serious and displeased gaze. The look that flashed from its eyes was: "You had better behave yourself! The way in which you are talking to those people shows terrible manners. You know better!" Whatever the message really was, the raven's presence scared the hell out of me and I woke up. I couldn't get to sleep again. I have tried to make sense of why I was given such a powerful dream. I got to thinking that the only ravens I knew really well that might be in the dream/spirit world are my Grandmother and her son, my Uncle Art, a sub-chief in her tribe[21]. The raven is the primary crest and guardian spirit of the Gitsiis Tribe to whom my Granny and uncle belonged. Was this dream a message from them?

After much contemplation, I have interpreted the dream in this way. My grandmother wanted me to dedicate my efforts to seeking genuine solutions, to being a soldier in the effort to provide that glimmer of hope to lost Aboriginal generations. At one point, I got sidetracked by the glitz of the business world and started chasing money solely for its own sake. For reasons which I did not understand at the time, everything that I undertook seemed to run into problems. My belief is that my grandmother visited me in the dream to tell me that I had lost my way. I had lost my *raison d'être*—a purpose important not only to my Grandmother, but to my own well-being.

I also believe there was a moral message in the nocturnal visit from the raven. In seeking answers to my grandmother's question regarding how to improve the lot of Aboriginal people, it is of utmost importance to be principled and humble. A friend told me that Cree people begin all prayers with the invocation that I have translated as: "Thank you Creator for giving me, such a pitiful little creature, another day and much to be thankful for." Repeating this is intended to acknowledge the miniscule role played by individuals in the greater cosmic order and to show thankfulness and respect to Nature for what we have been given. It is important to keep this in mind in our search to find the target—solutions to Aboriginal problems. Perhaps the raven's message is that, in order to find the target, our arrow must be straight, our aim true, and our vision unclouded by arrogance, self-interest or fear.

COURAGE TO FACE THE UNPLEASANT

> You must speak straight so that your words may go as sunlight to our hearts.
> COCHISE, Apache Leader (1815 – 1874)[22]

Finally, if lasting solutions are to be found, the *real* Aboriginal social and political problems must be discussed openly and frankly. Aboriginal people need to declare an Aboriginal "glasnost" similar to that in the Soviet Union under Mikhail Gorbachev. The removal of government censorship allowed the problems of the Soviet Union to be discussed and addressed in an environment of openness. Aboriginal citizens must also squarely face the Industry of Non-Aboriginal Hucksters, and "consultants", and those Aboriginal politicians who are openly profiting from this sea of despair and poverty. In spite of what they say, this "Indian Industry" has no real interest in changing a system from which they are profiting. Without such resolve it will be difficult, if not impossible, to deal with the myriad of problems that must be tackled.

If manners and common civilities stand in the way of finding solutions, then these must be set aside. It is also time to put questions of self-interest and

GAAX FLIES

The Raven (*Gaax*) was the first symbol and crest of the Northwest Coastal peoples. As the Creator's assistant, he created all things that exist, with mysterious trickery. This mystical bird is a symbol of prestige—a cultural hero.

political correctness aside while real solutions are explored in the name of a higher purpose. The tears and broken hearts of thousands of mothers and grandmothers should be enough to convince anyone that we must take action *now*. How long are we prepared to leave the plight of Aboriginal children and youth in the unkind hands of the welfare trap? How many more families need to fall as casualties of a fatal "welfare syndrome"—one that is literally stealing the lives and hopes of our future generations? We must shake off the apathy of an all too comfortable "cloak of welfare" and act to fix the problems now.

A solution to the problems plaguing Aboriginal people in Canada will ultimately take a more workable policy framework, and likely several generations of reform. In the meantime, there are effective economic and business resolutions that, if pursued, can have a huge impact right now. To exploit these opportunities will require a fundamental change in the dependency mindset of Aboriginal people. For lasting solutions, decisions have to come from Aboriginal people themselves. Aboriginals have to consciously choose a more beneficial path than the dependency course they are currently on—and have the conviction to live with the consequences.

Aboriginal citizens must take ownership of these problems and assert control over their own destinies. We must look immediately to opportunities to generate our own sources of wealth and employment that could lead to the Holy Grail of rediscovered independence and self-reliance. It is time to re-take control of our lives from government departments, bureaucrats, and the Indian Industry. To do this, we must create our own wealth, develop a focussed strategy to educate youth, and control our own purse strings. Reasserting control with a strategic plan for moving forward should ultimately lead to more basic personal happiness. The object is to ensure that larger numbers of Aboriginal people are leading enriched, rewarding lives. Wealth (or money), although needed to provide opportunities, in itself is not the goal, but only a means to this greater end. Successfully implemented, this process in turn should pay huge economic and social dividends for Canada as a country.

A UNIVERSAL MESSAGE OF SELF-RELIANCE

The inevitable consequence of poverty is dependence.
SAMUEL JOHNSON

The situation involving Canada's indigenous people can be seen as a microcosm representing any population going through a condition of enforced dependency. It seems government-sponsored welfare dependency results in astonishingly similar behavior and attitudes regardless of a population's ethnicity. Indeed, throughout the world, societies with long-ingrained entitlement cultures are questioning the wisdom of having created attitudes of expectation.

While welfare payments provide valuable assistance to many individuals in short–term need, the long-term question is: *How can we liberate from poverty a population that has been socialized into a dependency mindset over a long period of time?* Africans, for example, are beginning to openly question the distorting impact of aid, which is a form of welfare, on their long-term well-being. In a recent online posting titled "Africans to Bono: 'For God's sake please stop!'" author Jennifer Brea points out the crippling dependency and corruption created by aid given with the best of intentions.[23] She alludes to the growing chorus of African voices asserting, "We can continue the endless cycle of need and dependency, or you can create jobs, develop indigenous capacity, and build a sustainable future."[24] Such aid further crowds out local entrepreneurship, makes governments lazy, and deprives countries of the incentive to build effective institutions. She notes: "Public revenue derived from taxes makes governments directly responsible to their citizens. Free money builds white elephants and bloated bureaucracies, it being far easier to create new government jobs than implement policies to fight unemployment, especially when someone else is footing the bill."[25] She concludes, "If we really want to help, why not ask Africans, not their governments, how they perceive the challenges before them, the dreams they have for the future, and the resources they think they need to realize them?"[26]

Germans, as well, are intimately acquainted with the ways in which dependency, enforced through government policy, can quickly manifest in a formerly self-reliant population. The subsequent cost of unification and the deeply-ingrained attitudes regarding dependency of their East German counterparts ultimately came as an enormous shock to West Germans. The terms *Wessi* ("westerner") and *Ossi* ("easterner") came to imply their different approaches to the world. *Wessi* refers to a competitive and aggressive nature, the product of what former East Germans call the West's "elbow society." *Ossi* refers to passivity, indolence, and dependence—in effect, the West German view of the East Germans as products of communism.[27]

Similar observations regarding long-term dependency fostered by social welfare systems are being made around the world. Certainly, the creation of long-term welfare dependency in any former colonial population or developing country needs to be reexamined in light of the massive harm caused.

{ I }

THE DEMOGRAPHIC TSUNAMI:
MAJOR PROBLEM OR URGENT OPPORTUNITY?

2

THE LOOMING CRISIS NO ONE KNOWS ABOUT

Chinese Sinogram for the word "crisis"

THE DEMOGRAPHIC TSUNAMI

The Chinese word for crisis is represented by two characters (referred to collectively as a "sinogram"): wēi and jī. These are translated respectively to mean "danger" at a "critical moment":[28]

Crisis = Danger + Critical Moment

I use the sinogram to represent an unfolding moment of danger in Canadian history underscored by current demographic trends. The use of the sinogram "crisis" is appropriate in the context where most North Americans are unaware of the seriousness of ignoring these developments.

    The circumstances in Canada are comparable to the United States where 77 million baby boomers (10 million in Canada) are getting set to retire. David Walker, U.S. comptroller general (counterpart to Canada's Auditor General), calls this group the "demographic tidal wave" coming to swamp the country's finances as the costs for social programs and health care costs soar.[29]

The American financial situation is so serious according to the U.S. comptroller that: "when you take into account the unfunded liabilities of Social Security, Medicare and Medicaid—programs that together comprise the heart of the U.S. social safety net, paying pension and health-care costs for the elderly, as well as providing medical coverage for the poor—America's long-term budget shortfall is approximately U.S. $43 trillion, about four times the size of the nation's economy, and more than 20 times the federal government's annual tax revenues."[30] While Canada's finances are comparatively better, there is an equally surprising "Aboriginal demographic tidal wave" that also could contribute significantly to swamping Canada's finances. The impact of these two demographic realities must be considered carefully.

In the past, Canadians have been content to put Aboriginal challenges out-of-mind and into the backwater bureaucracy of the Department of Indian and Northern Affairs since, other than increasing government expenditures, these issues have not yet impacted the public directly. Whether anyone likes it or not, this issue is forcing its way to the top of the national agenda in a manner that is likely to surprise the public. The issue has grown far beyond being just an Aboriginal problem, and is looming as possibly the number one "Canadian" problem—or *opportunity*, depending on how it is approached.

OPPOSING DEMOGRAPHIC TRENDS

The demographic trends in the mainstream and Aboriginal communities are intersecting in a manner that has sombre implications for the national work force and ultimately the health of the public purse. Census data from 2001 shows Canada's Aboriginal population is on a very steep rise. Of the 1.3 million people that reported having at least some Aboriginal ancestry, nearly 1 million persons identified themselves with one or more of the Status, non-Status, Inuit or Métis Aboriginal groups.[31] That is a comparative increase to 3.3 percent from 2.8 percent of the total population from the previous census five years earlier. By comparison, Canada's overall population was approximately 30 million, and has experienced a steep decline in rate of growth from the baby boom era.[32] It is clear that the two populations are going in opposite demographic directions with the Aboriginal population rapidly rising while the mainstream population is in dramatic decline.[33]

Comparing the median ages (the point where exactly one-half of the population is older, and the other half is younger) between the two population

EAGLE (XSGYIIK) TRANSFORMING TOTEM

Tsimshian mythology tells of the spirit world where animals and people co-existed and communicated. In such a mystical world view it was possible for animals, humans, spirits, and objects to cross boundaries from animate to inanimate and material to spiritual. In this painting, an *xsgyiik* (eagle), the spirit guardian of his tribe, transforms out of the cedar totem to warn Laxsgiik (eagle clan) of impending danger.

Census to Census Population Growth Rate Change 1956–2001

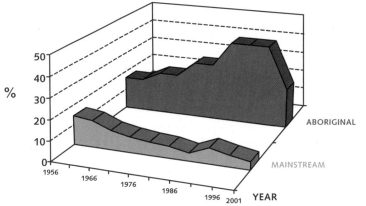

Source of data: Statistics Canada

groups quickly reveals that the mainstream population is much older. The graphic below shows that, in fact, the mainstream population is **13 years older** than the Aboriginal population.

Comparison of Aboriginal vs Non-Aboriginal Median Age

Non-Aboriginal Median Age (37.7 years)

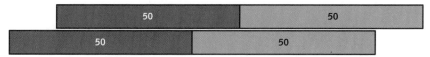

Aboriginal Median Age (24.7 years)

Source of data: Statistics Canada

The difference in growth trends is the result of the high birth rate in the Aboriginal population and the corresponding low birth rates in the mainstream. This divergence further reflects the different times in which the baby boomer generation (those born from 1946 to 1966), peaked in each population group. The overall Canadian and Aboriginal baby boom populations peaked in 1957 and 1967, respectively. It is also interesting to note that mainstream baby boomers (those between 39–59 years of age in 2005) still make up the largest segment of the population—representing almost one-third of the national total. Over the last census period, the Aboriginal population grew at a rate 1.5 times faster than the mainstream population, and outgrew the mainstream population by almost 19 percent. From 1951 to 2001, the growth is even more dramatic, with the Aboriginal population growing sevenfold, while the Canadian population as a whole only doubled.

Times Population Multiplied; Comparison between 1951–2001

2

7

■ Aboriginal Population   □ Non-Aboriginal Population

Source of data: Statistics Canada

The Aboriginal population is not only growing more rapidly, but is much younger than the mainstream population. One-third of the Aboriginal population is aged 14 and under—almost double the corresponding share of 19 percent in the non-Aboriginal population. Looked at another way, although

Relative Percentage of Population under 14 Years of Age

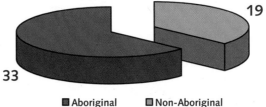

19

33

■ Aboriginal   □ Non-Aboriginal

Source of data: Statistics Canada

the Aboriginal population accounted for only 3.3 percent of Canada's total population, Aboriginal children represented 5.6 percent of all children in Canada.[34]

Demographic trends also illustrate that the Aboriginal population:
• is largely concentrated in Western and Northern Canada;
• must now also be recognized as urban as much as rural with almost 50 percent of the population now based in urban areas;
• is more mobile due to frequent changes in residences; and
• will represent an ever increasing portion of the national labor force.

In comparison, the mainstream population:[35]
• has a low birth rate as well as substantial declines in the number of children;[36]
• is growing fastest among the oldest age group;[37]
• has a "greying" working population as the number of older workers increases;[38]
• beginning in 2011, the proportion of the population age 65 and over will expand rapidly[39], reinforced by low birth rate and longer life expectancy;
• has the potential for significant shortages of workers in certain occupations such as health care, education, skilled trades (such as pipe fitters, carpenters, brick layers, plumbers, electricians, etc.); and
• will have fewer young people entering the labor force to replace those retiring due to low fertility rates in the past few 30 years.

In the U.S., demographic trends mirror those in Canada. According to 2005 Census Bureau data projections, by 2020 the white population is expected to increase by 1 percent compared to 26 percent for Native Americans, 77 percent for Hispanics, and 32 percent for African Americans.[40] The Native American demographic trend in the U.S. is consistent with the growth patterns of indigenous and poor populations in Asia, South America, Africa, the Middle East, and Europe. And everywhere the greatest population growth occurs among ethnic groups that are least educated. As well, Census data from 2000 confirms that Native Americans and Alaska Natives have the highest poverty rates in the nation, at more than two times the national average of 11.7 percent.[41]

Combined with these demographic developments are societal trends indicating that an enormous demographic tsunami is coming to swamp the finances of America. First, the fact that 80 million Americans are set to retire

American Demographic Tsunami (Approximately 80 million retirees by 2050)

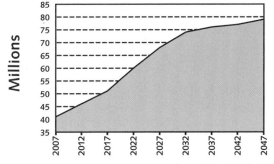

Source of data: 2007 Social Security Trustees Report

has enormous financial implications.[42] A major area of impact is the pension system. In 1950, there were 16.5 U.S. workers for every retiree, while by 2032 only 2.1 workers will be paying for each beneficiary. By 2041, experts say the

Ratio of Workers to Retirees

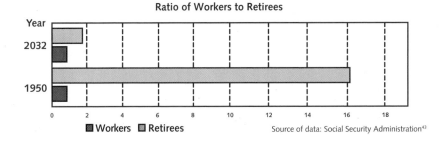

■ Workers ■ Retirees   Source of data: Social Security Administration[43]

U.S. pension system will be exhausted.[44] The prospect of losing one's pension does not weigh lightly on the minds of American elders or of families already under economic pressure.

Another trend indicative of an ensuing financial tsunami in America is the escalating national debt. Currently amounting to 37 percent of the entire U.S. economy, the national debt is projected to soar to 231 percent by 2050 if current budget policies—including laws governing entitlement programs and extensions of the administration's tax cuts—are continued.[45] At that point, interest payments alone would soak up more than half of the federal rev-

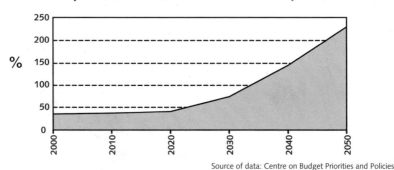

Projections for U.S. National Debt (231% of GDP by 2050)

Source of data: Centre on Budget Priorities and Policies

enues.[46] According to a recent report, the U.S. national debt is now $9 trillion and approaching 70 percent of the gross domestic product (GDP), with forecasters predicting $11 trillion by 2010.[47] Significantly, the biggest budgetary problem increasing the national debt has been identified as rising healthcare costs, predicted to increase radically.

Another major source of financial pressure is the country's long-term budget shortfall. The American financial situation is so serious, according to U.S. comptroller David Walker, that "when you take into account the unfunded liabilities of Social Security Medicare and Medicaid programs that together comprise the heart of the U.S. social safety net, paying pension and healthcare costs for the elderly, as well as providing medical coverage for the poor—America's long-term budget shortfall is approximately $43 trillion."[48] This amount, Mr. Walker notes, is four times the size of the nation's economy, and more than 20 times the federal government's annual tax revenues.

CHIEF AND WIFE LOOK OUT TO SEA IN FRONT OF TRIBAL LONG HOUSE

"When will the storm come?" Sm'ooygit (Chief) wonders as he looks out to sea. In the background is a traditional Tsimshian long house with a totem pole in front of it. In some ways, the totem pole is akin to a coat of arms—full of symbolism that is understood within the culture. The creatures or totems carved in the pole represent the clan's kinship system, dignity, accomplishments, prestige, adventures, stories, and rights.

3

IMPLICATIONS OF DEMOGRAPHIC TRENDS

Demography, the study of human populations, is the most powerful—and most underutilized—tool we have to understand the past and foretell the future. Demographics affect every one of us as individuals…[and] also play a pivotal role in the economic and social life of our country. … Demographics explain about two-thirds of everything. … Demographics are about everyone. …Demographics are critically important for business.

DAVE K. FOOT, *Boom, Bust and Echo 2000* [49]

THE ECONOMIC BOMB

So what does this data illustrate? There are specific implications for Aboriginal leaders, and the national labor force. These trends could also translate into looming potential costs which, unless addressed, will impact individual taxpayers directly in their wallets and will have serious long-term repercussions to the well-being of Canada generally.

Even without considering the additional impact of the Aboriginal demographic tsunami, alarm bells are being sounded about the general demographic predicament. A very recent Statistics Canada report advises that "In 25 years, Canada's population of seniors 65 and older could be more than double the number of children under 15."[50] High level sources are warning of the dire need for political leaders to compel corporations and unions to extend retirement past the age of 60 (the age at which Canadians can retire early under the Canada Pension Plan) so that older workers can help meet the desperate need to deal with what has been called the mainstream demographic time bomb. The Finance department has warned that Canada will need to boost its lacklustre productivity due to the shrinking labor force as the growing number of retirees "exert a downward pressure on the growth of living standards."[51] Unless corrective measures are taken immediately, David Dodge, governor of the Bank of Canada, sums up the impact this way:

"What's critical then, if we are going to increase our standards of living, is the amount, or value, of what we produce in a given hour of work rises. It's the only way we will be able to maintain our real incomes. It is absolutely critical."[52]

In a recent article, Jerry Grafstein, Chairman of the Senate Banking Committee, stated:

"There is a huge [demographic] economic bomb that's about to explode [caused by retiring baby boomers]. Governments, to be fair, are looking at it or nibbling at it. But their problem is that public opinion is in exactly the opposite direction.

It is one thing to change policies, but you have to lead the change in public attitudes about this. And you have business and the unions who are working in exactly the wrong direction."[53]

In the same vein, Canadians are also largely ignorant of the huge impact on the economy and public purse that the Aboriginal demographic tsunami may have.

A CLEAR MESSAGE TO ABORIGINAL LEADERS

On the one hand, there is no question that Aboriginal leaders should take notice of these trends because:

- If no action is taken now the rapidly growing and young Aboriginal population will require a huge increase in government spending to keep up with current per capita payments (which are now widely regarded by Aboriginal leaders as being woefully inadequate).
- This growth trend is occurring precisely at a time when there is diminishing public support for increased public spending on Aboriginal people—federal Aboriginal programming expenditures in 2005–2006 are estimated to be approximately $9 billion.[54]
- The growth trend is occurring when there is also greater demand for accountability, transparency,[55] and better value for the huge amount of monies being spent.[56]
- Huge reserve population increases will exacerbate existing problems with overcrowding, unemployment, inadequate educational opportunities, and related social pathologies. If Aboriginal leaders think they may be facing community pressure now, the pressure is guaranteed to rise with a rapidly increasing young population clamouring for more programs, services, and real opportunities.

- Currently, while only 29 percent of the Aboriginal population live on reserves, they receive (according to one study released in 2003[57]), 88 percent of the federal government program spending. The 50 percent that live in cities receive only 3.5 percent of this amount (and the rest of the population live off-reserve in rural areas)—a huge inequity no matter how you look at it.

  There appears to be growing support for either redirecting more current federal spending to the enormous urban Aboriginal populations (which can only increase fiscal pressures on Aboriginal communities) or increasing overall spending to provide for this group in areas such as healthcare, education, etc.[58]

- Métis are the fastest-growing Aboriginal population by far.[59] If Métis case law develops to the point where Aboriginal legal rights are achieved that are comparable to First Nation and Inuit Aboriginal rights, the case will be made that their population base should also be served by similar government programming.[60] This could add billions to existing federal government spending. In fact, if the governments have to provide equivalent programs and services to the Métis population (estimated to be between 300,000–800,000[61]), this could increase total annual government spending for Aboriginal people from 50 percent to over 100 percent!

THE URGENT NEED FOR ABORIGINAL LABOR

From the Aboriginal perspective, unemployment is one of the biggest problems to overcome. Such unemployment is occurring at a time when the mainstream desperately needs trained Aboriginal employees. Though the Aboriginal rate of unemployment has slowly fallen since 1991, the chart below shows that it is almost three times that of the total population.[62] This level of unemployment is one of the most significant costs relating to Aboriginal people.[63]

Aboriginal vs Total Population Unemployment

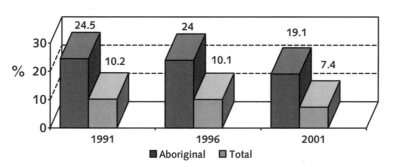

Source of data: Canadian Labor and Business Centre Report

The challenge facing Canada is that this high rate of Aboriginal unemployment is occurring precisely at the time when Canada needs the workers most. The conclusions from a recent study confirmed that:

> Aboriginal success in Canada's labour market is, or should be, of great interest to all Canadians. Our interest stems not only from the value we place on equitable treatment of all of our residents, but it is also rooted in self-interest. Canada cannot have a high quality of life if there is a significant minority forming an impoverished underclass. Moreover... **Aboriginal entrants into the labour market will be absolutely vital in filling labour demand requirements. To a larger extent than is generally recognized, Canada's future prosperity depends on how successful we are in achieving equitable results in our labour market for Aboriginal Canadians** [Emphasis added].[64]

The study further concludes that to close the gap in unemployment in 2006 would have required the employment of an additional 103,093 Aboriginal workers; by 2016 this number will rise to 189,842 jobs.

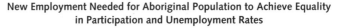

New Employment Needed for Aboriginal Population to Achieve Equality
in Participation and Unemployment Rates

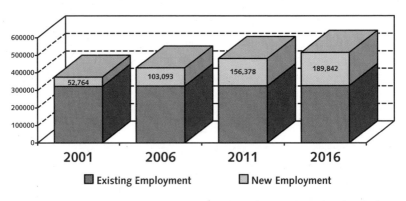

Source of data: Caledon Institute of Social Policy Report

Over the next ten years, the Aboriginal working-age population is expected to grow 3–5 times as fast as its non-Aboriginal counterpart.[65] This rapidly-growing workforce will provide a large pool of potential employees at a time when the broader Canadian population is aging into retirement. The importance of the Aboriginal workforce will be felt most acutely in Western and Northern Canada where the Aboriginal population is highest and there is considerable dependence on a supply of Aboriginal workers for an economy largely based on natural resource extraction.

A report prepared by the British Columbia Chamber of Commerce states the challenge as follows:

> A recent newspaper story warned that, "A crisis looms if we do nothing to train and employ the 920,000 working-age Aboriginal Canadians who will enter the work force by 2006." The Aboriginal working-age population is growing three time faster than any other group in Canada. The story concluded with two choices: "We can accept the status quo and do nothing, or we can seize the unprecedented opportunity for both Aboriginal youth and corporate Canada. ... [Altruism aside] **it is now an economic imperative**—businesses, unions and governments need to consider all sources of skilled workers and ensure the retention and development of human resources [Emphasis added].[66]

For Western and Northern Canada, the crisis is here now! A booming resource economy and the prospect of the 2010 Olympics in British Columbia are fuelling approximately $80 billion in infrastructure projects.[67] Today, $87 billion dollars worth of investment is either proposed, underway or recently committed in Alberta's oil sands alone.[68] The economy of the Northwest Territories is booming with both Ekati and Diavik diamond mines in production. The Jericho diamond project in Nunavut is in production and the Snap Lake diamond project is in progress.[69] Oil and gas activity in the Northwest Territories, British Columbia, and the Yukon, with the proposed Mackenzie Valley and Alaska Highway Pipeline projects will ensure a requirement for large workforces. Alarm bells are sounding, demanding who will build the projects that will largely pay for our future. With billions of investment "in the ground," major corporations are wondering publicly where the work force will be found. A front page article in the *Vancouver Sun* disclosed that companies are now looking to India and China to fulfill skilled labor needs, announcing, "Contractors hiring globally: Not enough trades people in Canada to fill BC's growing demand...."[70] It is worth keeping in mind this shortage is already occurring before the period of 2011 and onward, when baby boomers will begin to leave the work force in huge numbers.

The 1996 Royal Commission Report makes the case that there is a negative cost to doing nothing and maintaining the Aboriginal status quo. Costs are summarized to comprise: (a) the cost of Aboriginal peoples' inability to obtain good jobs and earn reasonable incomes;[71] and (b) a significant financial burden on taxpayers arising from remedial services to help Aboriginal people cope with the negative effects of their history of domination (such as higher than average use of welfare programs, housing subsidies, health and justice services).[72] It has also been documented that while all governments spend money on all citizens, the amount spent per person for Aboriginal people is *57 percent higher* than for Canadians generally.[73]

Applying this analysis, the report contends the cost to taxpayers of failing to address Aboriginal problems would amount to $7.5 billion[74] in 1996 and $11 billion in 2016.[75] As a comparison, the entire budget to run the province of New Brunswick throughout all of 1996 was $4.6 billion![76]

Looked at more broadly, the following analysis might be applied to assess the real costs of failing to address squarely the Aboriginal social and economic pathologies and direct costs associated with the Aboriginal demographic tidal wave. The Royal Commission Report reveals that federal spending on Aboriginal programs in 1992–1993 represented approximately $6 billion. Other governments (mostly provincial governments) spent an additional $5.6 billion, almost matching the federal contribution. This amounted to $11.6 billion for that year.[77]

It has already been noted that federal government spending for the registered Indian and Inuit populations in 2005 was $9 billion. If the same provincial spending levels for 1992–1993 are extrapolated to 2005, total government spending for Aboriginal programs will approach $18 billion. On top of this, if, as they are seeking, the Métis population achieves full parity in the level of programs and services provided to the First Nations and Inuit populations in 2005, this could conceivably increase required spending to $24 billion (if there are 300,000 Métis) or over $36 billion (if there are more than 800,000)! Amazingly, these amounts represent between 11 to 22 percent of all provincial own-source revenue for all Canadian provinces for 2002–2003[78], or (the high end of the estimate) represents about half of the GDP for a country like New Zealand in fiscal year 2004.[79] And these estimates still do not include potential increased spending estimates for the 50% of Aboriginal people living in the cities (now receiving only 3.5 percent of spending for Aboriginal people).

If these figures are not sufficient to cause serious concern about Aboriginal issues in the average Canadian's mind, the situation could be made worse by the intersection of mainstream demographic trends. In the rapidly greying mainstream Canadian population:

- The large aging baby boom segment of the population, as it advances through the years, means a much larger segment of the population will be reliant on costly social programs, as well as health care spending (one of the largest single line items in the federal budget).[80] As suggested by the American comptroller general, David Walker, this will escalate government spending on programs and services in these areas enormously.
- This older population will be reliant on such spending at a time when a huge number of the working age population will be retiring and not contributing to the revenue base, and these costs will be longer-term given the longer life expectancy of the general Canadian population.
- Canada needs to replenish its working age segment of skilled workers not only to ensure a healthy tax base to pay the costs of baby boomer retirees, but to ensure that Canada as a nation remains competitive and prosperous.
- The aging population and dramatically declining fertility rate mean that Canada has to look elsewhere for a huge working age population to sustain its current social and economic status quo.

IMPACT ON TAXPAYERS: THE DEMOGRAPHIC TSUNAMI

If the situation of Aboriginal people is not collectively addressed, Canada's finances could literally be swamped in the combined impact of the demographic tsunami. On the one hand, huge numbers of the workforce are retiring, are no longer contributing to the country's tax base, are utilizing expensive health care and social programs, and living much longer.[81] This trend will accelerate rapidly from 2011 onward as baby boomers (representing one third of the Canadian population) retire at an ever-increasing rate. In sum, the scenario emerging from mainstream demographic trends is of dramatically falling source revenues while social program and health care expenditures rise sharply. This is precisely the situation that caused such great alarm for the U.S. Comptroller General about looming demographics and fiscal fallout of retiring baby boomers.

The question for Canadians is really simple. If no effort is made to resolve the Aboriginal situation, the two demographic trends will combine to create a fiscal demographic tsunami on a scale never before seen in Canada. The question for Aboriginal leaders and people is equally simple: without taking immediate action to reform the current dependency system, the host of social and economic pathologies plaguing the Aboriginal population will increase sharply. On the other hand, if effective measures are taken now to develop and implement a strategy which results in wide-scale Aboriginal employment and wealth creation, instead of the destructive impact of a tsunami, when the tide comes in naturally, the Canadian boat and Aboriginal canoe will be lifted in an equally beneficial manner. In the end, with a little careful planning and the right spirit of partnership, the Canadian economy and nation will be the beneficiary of such cooperation.

A WAKE-UP CALL FOR AMERICA

Given the precarious financial exposure of the country, the threatening tsunami is likely to be much more intense when it comes to America. The rapidly growing legions of poor relying on expensive government entitlement programs, combined with the massive population of retiring baby boomers, will tax the resources of the nation in an unprecedented manner, surely testing the resiliency for which America is renowned.

As if government debt were not enough fiscal pressure, in 2007 average Americans were up to their eyeballs in mortgage debt, car loans and credit-card spending. According to some experts, the U.S. savings rate is now below zero, meaning more money is being spent than earned.[82] To maintain a lifestyle that would ordinarily be unattainable, Americans owe a staggering $16 trillion dollars—$2.4 trillion in personal debt and $13.6 trillion borrowed against homes—a financial house of cards that has been partially exposed by the "subprime" mortgage debacle.[83] Home foreclosures in 2007 leaped 93 percent from the previous year.[84] Yet, this may be only the beginning of a terrible downward trend caused by the fallout of the subprime mortgage disaster that has placed an estimated 2 million Americans in danger of losing their homes.[85] One writer summarizes America's overall financial predicament this way:

> The United States might be the only superpower but we still owe Japan and China each about a trillion dollars. (We owe even more to the Gulf Arabs.) With no savings, America continues to run an $800 billion dollar trade deficit. We are effectively *giving America away to our creditors*, and if we continue to give more and more away, we will lose the ability and the

Demographic Tsunami: Worst-Case Fiscal Impact

NON-ABORIGINAL FACTORS

ABORIGINAL FACTORS

MÉTIS FACTORS

ABORIGINAL DEMOGRAPHIC FACTOR

1) Continued high cost for per capita spending

2) Huge rapidly-growing, young population

3) If current course not altered, could be huge cost to Canada for future delivery of programs and services at a time when more resources are needed for aging population

4) 50% of the population living in urban areas receive only 3.5% of existing spending: enormous gap must be addressed to maximize impact of spending.

NON-ABORIGINAL DEMOGRAPHIC FACTOR

1) Increased numbers of Baby Boomers retiring from work-force by 2011

2) Retirees living longer and requiring expensive social and health care spending

3) No longer contributing to tax base

4) Many skilled workers needed to replace retirees just to keep Canada competitive and prosperous.

MÉTIS FACTOR

1) 300,000 Métis in 2001 (perhaps as many as 800,000)

2) Métis currently receive very limited government program $;

3) Métis the fastest-growing Aboriginal population at 43% vs. approximately 13% for Indian and Inuit

4) If Métis rights develop further in law, there is some speculation government could be legally bound to provide per capita level of spending similar to registered Indians and Inuit.

will to take back control and ownership of our own economy. *Not only are Americans, individually, becoming debt slaves,* but the country on a national level is losing its independence... [Emphasis added].[86]

While much attention is justifiably being paid to the serious problem of global warming, the nation would be well advised to turn its attention as well to the serious economic cooling from the tidal wave of debt that threatens the well-being of every American citizen.

At some point everyone has to "pay the piper" and come clean on their debts. To avoid crisis management scenarios and increasing stress on a population—two-thirds of whom are already likely to seek help for stress[87]—discussion and long-term planning need to be put in place now. The poorest populations in America will unquestionably be hardest hit by the oncoming tsunami. With the implementation of long-term strategic planning, however, it is likely that the economic and social disadvantages of the poor can be alleviated so these people may better withstand the trauma of oncoming change.

If the demographic tsunami, and the response to it are part of the fourth wave, the remainder of this book will be divided into four parts, the first, second, third, and fourth wave.

{ 2 }

**A FIRST AND SECOND WAVE:
FROM SELF-RELIANCE TO COLONIALISM**

4

THE FIRST WAVE:
INDIGENOUS DEVELOPMENT PRIOR TO CONTACT

Walking Eagle tells the weather
If it's cold or it's warm
If the day will be cloudy
Or the stars will shine in the sky
There's a language within nature
Written on the forest floor
On every leaf, root and creeper
In every lake or sandy shore
What can he see for his people?
Will there be dark clouds on the way
Will the storms come pounding, crashing?
As it's been since long before.

> WILLIE DUNN, Aboriginal "topical folksinger,"
> excerpted from the song *Walking Eagle*

ABORIGINAL EXISTENCE PRIOR TO EUROPEAN CONTACT: 9,600 YEAR CANOE JOURNEY

There is nothing like returning to a place that remains unchanged to find the ways in which you yourself have altered.

NELSON MANDELA (1918–), *A Long Walk to Freedom*

There is evidence that Aboriginal people have occupied certain parts of North America for at least 20,000 years.[88] For purposes of this discussion, I will assume that Aboriginals have sailed through mists of antiquity on a canoe journey of at least 10,000 years. So, prior to European contact, for at least perhaps 9,600 years, the Aboriginal canoe sailed along just fine.[89]

By necessity Aboriginal societies were self-reliant, socially-coherent, healthy, and had a clear direction. They evidently thrived without welfare, without unemployment insurance and without government transfer payments. Only in the last 400 years has the canoe been caught in a terrible storm and Aboriginal people undergone a calamitous decline. The vision and clear direction of our ancestral leaders that might have taken the Aboriginal canoe out of trouble, seems to be lost in the haze of a comparatively recent storm of colonialism.

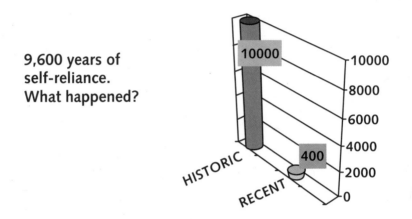

9,600 years of self-reliance. What happened?

Why? What happened? In trying to guide the Aboriginal canoe out of this storm, it may be useful to look back before looking ahead in an attempt to discern the course navigated by the ancient Aboriginal mariners. The elements that for millennia contributed to the survival and success of Aboriginal societies may provide some clues to solutions in the present situation. This chapter surveys key elements of indigenous societies that ensured their survival. It is intended to provide the reader with a sense of the societies that existed and the degree of complexity of social organization. From these the writer then draws his own conclusions.

Populations and Social Structures Maintained by Natural Resources

Prior to contact with European peoples, there is evidence that indigenous tribes flourished in varying degrees throughout North America. According to Professor Olive Dickason, in the fifteenth century (on the eve of European arrival), estimates of the North and South American population have been

AURORA HARMONY

A family of Orcas, known to Tsimshian ancestors as *'neext* (otherwise known as black fish or killer whales), swim and frolic in the evening Northern Lights. Behind them is a Nisga'a village called Kincolith. The Aurora outlines a heart shape that symbolizes love and unity. Orca populations are diminishing everywhere. We must protect them and their habitats before it is too late. A limited edition of giclee method prints was made.

going steadily upward and reached a high of 112.5 million.[90] The population estimates for North America itself (north of the Rio Grande) in the sixteenth century range up to an unlikely 18 million and even higher.[91] In relation to Canada, Dickason describes the population as thinly-scattered, since the mode of subsistence for hunter/gatherer societies was land intensive.[92] She suggests further that the most widely-accepted population estimate is about 500,000, though recent demographic studies have pushed the possible figure to well over 2 million.[93] She also notes that: "principal population concentrations were on the Northwest Coast, where abundant and easily available resources allowed a sedentary life, and in what is today's southern Ontario, where various branches of Iroquoians practiced farming. The Iroquoian groups may have totalled about 60,000 if not more, and the Northwest Coast could have counted as many as 200,000 souls, making it "one of the most densely populated non-agricultural regions in the world."[94]

As suggested, in British Columbia alone the bounty of nature sustained approximately 30 completely different Aboriginal groups. Professor Paul Tennant, a recently retired political science professor from the University of British Columbia, comments further: "Each had a unique linguistic and cultural identity, as well as a name for itself and a territory which it made use of. The groups were as distinct from one another as were the various European nations of the time. While several of the smaller groups died out after contact, most survived."[95]

In relation to British Columbia, anthropologist Philip Drucker comments: "That they [Northwest Coast Aboriginal people] were able to attain their high level of civilization is due largely to the amazing wealth of natural resources of their area. From the sea and rivers—[came] five species of Pacific Salmon, halibut, cod, herring, smelt and the famous olachen or "candle fish." and other species too numerous to mention."[96] Prolific sea life on the coast, and salmon and freshwater fish in the interior, led to the development of highly formalized artistic traditions and complex social structures.

Professor Tennant notes further that on the coast of British Columbia the giant red cedar tree provided, in addition to large plank houses, the world's largest dug-out canoes. These allowed full use of the coastal environment, and exploitation of areas extensive enough to provision sedentary winter villages with populations of several thousand. "The canoes permitted ready communication among the villages composing a tribal group, and they enabled travel and trade up and down the entire coast. The cedar houses enabled a large number of people, usually family groups, to live under one roof, and many people could thus live compactly together in winter villages."[97]

Other tribes in Canada sustained themselves with the various resources available in their regions. The Iroquois and the Odawa (Ottawa) were the only farmer-hunters in Canada.[98] There was some reliance by the Ojibwa on uncultivated crops such as wild rice. For the most part, all other Aboriginal groups in Canada were hunters and gatherers. In the Northwestern plains, nomadic tribes survived on the communal bison hunt. Dickason suggests that both bison drives and jumps were practised depending on the conformity of the land and that: "These forms of hunting called for a **high degree of co-operation and organization**, not only within bands but also between them and sometimes intertribally. Impounding or corralling was the more complex method, and has been described by archaeologist Thomas F. Kehoe as a form of food production rather than hunting—a precursor, if not an early form, of domestication [Emphasis added]."[99]

Political Institutions

There were varying degrees of political organization amongst the North American tribes. Wilson Duff has commented that: "The Indians, especially those of the coast tribes [of British Columbia] had rich and elaborate patterns of social organization. In the virtual absence of political institutions, they regulated their lives by social institutions."[100]

Anthropologists identify two main types of traditional or indigenous society.[101] One type is highly structured with distinct politics based on rank, status and hierarchy (as is found in the Tsimshian previously discussed). This type emerges only from bountiful natural environment which can sustain a substantial population. The other type is less structured and much more egalitarian; it is associated with small populations, often those having to gather food over extensive territories.[102] Professor Tennant comments that: "Morton Fried distinguishes the two as 'rank societies' and 'band equalitarian societies.' The British Columbia tribal groups provide examples of each. ... [C]oastal groups were highly structured societies having clearly evident and permanent positions of political leadership. The interior groups were typically composed of small communities having little need for specialized politics."[103]

Along the eastern seaboard, the famous Iroquois Confederacy was a well-organized group initially covering much of New York state. In the early years, this group was such a military power that it threatened the very existence of the colonies.[104] A famous chief, Dekanawida, united the formerly-warring tribes (which shared similar customs and languages) through the creation of

GWIS'NAGMGYEMK

This artwork is a design for a *gwis'nagmgyemk* (Sm'algyax word for what is commonly known as a Chilkat blanket). The origin story is attributed to an ancient Tsimshian woman, from the village of Kitkatla, who lived long ago on the Skeena River in northern British Columbia. It purportedly spread from the Tsimshian to the Tlingits through trade and marriage. Traditionally, only the wealthy could make or own a blanket. Both men and women played a role in the creation of the blankets and both considered it a great privilege to wear one. The blanket was made of mountain goat wool spun over a core of cedar-bark string. The men hunted the goat, constructed the frame on which the weaving was done and painted the design board from which the women, who did the weaving, took the design. The patterns were a highly stylized form or art often representing clan symbols and natural forms in an abstract geometric pattern. Animals were portrayed as if sliced down the center and laid out flat. The small circles are ball and socket joints. Eyes were often used as space fillers. The men designed the pattern and painted the abstract figures on a wooden "pattern board." As the blanket was bilateral, only half the pattern was painted in life-size dimensions. The blanket pattern could be interpreted in a variety of ways, however only the man who designed the blanket knew the true legend. The blankets represent the high point of Northwest Coast art and are almost always black, yellow, white, and blue in colour.

a code of laws he named the Great Binding Law. Now called the "Iroquois Constitution," it was a remarkable civil and social system, and one of the first attempts to establish a confederacy of independent states. It sets out:

> The relation of the confederacy to these independent states as well as the mechanism for making decisions collectively would form the basis of the governing body of the Iroquois League. But the Iroquois Constitution goes beyond simply outlining the structure of a confederate government; nearly every aspect of tribal life is included in "the great binding law." For the practice of government infused every aspect of life: religion, birth, adoption, and death; no neat boundaries separated these other aspects of life from government and the practice of authority.[105]

The Iroquois system of government is widely thought to have influenced the drafting of the American constitution. Benjamin Franklin, a founding father of early American colonial confederation, freely acknowledged the Iroquois Confederacy as a model to build upon in his observation that: "It would be a strange thing...if Six Nations of ignorant savages should be capable of forming such a union and be able to execute it in such a manner that it has subsisted for ages and appears indissoluble, and yet that a like union should be impractical for ten or a dozen English colonies, to whom it is more necessary and must be more advantageous, and who cannot be supposed to want an equal understanding of their interest."[106]

There were many forms of political institutions in the many tribes that occupied North America with varying degrees of formality and sophistication. In the views of most tribes, they were self-governing nations. This view was partially recognized in law by the United States Supreme Court in the famous Marshall decisions of the early 1800's where, in recognizing the land and self-government rights of the Cherokee Indians from Georgia, the court characterized those tribes as "domestic, dependent nations."[107]

The differing contemporary views relating to sovereignty between state governments and indigenous peoples is at the root of disagreements relating to a host of contentious issues in Canada. The legitimacy of these governments is questioned because: (1) under international law,[108] all peoples have the right to decide how they will be governed, and no government can be imposed upon a people without their consent; (2) Aboriginal people in Canada say that they never consented to be governed by the French or British or the government of Canada; (3) European powers did not assert authority over Aboriginals on any valid grounds;[109] and (4) title to the land cannot be claimed by conquest since there was no conquest.[110, 111]

Social Structure

Tribes throughout North America were largely organized in terms of communities consisting of kinship units. The most important element of tribal life was the family, followed by the extended family and tribal unit. The traditional views of the importance of the family unit to indigenous lives were restated in the 1996 hearings of the Report of the Royal Commission on Aboriginal Peoples:[112] "the family is the foundation of Inuit culture, society and economy. All of our social and economic structures, customary laws, traditions and actions have tried to recognize and affirm the strength of the family unit."[113]

In discussing coastal indigenous groups of BC, Professor Tennant reveals: "The 'houses' or [family] households, indeed became the basic social unit in all the coastal groups. ... The households possessed property...land...buildings, canoes. ... Houses could have rights to fish in certain waters...engage in certain [subsistence and economic] activities. ... Houses also owned 'a host of ritual and intangible possessions,' including crests, stories, songs, dances and names. ... Among the coastal peoples the households were grouped into lineages having common ancestry."[114]

In general, even though there were sophisticated political institutions in some of the North American tribal groups, there was a fundamental difference in the manner in which tribes looked at their own organization. Viewed from this perspective, the political, social and economic dichotomy that evolved in the Western world simply didn't occur or exist in most tribal groups. For example, there was no such notion as the separation of church (i.e., spiritual life) and state (i.e., decisions in Western society that would be considered government-related). Most tribes had a more holistic worldview that placed social concerns at the centre of everything, including religious, economic and political aspects of the society.

It has also been suggested that the difference between the views and approach of Western and traditional indigenous societies is really a question of two cultures at two differing stages of development. Brian Cowley argues that the simplicity of the form of life attributed to pre-contact Aboriginals arose out of a different order of social complexity and population density.[115] He contends the Aboriginal civilizations were face-to-face traditional societies based on a concrete, shared end built around sustenance activities. All of

TXADOX (TSIMSHIAN POTLATCH)

The large coastal long houses enabled the holding of elaborate feasts and performances known as potlatches. These events made the coastal societies distinctive from all others in North America. Their purpose was to provide a formal means of recognition for a host of tribal businesses. These could include the taking on of new names by individuals, legitimizing political rank and authority. The holding of such events validated the rightful possession of prestige, and the use of Chiefly power and influence. Chiefs would hold periodic potlatches to demonstrate their rank and wealth, giving away large amounts of tools, personal goods, and food. What they gained in status, they lost in material wealth, but this ensured the circulation of wealth within the community.

tribal life was therefore organized as a function of this reality of common purpose. Playing one's assigned role within this overarching social organization constituted the conditions of sharing on which the cooperative nature of Aboriginal society was founded, he suggests. Conversely, he proposes that Europeans were already moving to the vast, extended order of social cooperation that the West enjoys today (without having to agree on a common purpose to pursue as a society).[116]

He goes on to suggest:

> What transformed Western society, making it so different culturally from many traditional societies, was that, under pressures such as scarcity, urbanization, the growth of technological diversity, and the emergence of the concept of individuality, acceptance of a shared, concrete social project began to break down. *People could no longer achieve social solidarity and mutual cooperation merely on the grounds that all could see that their material survival and spiritual salvation depended on their playing a predetermined role or function.* Nor could life continue to be based on a shared belief in a divinely directed unfolding of human affairs. The Reformation among other things saw to that [Emphasis added].

Philosophical and Spiritual Views

> This we know: the earth does not belong to man, man belongs to the earth. All things are connected like the blood that unites us all. Man did not weave the web of life, he is merely a strand in it. Whatever he does to the web, he does to himself.[117]

The excerpt above is from a version of a controversial speech attributed to Chief Seattle of the Salishan Nation (in what is now Washington State) in January of 1854. Although some controversy surrounds the historical accuracy of this speech, the excerpt quoted above captures somewhat the views of most indigenous groups towards nature and the cosmos.

At the root of indigenous cultures are deeply-held spiritual views based on a profound respect for nature. Professor Dickason comments that indigenous people perceived the universe as an intricate meshing of personalized powers great and small, beneficial and dangerous, whose equilibrium was based on reciprocity.[118] It was thought that while humans could not control the system, they could influence particular manifestations through alliances with spiritual powers, combined with their knowledge of how these powers worked. Dickason notes that:

Such alliances had to be approached judiciously, as some spirits were more powerful than others, just as some were beneficent and others malevolent; every force had a counterforce. Things were not always as they seemed at first sight; with stones, even inanimate objects could have unexpected hidden attributes. Keeping the cosmos in tune and staying in tune with the cosmos called for ceremonials, rituals, and taboos that had to be properly observed or performed if they were to be effective. **Attention to detail** could be so close that a missed step in a dance would result in chastisement. Even construction of dwellings and the layout of villages and encampments (not to mention cities and temple complexes of the south) reflected this sense of spiritual order, with its emphasis on centres rather than boundaries[119] [Emphasis added].

In rejecting an inquiry to establish a missionary post among the Seneca, the famous Chief Red Jacket responded in a manner descriptive of indigenous spirituality and the manner in which many tribes perceived Christianity:

"Brother: Continue to listen. You say that you are sent to instruct us how to worship the Great Spirit agreeably to his mind, and if we do not take hold of the religion which you white people teach, we shall be unhappy hereafter. ... How do we know this to be true? We understand that your religion is written in a book. If it was intended for us as well as you, why has not the Great Spirit given to us, and not only to us, but why did he not give our forefathers, the knowledge of that book [the Bible], with the means of understanding it rightly? We only know what you tell us about it. ...

"Brother:...We also have a religion, which was given to our forefathers, and has been handed down to us their children. We worship in that way. It teaches us to be thankful for all the favours we receive; to love each other, and to be united. We never quarrel about religion. ...

"...The Great Spirit does right. He knows what is best for his children; we are satisfied."[120]

Another writer elaborates further on the considerable evidence of the deep spirituality of indigenous people. This view is contrary to the popular

Euro-centric notion of the time that indigenous people were essentially uncivilized "savages" without their own forms of spirituality, and what might be characterized as deeply-held religious convictions.

Everyone nowadays has heard of the Bible and knows from the Old Testament how religious the Israelites were. Yet way back in 1893, the official report of the Bureau of Ethnography wrote: "The most surprising fact relating to the North American Indians which until lately had not been realized, is that they habitually lived in and by religion to a degree comparable with the old Israelites under the theocracy."

Even earlier than 1893, the famous author Washington Irving, wrote in 1837, over 130 years ago: "Simply to call these people religious would convey but a faint idea of the DEEP HUE OF PIETY AND DEVOTION WHICH PERVADES THEIR WHOLE CONDUCT. THEIR HONESTY IS IMMACULATE and their purity of purpose in their observance of the rites of their religion are most uniform and remarkable. THEY ARE CERTAINLY MORE LIKE A NATION OF SAINTS THAN A HORDE OF SAVAGES."

A non-Indian who lived among the Indians for sixty years wrote back in 1925, "I claim for the Indian of North America the purest religion and THE MOST LOFTY CONCEPTIONS OF THE GREAT CREATOR." The famous George Bird Grinnel wrote about the notion of God in the lives of the Indians: "He is an intangible spirit, omnipotent and beneficent. He pervades the universe and is the supreme ruler. Upon his will depends everything that happens. He can bring good luck or bad; can give success or failure. Everything rests on him. As a natural consequence of this conception of the Deity, they are very religious people. NOTHING IS UNDERTAKEN WITHOUT PRAYER TO THE FATHER FOR ASSISTANCE." Another writer wrote in 1910: "The Great Spirit, or Great Mystery, or Good Power is everywhere and in all things."[121]

The indigenous philosophical perspective was intimately tied to survival. In turn, survival was intimately connected to nature and what were viewed as precious gifts yielded up from land and resources. The intense philosophical view of nature grew out of the realization that mankind was almost totally dependent upon Nature's grace for survival. In the indigenous view, the position of mankind in the cosmos was one of relative insignificance. In varying degrees of complexity, rituals arose to remind tribal people that their existence was dependent upon nature (referred to by some indigenous groups as the

"Creator") and that a substantial degree of humility and very careful steward-ship was required in dealing with lands and resources. In keeping with the holistic view partially described above, indigenous people generally viewed their existence as part of the "web" of nature: in order to survive, tribal peo-ple were of the view that they had to be extremely careful about what they did to nature, its lands and resources such as water and wildlife.[122]

It is also well-known that self-discipline and humour played an important role in survival. Dickason comments that: "Although local conditions and subsistence bases ensured that peoples spread across Canada lead different lives within distinctive cultural frameworks at various levels of complexity, yet **they all practised severe self-discipline** to stand alone against an uncertain world, along with the acquisition of as much personal power as possible [Emphasis added]."[123] According to Dickason, "Humour was highly valued, and they thoroughly approved of anything that provoked laughter. This char-acteristic was one of the first to be reported of New World peoples…[as] Hwui Shan …[told] the Chinese court [in the fifteenth century]…."[124]

There were also some significant differences between the philosophical views of the various indigenous groups. The coastal groups of BC, for exam-ple, were more material-, status-, and rank-oriented than the plains Cree who were comparatively more philosophically egalitarian and less concerned with mere material possessions. The differences in worldviews and the cultural framework that emerged were unquestionably influenced by the availability of natural resources and whether the tribes fell into the "rank societies" or "band equalitarian societies" as discussed by Professor Tennant above.

Indigenous Economies

The nature of indigenous economies in North America depended on the avail-ability of natural resources from one region to another. Prior to contact with Europeans, most Aboriginal people in the northern half of North America were hunters, fishers, gatherers. The economy of those with access to the Pacific, Arctic and Atlantic coasts included substantial sea harvesting while those living on the St. Lawrence Valley and Great Lakes region engaged in agri-culture.[125] Where there was a surplus of product, it provided a basis for trade with and among Aboriginal nations. Agricultural producing tribes in southern Ontario and the St. Lawrence valley supplied corn and other products to those without an agricultural base, exchanging them for fish or furs.[126] The extensive commercial networks that also existed in areas such as the northwest coast of

British Columbia have already been discussed (where foodstuffs were transported between the coast and the interior). Such trade routes were also used to exchange technology. In British Columbia, potlatches were a central cultural institution that ensured the circulation of wealth in the coastal tribes.[127]

Contrary to the view that Aboriginal goods could be had for trinkets, Helen Meilleur, whose father ran the general store for the Hudson's Bay Company, points out that: "Without a doubt, in some parts of Canada, at some time, Indians exchanged valuable furs for trinkets, but not the Tsimshians. They were shrewd and sophisticated traders before the Russian American Company and the Hudson's Bay Company broke into their trade routes that wound back to time beyond our reckoning."[128]

In fact, the Tsimshian would often seek higher "retail" prices for their furs and would include the middleman's profit in the price the furs were offered to the fort. Furthermore, the Tsimshian Chiefs exacted a tribute that amounted to a tariff from other tribes who wanted to trade furs to the fort within their territory.[129] If there was resistance to paying the tribute it would be enforced by force of arms. Ms. Meilleur gives the following account of an actual bargaining session between her father and a Tsimshian trapper:

> Fur trading in Port Simpson was unlike the active vociferous bargaining that we associate with the marketplaces the world over. It consisted chiefly of supercharged silences. On this occasion the foxes were heaped on the counter and beside them a growing pile of ten dollar bills. On one side of the counter the Indian trapper stood immobile and on the other side, Dad paced. When the particular silence reached a climax that threatened to explode, Dad opened the till, withdrew another ten-dollar bill, placed it on top of the pile and closed the till. That launched a further silence, and so trading continued while the store clock clattered. After many openings and closings of the till the trapper nodded, picked up the stack of bills and then Dad shook his hand and conversed.[130]

LESSONS FROM ABORIGINAL ANCESTORS

There are several important traits and characteristics of pre-contact Aboriginal populations that ensured they survived in an extremely harsh environment. An attempt will be made to glean some understanding of these overarching traits and characteristics, in an effort to distil clues necessary to finding a solution and new directions to the problems of contemporary Aboriginal peoples.

> A leader takes people where they want to go. A great leader takes people
> where they don't necessarily want to go, but ought to be.
> ROSALYNN CARTER

So what we can conclude about Aboriginal societies prior to contact was
that they were **completely self-reliant**—a fact of life borne of necessity.
Tribes were fiercely self-reliant because they simply had to be—there was no
alternative that did not involve starvation and demise. One writer
comments:

> In the old times, once a person stepped outside of the camp circle, he was
> on his own and, if he wanted to survive, **he himself** had to make the right
> decisions. He had to stand on his own two feet because often there was no
> one else around **to force him** to do the right thing. One of the main rules
> he had to learn was **never depend upon anybody**. He had to depend on
> himself, whether on the warpath or hunting [Emphasis added].[131]

Self-reliance was backed (to paraphrase Professor Dickason) by the severe
self-discipline needed to stand alone against an uncertain world. There were
no government transfer payments, welfare cheques or employment insurance.
This stark reality ensured that a fundamental level of organization and understanding pervaded the very grassroots of the tribal structure

Interdependence, that is, mutual dependence by individual tribal members on each other, was also essential for survival. Without organizing and
working with the common purpose of mutual protection and obtaining
sustenance, starvation or domination by the next tribe always tempered conduct. So a key reason that the Aboriginal canoe of antiquity survived storms
was that mutual survival ensured a high degree of social cohesion and cooperation that kept the entire tribal "crew" in cultural synch and paddling in a
common direction.

Material survival and spiritual salvation depended on each tribal member
playing a predetermined role. One of the most important roles was that of
leader. Leadership meant assuming enormous responsibility. A high code of
moral conduct was essential to real leadership—otherwise, in their worldview, the tribe may "go out of tune with the cosmos" and this might bring
spiritual and potential material ruin to a tribe.

MYSTERY CHIEF

This painting was inspired by an old archival photo of a proud Kwakwaka'wakw chief of the Tsawatainuk Nation. The portrait captures the steely stare, resolve and conviction to take the right path in the face of an uncertain future. The Chief is wearing a loon and two-headed serpent head dress, and the two feathers he holds are symbols of peace and friendship. The original, an acrylic on 100% rag, was painted in 2000 and used by Indian Motorcyles of Los Angeles as a promotion for their new Chief motorbikes.

American philosopher Ralph Waldo Emerson underscored the general importance of leadership to any society with his comment: "leadership, must be had, and we are not allowed to be nice in choosing. We must fetch [prime] the pump with dirty water, if clean cannot be had."[132] Leadership required vision, a sense of where safety from a storm might be (as provided by Walking Eagle in Willie Dunn's song), and a carefully considered strategy for how to get there. Would going in one particular direction over another take your tribe into or out of a storm? The collective experience of a tribe, including the elders, was brought to bear through its leadership in making important decisions. Decisions did matter—often the difference between life and death hung in the balance of key tribal decisions.

Real leaders paid close attention to the state and condition of their people and provided good advice when needed. One writer elaborates on what this means:

"What kind of person did the old Indians regard as a good man, the 'wicasa waste'[?] [A]gain and again the answers would be like this: "He could always provide you good advice." They would say that if you were in trouble and didn't know what to do, this particular kind of good, wise person could always tell you the right thing to do. He could advise you wisely. The kind of knowledge possessed by such a person and admired by the people was not the kind of knowledge used for making money or becoming powerful or famous. The kind of knowledge he possessed was directed toward: a) understanding and getting along with people, and b) understanding the world around us.[133]

Mindset or Attitude

Another striking difference between pre-contact Aboriginal people and those of more recent vintage is the difference in attitude. This shift started initially with the decimation of resources on which tribes initially relied for sustenance, such as the bison of the northwestern plains. Since tribes were largely organized around the necessary activity of eking out material sustenance, taking that activity away either purposely or in the course of unfolding events, made it easier to control and "civilize" tribes by placing them on reserves.

Throughout the period of colonization, dependency shifted from the tribal unit to the government. This shift from self-reliance to government-reliance accelerated rapidly from the 1960s onward as a result of an increasingly generous baby boom social safety net. While this may seem a trite observation, it has had an enormous impact on how Aboriginal people view the solving of their problems. It will be difficult, if not impossible, to find a solution to Aboriginal problems if reliance for answers were placed entirely on the government, as has been the case in the past.

Cultural Cooperation or Synchronization

Tribal people developed cultures that reinforced the interdependence of tribal members on each other to a very high degree. What modern management gurus refer to as "teamwork" or "team players" was a characteristic consciously encouraged through games, rituals and the most fundamental of tribal practices. In the coastal Tsimshian language, Sm'algyax, the expression, "sayt k,ilim goot," which literally means "all tribal members are being of one heart, one path, and one mind," was intended to capture the importance of this notion. In other words, long experience had taught that successful survival required tribal members to be in tune with each other emotionally and socially. We have already seen that successfully executing the complex bison hunts, as by the Northwestern plains nomadic tribes, required enormous organization, cooperation and deliberate cultural synchronization. Similarly, successfully manoeuvring an open cedar dugout canoe through huge breakers in a Pacific coast storm requires split-second timing, anticipation and synchronization to avoid foundering and almost certain death. Aboriginal crews understood from experience how their immediate survival depended upon their being culturally attuned. Cooperation of the unit insured the survival of the individual.

SUMMARY

What emerges from looking back to the 9,600 years prior to contact is a picture of a metaphorical Aboriginal tribal canoe whose occupants were tribally and culturally synchronized to survive the vagaries of Nature. Self-reliance, self-discipline, complete interdependence, teamwork and moral leadership ensured the Aboriginal canoe weathered stormy weather. These are fundamental elements key to the past well-being of Aboriginal people. In the search for practical solutions to problems confronting indigenous peoples today, it is important to keep these inherent traits and strengths in mind.

5

THE SECOND WAVE:
AT SEA IN THE COLONIAL STORM

"Brothers: you have talked to us about concessions. It appears strange that you expect any from us, who have been defending our just rights against your invasions. We want peace. Restore to us our country, and we shall be enemies no longer. ...

"Brothers: we desire you to consider that our only demand is the peaceable possession of a small part of our once great country. Look back and view the lands from whence we have been driven to this spot. We can retreat no farther, because the country behind hardly affords food for its present inhabitants; and we have therefore resolved to leave our bones in this small space to which we now are consigned."

THAYENDANEGEA (JOSEPH BRANT), Mohawk Chief [134]

IMPACT OF CONTACT

The Aboriginal canoe of antiquity began to lose its way some time after contact with Europeans. This chapter will examine exactly how the flourishing indigenous societies were to encounter and subsequently founder on a submerged shoal of colonialism. Aboriginal cultures and languages were targeted at a time when indigenous societies were completely decimated by disease introduced by Europeans to which they had no natural immunity. The tools of the colonial interests were law and policy. This machinery of colonial government was wielded with the single-minded purpose of dismantling and assimilating the once-vigorous and ancient societies and cultures. While the intention of assimilation was an unmitigated disaster, the assault on Aboriginal languages, governments, and culture was much more successful in achieving its ends.

An old and respected philosopher acquaintance used to say, "When a culture falls apart, booze seeps into its cracks." It was his way of summarizing the collision between European and indigenous cultures the world over. "Booze," a subject he knew perhaps too intimately, was his way of describing the host of social pathologies, confusion, and dysfunction that afflict indigenous people as a result of the impact of contact with Europeans. The consequences of such a conflict have been catastrophic. The prevailing assumption at the time colonization took place was that indigenous cultures were simply inferior. It was thought that the best way to deal with the indigenous peoples was to systematically assimilate succeeding generations in the hopes of obliterating what were perceived to be backward cultures of limited value. Assimilation—that is, the imposition of European customs and values on indigenous peoples—became the fundamental objective of European and colonial governments. Indigenous people throughout the world were the hapless recipients of the fallout of such attitudes and policies.

Colonization

> "I am ready. I do not wish to be put in irons. Let me be free. I have given away my life. It is gone like that [with the wave of his hand]. I would not take it back. It is gone."
>
> RED BIRD, Chief of the Winnebago (*rather than precipitate a hopeless struggle for his tribe, he sacrificed his personal freedom by giving himself up to colonial authorities.*)[135]

While colonial attitudes differed somewhat from nation to nation, their impacts have largely wrought similar destruction on the Aboriginal populations that were contacted.

In North America, colonial attitudes varied towards tribes, at times running the gamut from war allies, partners in trade, to an impediment to progress that had to be exterminated. Andrew Armitage, an author, and associate professor and director of the School of Social Work at the University of Victoria, comments: "Race relations between Aboriginal and European peoples were not conducted on an equal and respectful basis once the latter gained the unquestioned dominance. At that point they became subsumed within the numerous relationships existing between Britain and its colonies. For European settlers, the colonial era ended in the nineteenth century with the establishment of self-government."[136] Notwithstanding the fact that the colonial era ended with the formation of Canada, the policies of the colonial period continue to be applied today in the modern state.

GAAX VILLAGE

This is the village of *gaax* (raven). Are they ravens or are they people?

It does not matter if you are *gaax*. If you enter this village, pay attention! *Gaax* will be looking to trick or tease you.

At first tribes were considered essential in the execution of the fur trade and for providing food supplies to early colonialists. As colonial settlements grew and hostilities erupted with various groups over land, colonial attitudes changed. Armitage comments further:

> The first period [of colonialism] was mercantilist, and it began with a primary interest in the extraction of wealth. This interest expanded to include the establishment of settlements and the direct exploitation of the resources of the colonial territories. The second was acquisitive, and competition among colonial powers was a major factor. Territory was taken not because it was considered valuable but to prevent it being taken by another European power. Commercial exploitation, settlement, and missionary activity followed acquisition. The pre-eminence of British naval power in the nineteenth century ensured that Britain acquired more territory than any other European power.[137]

For the British Empire, the early nineteenth century was not only a period of major colonial expansion, but also a period of major social reform. Armitage suggests: "The ideals of both [colonial expansion and social reform]…were interrelated…. In 1834 the House of Commons received the royal commission report on the Poor Law…[which subsequently] provided fundamental principles of British policy and practice in relation to the indigent."[138] Later in 1835, the House of Commons appointed a select committee on Aborigines. The subsequent 1837 report of this committee shared ideals and methods with the earlier report which had been produced on the Poor Law in relation to how best to deal with Aboriginal populations in countries which the British Empire had colonized.[139] Armitage notes: "Both reports dealt with policies concerning [what was understood at the time to be] the 'correct' way to deal with a population that operated outside the accepted economic structure and which might become a source of disorder."[140] Such policies included:[141]

- The assertion of control, that is to say, the assumption that an orderly, managed world was needed and that Britain was to provide it—both at home and overseas;
- An assumption that the purpose of the policy was to bring "outsiders" whether [Britain's] poor or Aboriginals, within the established institutions of British society and, particularly, the wage economy (albeit at the level of the lowest paid independent laborer);

- A commitment to a legal and regulatory process anchored in separate law for those outside mainstream society, pending their full citizenship;
- Appointment of "protectors" (who could provide Aboriginal peoples with restricted status under the law and subject them to summary discipline) and of "overseers" (who could do the same for paupers);
- Special recognition for the situation of children, who were considered particularly open to change, education, and salvation;
- Special recognition of the elderly, for whom change seemed unlikely;
- A recognized place for organized Christianity as an essential element of producing citizens: and
- An obligation to provide orderly reports on the progress of the administration and the welfare of Aboriginal peoples and/or paupers.

These principles gradually found their way into the administration of Aboriginal people in Canada and are still recognizable in current government policy.

On the one hand, while Victorians viewed what came to be known as the Doctrine of Assimilation (as it evolved in Canada) as an enlightened new direction in social policy, it was subsequently criticized as being based on four dehumanizing and incorrect ideas about Aboriginal peoples. These assumptions were that:[142]

- Aboriginals were inferior peoples;
- Aboriginal peoples were unable to govern themselves and that colonial and Canadian authorities knew best how to protect their well-being;
- the special relationship of respect and sharing that was enshrined in treaties was an historical anomaly with no more force and meaning; and
- European ideas about progress and development were self-evidently correct and could be imposed on Aboriginal people without reference to any other values and opinions—let alone rights they might possess.

Regrettably, most Aboriginal people would recognize how such principles have been expressed in the context of the Canadian experience. Remnants of the paternalistic attitude that stemmed from these early ideas of social reform are still present in the current legal and regulatory regime governing Aboriginal people in Canada.

The strictest law sometimes becomes the severest injustice.
BENJAMIN FRANKLIN

Prior to Confederation, the tenor of Indian policy in Canada was established by the Royal Proclamation of 1763 and a variety of colonial ordinances.[143] The Royal Proclamation of 1763 is a key document in the relationship that was to develop between Aboriginal and non-Aboriginal people. Firstly, it summarized the rules governing British dealings with Aboriginal people—particularly in relation to how land was to be acquired (i.e., by fair dealing, by treaty or purchase by the Crown). Secondly, the Royal Proclamation portrayed Indian nations as autonomous political entities, living under the protection of the Crown, but retaining their own internal political authority.

In Canada, Confederation, which was declared in 1867, was viewed as a new partnership between English and French colonists to manage lands and resources north of the 49th parallel. It was negotiated without reference to the Aboriginal nations (the first partners of both the French and English). Indeed (consistent with the early policy of the British government), the newly-elected Prime Minister of Canada, John A. McDonald, announced that it would be his government's goal to "do away with the tribal system," and assimilate Indian people in all respects with the inhabitants of the Dominion."[144]

Since Confederation, Indians in Canada have had a special constitutional status since they represent the only ethnic group in Canada for which exclusive federal authority over their matters is constitutionally mandated. The essence of the British Empire's social reform and policy outcomes (resulting from the earlier Royal Commission Report on the Poor Law and select committee report on Aborigines) were essentially applied to the "backward" Indians of Canada to ensure that they "operated within the accepted economic structure and did not become a source of disorder." Section 91(24) of the Constitution Act, 1867 (also known as the "BNA Act") confers upon the federal Parliament the power to legislate on the subject of "Indians, and Lands reserved for the Indians."[145] The federal government has exercised its authority under section 91(24) through the *Indian Act*.[146] The *Indian Act* itself has its roots in the pre-Confederation legislation of the Province of Canada and the enactments of the Province of Upper Canada.[147]

The *Indian Act* of 1876 essentially set up Indian communities as rural municipalities with simple governmental structures. It effectively isolated

Aboriginal people on reserve lands outside the mainstream society and made it much easier to control these populations. Its intent was to replace traditional Aboriginal governments with band councils with comparatively insignificant powers, to take control of valuable resources located on reserves, to take charge of reserve finances, to impose what was an unfamiliar system of land tenure, and to apply non-Aboriginal concepts of marriage and parenting.[148]

Achieving "Social Reform" through Law and Policy

> Every reform, however necessary, will by weak minds be carried to an excess, that itself will need reforming.
> SAMUEL TAYLOR COLERIDGE

From the government's perspective, the *Indian Act* was the primary legal instrument of its assimilationist policy—a policy designed to bring Indians in Canada into "full citizenship." It was thought, however, that Indians had to be civilized first by clustering them on reserves and giving various religious denominations an opportunity to save their "savage" souls. As previously pointed out, the Act basically set up a separate reserve system with a rural system of municipal government. The recent Royal Commission Report points out that colonial and Canadian governments established reserves of land for Aboriginal people—usually of inadequate size and resources—with or without treaty agreements.[149] The system of establishing reserves began in 1637, with a Jesuit settlement at Sillery in New France. Though reserves were designed supposedly to protect Aboriginal people, they operated instead, largely to continue to isolate and impoverish them.[150] The fundamental purpose of assimilating Aboriginal people remained constant through various incarnations of the *Indian Act* subsequently passed.[151]

One of the first impacts of related legislation struck a crippling blow to the Aboriginals and the relationship to their lands. In an effort to encourage European immigration to Canada, colonial and provincial governments pursued a policy of land pre-emptions or grants. In British Columbia, a European male over the age of eighteen could simply occupy 320 acres of land and ultimately claim legal title to it.[152] This could be done regardless of pre-existing Aboriginal rights to such lands (as had been acknowledged previously by the British Crown in North America through the Royal Proclamation of 1763). The federal *Indian Act* of 1876 specifically prohibited

Indians from similarly acquiring or pre-empting lands in Manitoba or the Northwest Territories.[153]

This impairment was compounded further by federal amendments to the *Indian Act* in 1927. These changes made it illegal for an Indian or Indian Nation to retain a lawyer to advance their claims to land, or even with the intention of retaining a lawyer.[154] Anyone convicted of this offence could be imprisoned. Finally, it should be pointed out that following the infamous McKenna-McBride Commission of 1916, whose mandate was to resolve questions about the nature and extent of Indian reserves in BC, the Federal and Provincial governments passed legislation removing extensive tracts of valuable land from many reserves in the province. This was done without approval of the Aboriginal governments, and until recently without compensation, and was contrary to express provisions of the *Indian Act* that required a surrender in order to alienate reserve lands.

The government's assault on Aboriginal culture and customs focused on the potlatch and practices of the longhouse in British Columbia. The longhouse was the heart of coastal Indian government, spiritual activity and focal point of the community. Almost every major event of community importance took place in the longhouse: the passing of laws, the giving of names, spiritual ceremonies and dancing. One of the most fundamental ceremonies of the longhouse was the potlatch. Through the ritual of the potlatch, the value systems by which coastal Aboriginal societies defined themselves were reinforced. Amongst other central functions, the potlatch served to legitimize political rank and authority. Additionally, the potlatch served the most important function of validating the rightful possession of prestige and the use of chiefly power and influence.[155] From 1880 to 1951, the *Indian Act* outlawed the potlatch and sacred dancing under the threat of a penalty of imprisonment for a two to six month period.[156] The 1927 *Indian Act* was even more prohibitive and invasive in its efforts to increase the powers of federal officials over the lives of Indian people.[157]

In 1885, the Sun Dance, central to the cultures of the prairie Aboriginal nations, was similarly outlawed. Again, participation was a criminal offence. In efforts to avoid criminal prosecution for seeking to preserve traditional political power, and to follow traditional religious practices, Aboriginal communities were forced to take the potlatch and sacred dance rituals to secluded locations. Even though these measures were taken, on occasions elders were still subsequently arrested and imprisoned for their participation in what were perceived to be heathen rituals that destabilized assimilation efforts.

As noted above, once such political institutions and traditional forms of Aboriginal government were outlawed, the federal government sought to impose its own form of Band Council government through the *Indian Act*. Former Chief of the Squamish Nation, Joe Mathias, commented: "The Band Council system…functioned on European perceptions of what constituted proper government. It was a system of government that had little meaning in Indian communities. Moreover, Band Councils were left with little or no ability to control the destiny of Indian political affairs. The jurisdiction of Band Councils was superficial. No substantive powers rested with these councils and any decisions made were subject to the ultimate approval of the Minister of Indian Affairs."[158] It is also worth noting that *Indian Acts* from the 1880's until the present have restrictively limited how band councils could allocate their own monies and resources.[159]

In addition to not having any real independent form of governmental power, Aboriginal people were not permitted participation in the mainstream political process since they were not allowed to vote. It was not until 1960 that Indians were allowed to vote in federal elections in Canada. In fact, every federal Elections Act up to and including the *Canada Elections Act* of 1952, specifically disqualified Indians from voting.[160] In British Columbia, Municipal Elections Acts up to and including the *Municipal Election Act* of 1948[161] and the *Provincial Elections Act* up to 1949[162] prohibited Indians (as well as Chinese and Japanese) from voting in municipal or provincial elections. In effect, "Indian Nations were denied the right and the means to function with any degree of independence and self-reliance, and at the same time, prohibited from functioning in the larger society with the rights and powers enjoyed by non-Indians."[163]

The government's assimilationist solution to the problem (of not being able to vote) was enfranchisement, a process under the *Indian Act* where Indians could give up their legal status as Indians and, in effect, become non-Indians by law. In a further effort to enforce assimilation on Aboriginal people, the 1880 version of the *Indian Act* provided for the enfranchisement of any Indian who obtained a university degree and became a lawyer, priest or minister.[164] In other words, if an Indian wanted a higher education or to pursue a professional calling, he had legally to become a non-Indian to do so. A further incentive for an Indian to become so enfranchised was the promise of the reward by Indian Affairs of a grant of land from the band's reserves.

While all of these measures were being imposed, a consistent effort was being focused on assimilating Aboriginal children. In 1849, the first of what would become a network of residential schools for Aboriginal children was opened in Alderville, Ontario. Residential schools continued until the late 1960s in Canada. In keeping with the initial social reform policy of the early nineteenth century British Empire, residential schools were generally entrusted to the administration and management of various Christian religious denominations. Church and government leaders of the time had come to the conclusion that the problem (as they saw it) of Aboriginal independence and "savagery" could be resolved by taking children from their families at an early age and instilling the ways of the dominant society during eight or nine years of residential schooling far from home. Attendance at such schools was compulsory. Aboriginal languages, customs, and habits of mind were often violently suppressed.

The critical kinship bonds examined previously in relation to pre-contact Aboriginal societies were bent and broken with disastrous results—particularly those between Aboriginal children and their families and nations. As recent lawsuits (against the churches that ran such schools and the federal government) reveal, Aboriginal children were often subjected to unspeakable humiliation, and physical and sexual abuse. Children were beaten for speaking their Aboriginal languages and practicing their traditions. A deliberate effort was made to make Aboriginal people feel ashamed of their Aboriginalness. To ensure attendance at residential schools, Indian children refusing to attend were prohibited from alternatively attending a provincial school near their own community. Given the importance of family to most Aboriginal cultures and the treatment they received at such schools, the devastating subsequent social dysfunction resulting from this tragic experiment should really be of no surprise to anyone.

Disease

As colonization spread across North America, tribes fell victim to a host of diseases which drastically reduced the population. Aboriginal people had to contend with the introduction of European diseases for which they had no natural immunity such as small pox, whooping cough, venereal disease, influenza, bubonic plague, measles, and yellow fever. Due to the manner in which settlement occurred in North America, European diseases were slower in appearing on the west coast than on the east coast.[165]

The Canadian pre-contact population that was estimated to be between 500,000 to over 2 million[166] fell to a low in 1871 of approximately 100,000.[167] By 1900, the population of all Indians in North America was below 1 million from one pre-contact estimate of 18 million. In some cases, diseases decimated up to 93 percent of the population.[168] To put this loss into perspective, if you assume the current North American population (i.e. Canada and the United States) is 330 million, a similar population decline at present would leave approximately 20 million people alive.

Some regions of the hemisphere were particularly hammered and had population drops of 95 percent.[169] In British Columbia, the population fell from one estimate of 500,000[170] and reached its nadir in 1929 when it touched 22,605.[171] The introduction of diseases was largely accidental, but there were some episodes of deliberate contamination or withholding of inoculations in what may perhaps best be described as an early use of natural weapons as a form of biological warfare.

SUMMARY

Over the period of the colonial storm, what Europeans effectively did was create a gulf between indigenous people and their past—a past which, over this period, became a distant world. In many ways the Aboriginal canoe was set adrift from everything that had made them unique: their deeply-ingrained traits that allowed them to survive for millennia, their languages and intricate cultural practices, and the variations of profound spirituality by which they lived their lives.

We have seen that colonial expansion across North America was largely dominated by the British Empire which enforced its claims through the superiority of its navy. The policies and legislation that emerged in Canada resulted from the ideas of social reform born out of the ethnocentric vim and vigour of the Victorian era. It was thought that the best way to civilize Aboriginal populations that operated outside the accepted economic structure of the time was through a systematic process of assimilation so that they would fit into the emerging industrial society and market economy. These early notions of social reform in Britain largely coloured how Aboriginal people would subsequently be treated as separate and distinct from the mainstream society in Canada.

The Royal Proclamation of 1763 and various colonial ordinances set the pre-Confederation stage as to how Aboriginal people would be dealt with in Canada. Following Confederation, the *Indian Act* and related regulations were to become the primary legislative tool whose ultimate purpose was the social re-engineering of Canadian Indians into brown-skinned white men.

The *Indian Act* purposely undermined traditional forms of Aboriginal government and replaced those with a government that had little jurisdiction or substantive powers. The act set up reserves that would serve to isolate the "Indian problem" and make it easier to control Indians for the larger purpose of assimilation. In addition to being the primary instrument in outlawing Aboriginal forms of government, the Act also served as the principal means of attacking and banning central Aboriginal traditions, customs, dances and forms of culture. Finally, the act and related legislation took specific aim at undermining the Aboriginal relationship with its traditional land base. It did this by, amongst other things, making it illegal (under threat of imprisonment) for an Indian to retain a lawyer with the intention of advancing their claims to land or even the intention of retaining a lawyer for this purpose.

The legislative assault was combined with the government and church effort focused on assimilating Aboriginal children by requiring mandatory attendance at residential schools. All this took place during a time when Indians could not vote in federal, provincial or municipal elections. To add further insult to the assimilationist injury, Indians were barred from pursuing university degrees or a professional calling without first becoming legally non-Indian through a process of enfranchisement. Aboriginal people had to endure such an onslaught at a time in their history when they were enormously weakened by drastic population decline due to the ravages of disease.

In the final analysis, what may have looked to Victorians like an enlightened new direction in social reform, was, in its execution in Canada, a tragedy of Homeric proportions. Those early pioneers that departed in their canoe 10,000 years ago unwittingly ran into the "perfect" colonial storm of cultural destruction. Aboriginal cultures were deliberately targeted and systematically dismantled at a time when they were weakest, having been decimated by communicable disease to which they had no natural immunity. While the intentions of subsequent generations of colonial and Canadian governments may have been good, Aboriginal people know, from several hundred years of bad experience, the place to which the road paved with good intentions has led.

Given this history and the dismal results of the early efforts at assimilation, it should not be surprising that Aboriginal people are highly suspicious of government attempts to promote a further agenda of assimilation. In 1969 the federal Liberal government of the time was not prepared for the vociferous and emotional opposition to their White Paper. This was self-described at the time as a "breath-taking governmental recipe for equality." It was intended by the then-Trudeau government (that rejected the concept of Aboriginal rights at the time) to simply assimilate Aboriginal people into mainstream society by making them legally like all other Canadians with no special status. The proposal suggested terminating the legal distinction between Indians and the rest of society, repealing the *Indian Act*, subjecting Indians to all provincial laws and phasing out the Department of Indian Affairs over a period of years. Sounds good on paper, right?

In light of the harm caused by the *Indian Act* and other assimilationist legislation and policies, it might have been expected that Indians would welcome the White Paper. What happened, however, was that there was very little consultation with Indian groups in the formulation of the White Paper, and Indians were highly suspicious about having another "white solution" to the "Indian Problem" crammed down their throats. Given the opposition that arose, the government retracted the White Paper in 1971. In retrospect, the White Paper became what was perceived to be yet another "breath-taking" example of governmental hubris and stupidity.

This history is provided in order to illustrate why the focus on assimilation by successive governments has become, for many, sadly confused with the notion of economic integration. This question and its implications will be the subject of more detailed exploration in relation to providing solutions to the current mess.

{3}

IMPACTS OF THE THIRD WAVE:
CULTURES AND COMMUNITIES IN DISARRAY

6

SOCIAL IMPACTS OF THE WELFARE TRAP

Years ago our people were self-reliant…[from] trapping and…whatever nature was able to provide us. Our life was hard… But we lived like men. Then the government came and offered welfare to our people…it was as if they had cut our throats. [Who]… would go out to work or trap and face hardships of making a living when all he had to do was sit at home and receive the food, and all he needed to live? The government had laid a trap for us, for they knew once we accepted welfare they would have us where they wanted us.[172]

HAROLD CARDINAL, *The Unjust Society*

GENERAL

For 9,600 years, the mythical Aboriginal canoe has journeyed through time, memory and culture. Its cargo has been the vigorous indigenous societies of a more dignified era, fiercely independent and self-sustaining. We have also witnessed the last 400 or so years, where the Aboriginal canoe has unwittingly navigated into a powerful storm of poverty, dysfunction and nauseating dependency. Given the statistics below, it is not surprising the financial relationship between Aboriginal people and mainstream societies has been conceptualized primarily as a form of welfare, determined by the need of the former.[173]

According to a recent UN report, Canada's high ranking on the United Nations' human development scale would dramatically drop from 7th to 48th (out of 174 countries) if the country were judged solely on the economic and social well-being of its First Nations people. According to the report: "Poverty, infant mortality, unemployment, morbidity, suicide, criminal detention, children on welfare, women victims of abuse, child prostitution, are all much higher among Aboriginal people than in any other sector of Canadian society."[174]

There appears to be no easy way out of this violent tempest—a period of chaos that has resulted in the modern day tragedy of the "welfare trap." In using this term, I am of the view that: "…Aboriginal welfare dependency is [not] limited to individual reliance on social assistance. But the dependency also extends to Aboriginal governments, which, with few exceptions, are financially dependent on transfers from the federal government."[175] Together, these serve to reinforce dependency and have directly resulted in a complex web of social and political pathologies. The welfare trap has created an artificial environment which has led to a dependency mindset that has slowly percolated into indigenous psyches over many generations.

In relation to discussing the welfare trap, there are several points that need to be made at the outset. Firstly, the mindset and terrible social pathologies that afflict Aboriginal people are not because they are Aboriginal, it is because they have been forced into a circumstance that creates dependency no matter what your race happens to be. Such dependency has been observed equally in non-Aboriginal populations where circumstances are comparable. In an article titled "Atlantic Canada's dole rots the soul," Brian Lee Crowley explains: "Each year they [non-Aboriginal maritime workers] worked briefly in a 'seasonal' job and then arranged to get laid off, drew EI, and spent the rest of the year doing their 'crafts', which they then sold (under the table of course!) …So now you know: The excess of bad crafts is your tax dollars at work."[176] He goes on to cite other examples of subsidization and concludes that "A cardinal rule of economics says if you subsidize something [such as seasonal work], you will get more of it."[177] The reason I mention this example is because the attitude of the non-Aboriginal Atlantic population discussed has similarly shifted to a dependency mindset.

Secondly, while Aboriginal people are not responsible for the conditions that have created the welfare trap, much of the currently prevailing mindset and the actions of the "Indian Industry" and a handful of leaders are contributing to keep Aboriginal people caught in the trap. Lastly, even if there were some perverse reason to want to preserve this condition, it should be equally clear from the previous discussion (in relation to the demographic tsunami) that Canada cannot financially afford to sustain the welfare trap—real reform has to be explored immediately.

While the Aboriginal canoe has been caught in the storm, there is also reason to lament the loss of vision of the ancient indigenous leaders, whose

GAAX AND 'NEEXT ASCEND

Traditional design of *gaax* (raven) and *'neext* (orca) rising in the sky above a salmon in the ocean.

time-honoured judgment had provided safe passage for millennia. As our ancestors were to learn, however, the colonial storm they encountered was not within their long experience and they would not have known what to expect. But we should also lament that, in the midst of this crisis, one of the only solutions repeatedly advanced by many contemporary Aboriginal leaders has been to put their hands out for more government money. Surely they should be able to see that this does little to solve the problem, may actually exacerbate existing pathologies, and instead reinforces existing dependency. For sure this approach will never lead to a solution to the current problems. What point is there in applying a small band-aid to a massive open wound when a more serious long-term healing is required?

To those that might defend the status quo, I would suggest they look carefully at the wholesale misery and poverty that the welfare trap is delivering now. The current statistics speak eloquently to the massive social dysfunction that is the result. These statistics tell of a situation so horrific that ordinary Canadians could not imagine the suffering of Aboriginal children on a daily basis. They clearly paint a picture of reserves across Canada that are, in many respects, the inner city ghettoes of America. One writer comments that "If apartheid were measured by results rather than intent, we would have it [on reserves today in Canada]."[178]

Some might argue that we are victims of a situation that is not of our creation. On the one hand, this is a true statement. There is, however, no reason to follow an unwise course particularly when it is so blatantly damaging to our own self-interest. We have to shake off the mantle of apathy that has descended on us. We have to do something different to what is being done because the status quo simply is not working. The welfare trap will never lead to basic human fulfillment or happiness, a state of existence that at one time did not cost a cent.

As with Alice in Wonderland, Aboriginal people have come to a crucial fork in the road of their history and need to make a decision:

> 'Cheshire Puss,'... [Alice] began, rather timidly... 'Would you tell me, please, which way I ought to go from here?'
> 'That depends a good deal on where you want to get to,' said the Cat.
> 'I don't much care where—' said Alice.
> 'Then it doesn't matter which way you go,' said the Cat.[179]

Aboriginal people are in a little better position than Alice though. We know that the welfare trap is one path we shouldn't continue to take. The

system of welfare and transfer payments have literally rotted the souls of many, and damaged their families beyond measure. Unlike Alice, however, it does matter which path we take. We must have the courage to make our own decisions. If Aboriginal people do not take charge of their own destiny now, future generations may be forced by the coming demographic tsunami on
a course that may once again not suit, and that will continue to harm their real interests.

A GOVERNMENT HISTORY OF ENCOURAGING DEPENDENCY

" ...Whatsoever a man soweth, that shall he also reap."
GALATIANS 6:7

We have seen how the Department of Indian and Northern Affairs Canada (INAC) assumed the detailed administration and control of Aboriginal lives and assets. In doing this, they often actively promoted welfare dependency. This has been done despite their fiduciary obligation in relation to First Nations people (i.e., their legally enforceable duty to act in the best Aboriginal interests). The reality in practice was often something far different. While the modern bureaucracy is at least paying lip-service to creating self-reliance, the historical record is replete with examples of INAC actively discouraging self-reliance and promoting welfare dependency. The approach taken by INAC is perhaps a good example of American economist Milton Friedman's dictum that "Nothing is so permanent as a temporary government program."

In an excellent book, *From Ploughs to Welfare*, Helen Buckley chronicles how federal neglect and discrimination led directly to Aboriginal poverty in the prairies following the western treaties in the 1870s.[180] At the time, many of the prairie Indian bands were strongly interested in agriculture and made some impressive starts—breaking sod, planting crops, experimenting with the latest farming techniques, and even winning prizes at agricultural fairs. Within a few years though, INAC had begun to systematically destroy their self-sufficiency. The scythes and wooden ploughs received as treaty payments soon became obsolete, and from that point onward the Indians were deliberately kept at a permanent disadvantage compared to their white farming neighbors.

Geoffrey York, a journalist who reviewed the book for *The Globe and Mail*, summarized what resulted as follows:

Federal agents took control of every aspect of the Indian reserves, often leasing out the best land at cheap rents to local white farmers, and requiring the Indians to get an official permit if they wanted to sell grain, buy cattle, or even to leave the reserve for a day. At a time when most settlers were getting 160 acres of land, the government had a policy of limiting the Indian families to a peasant-sized allotment of 40 acres each. While the white settlers were borrowing money from the banks to expand their operations, Indians could not legally mortgage their land. In the early years of the 20th century, much of the best land on Indian reserves was expropriated and given to nearby towns and cities.... Buckley... shows that the federal government helped to stimulate the economic development of non-native businesses on the prairies, while encouraging Indians to become dependent on welfare and social assistance. Only a tiny percentage of the Indian Affairs budget was spent on economic development; the vast majority of the federal money went to keeping Aboriginal people on the welfare rolls. Their schools were neglected, while millions of dollars were spent on useless manpower courses and temporary make-work projects that never led to permanent jobs. Even in the 1980s and 1990s, less than 5 percent of the department's budget was spent on economic development, while a growing percentage (as much as 27 percent) was spent on welfare.[181]

According to Chief Ruben Cantin of the Wabigoon First Nation, the self-reliance of his community members was similarly dashed when the province of Ontario flooded the forest areas that they traditionally worked: "Back then, most adult band members worked in the woods, usually cutting trees for local mills. Then in the 1960s, the government announced a new series of social initiatives, including income supplements, for every one on the reserve. 'The pride that was there to be self-sufficient, was all of a sudden taken away by these programs,' Cantin says."[182] Similarly, the Inuit: "Once shrewd hunters...were encouraged to stay home and collect welfare. They then were sold snowmobiles and the provincial government ordered the community's entire population of sled dogs slaughtered, claiming there was not enough food to go around."[183]

While total dependency has been sown by federal policy, the grim spectre of social pathologies is what Aboriginal people are reaping today. No matter what your race: "…the psychological effect on people from long-term dependence on transfer income is damaging. A 1992 report on a New Brunswick welfare reform program…appropriately starts by quoting a line from the famous *québécois* singer, Felix Leclerc: 'The best way to kill a man is to pay him to do nothing.' Among men, particularly, long-term welfare induces a loss of self-respect, increased rates of depression, and a tendency toward self-destructive activities (such as substance abuse and family violence)."[184] Many of the policies of the federal government, even though well-intentioned, continue to kill Aboriginal people by paying them to do nothing—the statistics below speak for themselves.

A major sociological study has concluded further that: "… the main problem is that lack of productive employment has undermined traditional role and status relationships, especially for male members, most of whom have lost their important role of food providers for their family or kin group. They are denied an opportunity to validate their self-worth by contributing to the survival and well-being of their family and community through work. The idleness of unemployment has devastated morale and undermined Indian cultures. This, in turn, has bred extraordinary levels of social pathologies [which are clearly exhibited in the following statistics]."[185]

So what are the social pathologies? Once again we must face the harsh reality that, no matter how horrific they appear, the statistics really provide only a remote glimpse of the real day-to-day conditions confronting many Aboriginal people in Canada. It is important to understand these though, because the Aboriginal condition has to be assessed realistically if solutions are to be found.

IMPACT ON YOUTH AND WOMEN

The impact of the welfare trap is most harsh on Aboriginal children, youth, and women.

Current best estimates are that there are between 22,500 and 28,000 Aboriginal children in the child welfare system (this is three times the highest enrolment figures of residential school in the 1940s).[186] Notwithstanding the fact that Aboriginal people represent 3.3 percent of the population in Canada, the low figure (22,500) represents an astonishing 30 percent of the total number of children in welfare care in Canada![187] The chances of a First Nations child going into child welfare care are 1 in 17 versus 1 in 200 for non-Aboriginal children.[188] It appears that the numbers of First Nations children entering into child care is rising at a tragic rate. According to recent data, the number of First Nations children resident on reserve in welfare care increased by a shocking *71.5 percent* nationally between 1995–2001.[189]

Poverty is also an enormous problem for Aboriginal youth and children. A 1999 report in the Vancouver area indicated that, of 4,300 Aboriginal children aged 0–6 years, fully 80 percent of them live in poverty.[190] A 2003 report card on poverty in Canada (Campaign 2000) reported further that 41 percent of Aboriginal children in off-reserve communities are living in poverty.[191] Furthermore: "In a document released by the First Nations Child and Family Caring Society of Canada (Blackstock et al, 2004), [it was revealed that] First Nations children die from injuries at disproportionate rates. The mortality rate from injury for First Nations infants is four times higher than non-Aboriginal infants and five times higher for First Nations preschoolers."[192]

In 1999 the suicide rate of Aboriginal people in general was 2.1 times the general population's. The suicide rates for youth and young adults are the most disturbing. First Nations males between 15 to 24 and 25 to 39 have a suicide rate that is an incredible five and four times the general Canadian rate, respectively. The situation is even worse for young First Nations women where the rates for females aged 15–24 and 25–39 are an intolerable eight and five times the general Canadian rate, respectively.[193]

First Nations Youth Aged 15–24 Suicide Rate vs Total Population

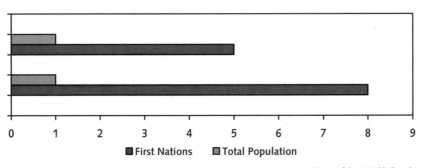

■ First Nations ▫ Total Population

Source of data: Health Canada

A 1991 survey reported that 73 and 59 percent of First Nations respondents said alcohol and drug abuse, respectively, was a problem in their communities. Twenty percent of Aboriginal youth reported that they have used solvents with 33 percent of those users under the age of 15.[194] Anecdotal reports suggest further that Aboriginal populations are rife with serious substance abuse problems with cheap and widely available drug abuse and addiction to such drugs as crystal meth and crack cocaine.

In relation to diseases, the following table sets out how many times higher the incidence of each disease is for the First Nations population. Diabetes, a disease virtually unknown amongst Aboriginal people fifty years ago, is now so prevalent it is considered an epidemic, with rates continuing to increase (again there appears higher rates for on-reserve as opposed to off-reserve populations).[195]

Times Higher Incidence of First Nations Disease vs Total Population

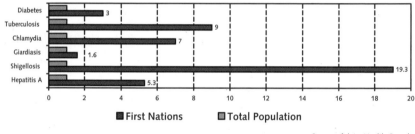

Source of data: Health Canada

The actual reliance on welfare or social assistance for the various Aboriginal groups is set out in the chart below (5 times higher than the mainstream on reserves).[196]

Aboriginal Welfare Rates vs Non-Aboriginal

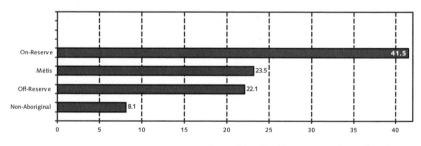

Source of data: Royal Commission on Aboriginal Peoples Report

The Aboriginal rate of incarceration is about 8 times that of non-Aboriginals. This situation has prompted the ordinarily ultra-conservative Supreme Court of Canada in a 1999 judgment to comment that this state of affairs constitutes a national disgrace since: a male treaty Indian is 25 times as likely to be admitted to a provincial jail than a non-native, and a female treaty Indian is 131 times as likely. This reality, the court said, is 'so stark and appalling that the magnitude of the problem can be neither understood nor interpreted away.'"[197] Information from Correctional Service Canada reveals that even though Aboriginal peoples account for about 3 percent of the Canadian population, they account for 18 percent of the incarcerated federal population. In the prairie region this level reaches 50–60 percent in some institutions (where the Aboriginal population represents a mere 14 percent of the population by comparison in those provinces).[198] Also, according to another report, the proportion of convicted Aboriginal sex offenders comprise a disproportionate 20–25 percent of the total number in Canada.[199]

The median incomes for Aboriginal people are set out in the table below. The Aboriginal population has a median income that is about $10,000 dollars less or about half of the median income for the non-Aboriginal population.[200]

Median Income for the Aboriginal and Non-Aboriginal Population (15 Years+)

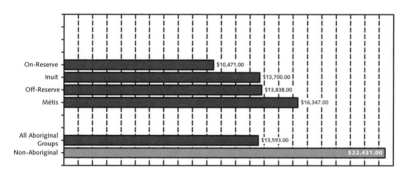

Source of data: Treasury Board of Canada Secretariat

Sadly, I could go on and on with more statistics that would simply provide more tragic colours to a painting of despair and poverty. The point I seek to make though, is that the situation is desperate and action needs to be taken immediately. The reasons for the welfare trap, and how this affected Aboriginal individuals and governments must be honestly examined by all parties in the cold light of day. Before solutions can be sought, we have to know what the problems are. Aboriginal people must take ownership of those problems and begin to roll up their sleeves and do something about it.

A LOOMING AMERICAN CRISIS

A similar situation exists in the United States, where rapidly growing Native and African American, as well as Hispanic, populations are heavily reliant on government entitlement programs and social welfare spending. Adding to the challenge, these generally poorer population segments are expanding at a time when a large portion of the mainstream population is retiring and becoming reliant on expensive government programs.

From a cost perspective, the most significant contributor to this looming crisis in America is health care. Not only will a disproportionate segment of the population be retiring, living longer, and relying on expensive health care, but the rapidly growing impoverished minorities are giving rise to epidemics likely to add immeasurably to the financial burden of the nation. For example, diabetes, which has been ravaging the health of indigenous communities, is said to be the most alarming social epidemic[201] (meaning it is widespread and growing in numbers) sweeping North America. Currently, 54 million Americans (approximately 20 percent of the population) are said to have pre-diabetes,[202] in addition to the 20.8 million with diabetes (7 percent of the population).[203] Experts now predict that more than one-third of American children born in this century may develop diabetes, largely as a result of obesity.

Although many people seem unaware of the toll this disease is taking on human life and well-being, the disease in so prevalent in working class and poor communities that its victims take it almost as a matter of course.[204] Similarly, in indigenous communities, the silent epidemic has been doing damage at such an alarming rate that, as has been noted, "one Elder speaks of diabetes as a killer because the disease is killing our people and destroying our communities."[205]

7

EXTERNAL EXPRESSIONS OF INTERNALIZED DEPENDENCY

"Learned helplessness" is another way in which the welfare trap has impacted Aboriginal people:

> Faced with inescapable situations, such as physical extermination, cultural genocide and colonial subjugation, individuals and groups often exhibit what social psychologists label "learned helplessness." ...this kind of behaviour occurs when an individual (or group) perceives that no action on his or her part will control outcomes of the future. Moreover, if the traumatic experience should endure across time (in the Aboriginal context, through three major periods of colonization and four hundred years of epidemics) and should be applicable across settings (or areas of impact: physical, economic, cultural and social), then failure in the present should create generalized expectations for failure in the future. Eventually, via the learned helplessness phenomenon, the trauma enters into the psychological makeup of people.[206]

As a result of this process, it is suggested further that "even if a person finds herself or himself in a situation where he or she could act and react to outside pressures, she or he fails to make an attempt to do so. A person or a group becomes passive, inactive and hostile, ascribing social failures to personal, internal causes and blaming themselves for their helplessness... It is this internal attribution of failure that results in decreased self- and social-esteem."[207]

At the heart of the matter is the question of controlling your own life. What has been given up by Aboriginals in exchange for paltry welfare crumbs is fundamental control over their lives. The real problem is *if you do not control your own purse strings, some one else does, and they have the power to control your destiny*. Aboriginal people must wrest control of their lives from government bureaucracy, from the Indian Industry and must have the courage to make their own decisions, even if they turn out to be mistakes.

The remainder of this chapter will examine some of the peculiar ways in which the welfare trap has impacted Aboriginal psyches and contributed to a dependency mindset over several generations.

When I was a kid on the reserve, we used the expression, "Nobody owes you nothing for nothing." Aside from really bad grammar, this expression was our childish way of expressing the idea that no one has the right to expect to receive anything when they haven't done anything to earn it. There is no free lunch.

Unfortunately, as the welfare state has emerged, views have changed. In the 1920s, "relief," as it was commonly called then, was the last resort for those individuals who needed financial aid on a temporary relief basis. It was "a demeaning and stigmatizing experience because it was widely regarded as clear evidence of personal incompetence and failure. Any help given was of a gratuitous nature, there being no thought to a right of assistance."[208] Over the years the notion of social security grew from a *residual* concept (i.e., one that provided minimal assistance, was temporary, and discretionary) to an *institutional* concept (i.e., was a right, based on the notion that a wealthy society should protect and compensate those who, for whatever reason, are economically unfortunate).[209]

Aboriginals' unhealthy focus on the federal government has further developed a deeply ingrained "culture of expectancy." In short, this is an expectation that all means for ordinary existence (social assistance, housing, education, medical and dental care, community infrastructure finance, and finance for operation of community governments, etc.) will be provided externally, with no expectation that effort must be expended or such items earned. Our Aboriginal ancestors of antiquity would find such an expectation utterly astonishing. How could they have built the beautiful, sophisticated societies that endured for so long with such an expectation? The question that my grandmother or grandfather might ask is, "What moral right does anyone have to something which they have done nothing for?" As a youth, if I were to suggest to my father, a hardworking commercial fisherman, that I deserved a fishing trip crew share when I had not done any of the work to earn it, I would quickly have been introduced to the business end of his gumboot.

Where is the Aboriginal or Canadian government leadership that will identify how unsustainable—and ultimately harmful—such an expectation is?

XSGYIIK RISING AT DUSK

The majestic *xsgiik* (eagle) slowly rises to have one last look for prey before the night falls. Photo collage. Photo taken by Sue Melito-Helin.

Aside from problems inherent in such an expectation, there is the question as to whether Canada will be in a fiscal position to continue to keep up such payments. Moreover, even if Canada were able to keep up with such per capita payments, it is clear from the recent public opinion poll cited in Chapter 3, that the Canadian public is becoming less sympathetic and less willing to continue to provide for such expectations. In fact, in the 2004 annual tracking poll conducted by the Centre for Research and Information on Canada titled *Portraits of Canada*, the question of improving Aboriginal quality of life was in second-last place on a list of 11 items that Canadians said should be a high priority for the federal government.[210]

The further problem with such an expectation is that, no matter what anyone tells you, no one but *you* can really have your own self-interest in mind. INAC has had a longstanding legal duty to look out for Aboriginal interests, and look where this has led? The current INAC bureaucracy has definitely improved in recent years, but even their best intentions cannot replace benevolent self-interest. Because, as Oscar Wilde is purported to have quipped, "It is always with the best intentions that the worst work is done." Can you imagine the Aboriginal leaders and communities of antiquity that survived for 9,600 years prior to European contact, putting *any* decisions concerning their well-being or futures in the hands of distant strangers?

If this weren't bad enough, many Aboriginal people simply expect that their problems will be taken care of by the federal government through its INAC bureaucracy. The fact is that a remote bureaucracy will *never, never* be able to solve Aboriginal problems. Individuals and communities *must* take ownership of the issue and problems. If past experience is any guide, rather than expecting the federal government to solve their problems, Aboriginal people should expect more of the same bad news. The only thing we have the right to expect is that we are the only people who can solve our problems.

Furthermore, even if you were to trust your fate to this faceless monolith, would you put further stock in the INAC bureaucracy which has historically proven to be possibly one of the most incompetent bureaucracies in Western history, as well as one that has a track record for being outright malicious to the true welfare of Aboriginal people? In Chapter 6 we have reviewed how INAC, through its policies and action, deliberately encouraged Aboriginal people onto welfare roles and, through its incompetence and related shortcomings, made it impossible for Aboriginal people to compete in the open marketplace. The situation as it exists is truly absurd. In this day and age, it might be asked what sane, practical person would put the fate of his or her family in the hands of any government, let alone a massive central government located in some distant city? Would you put the now-depleted East Coast cod stocks or West Coast salmon in these hands?

The further problem with this kind of argument is that, when you accept the baby in the bath, you must also accept the bathwater—by taking these kinds of payments without earning them, you are also implicitly accepting the horrendous results that flow from them. A more useful position would be to accept that the welfare dependency situation is a trap and begin from there to develop a strategy for escape. Only from this point can Aboriginal people begin to undo the massive harm reaped by government policy and its bureaucratic administration.

Finally, an incidental attitude that has arisen in relation to the culture of expectancy is that so many generations of Aboriginal people have been collecting welfare, many have been socialized into believing that the Aboriginal welfare trap is normal. Some argue that Aboriginal people *deserve* the transfer payments and welfare because of the historical injury, indignities, loss of land, resources, culture and language, etc. Granted, Aboriginal people had little input into how the current welfare system operates and are victims of a circumstance they did not create. But how can anyone, Aboriginal or otherwise, seek to defend or want to expand a system that is delivering such wholesale misery and despair? The current system is not justifiable no matter what your political, racial or other stripe happens to be.

As absurd as it sounds to those in the mainstream (who must work to survive), some Aboriginal community people have become so socialized into thinking that collecting welfare is normal, they see it, in effect, on a par with being gainfully employed. In the current reserve milieu, there is often no stigma or shame attached to collecting welfare as there would have been for our ancestors or for those today who have worked all their lives and are proud of their self-reliance. In fact, in some communities, there is often a stigma if you are *not* in the welfare ranks.

FREE MONEY? LOTTERY WINNERS WITHOUT THE WINDFALL

Some Aboriginals contend that we should take the welfare and transfer payments because they are "free." As seductive as this might appear, a resounding axiom of Nature is "nothing is ever free." Whatever comes to you without having to put out some effort always requires some compensation—just one that is not immediately visible.

Even lottery winners are said to pay a price for their winnings. According to a recent study[211] from Emory University in Atlanta, Georgia, lottery winners, trust-fund babies and others who obtain their money without working for it do not get as much satisfaction from their cash as those who earn it. The study examined pleasure centers in people's brains and measured brain activity in the striatum—the part of the brain associated with reward processing and pleasure. One group of volunteers had to work to receive money while playing a simple computer game; the other group was rewarded without having to earn it.

It was found that: "The brains of those who had to work for their money were more stimulated. 'When you have to do things for your reward, it's clearly more important to the brain,' said Greg Berns, associate professor of psychiatry and behavioural science. 'The subjects were more aroused when they had to do something to get the money relative to when they passively received the money.'...He said that other studies have shown 'there's substantial evidence that people who win the lottery are not happier a year after they win the lottery. It's also fairly clear from the psychological literature that people get a great deal of satisfaction out of the work they do.' Berns suggested that the brain is wired this way by nature. 'I don't think it ever evolved [for people] to sit back and sit on the couch and have things fall in our laps,' he said.

If the results of this study are accepted, it clearly provides some scientific basis for what has been known from experience about human behaviour in all cultures: money, in and of itself, does not make people happy. It is the process of doing something fulfilling to earn money that leads to happiness. This is clearly what is not happening through the institutional welfare model under which Aboriginal people exist in Canada. And it is leading to more misery than any other single impact in previous history. This is also the problem with the conditioned response of Aboriginal leaders simply asking the government for more money to solve problems. The problem is not entirely a shortage of money. In part, the problem is that the welfare trap system is providing money without Aboriginals having to do anything for it. What sense of pride, accomplishment, or self-worth can come from picking up a welfare cheque?

The dilemma of the situation has been described as follows:

Former chief Jerry Goodswimmer [of the Sturgeon Lake reserve in northern Alberta] may have come close to the answer on social ills. As a councillor in 1990, he wrote a letter to the editor of the *Valleyview* weekly. A multi-million dollar chopstick factory established on the reserve had recently gone bankrupt. Mr. Goodswimmer described the resulting infighting this way: "In my opinion [the problem is] not pride or dignity, **it's the millions of dollars which was given to us** [by the government]. **Along with the money comes jealousy and greed. ...How I wish that the money was never given to us, it is just tearing us apart.** Maybe the saying is right, 'Money is the root of all evil.'"[212] [Emphasis added]

The fact is that the money already paid out, has not been, by any stretch of the imagination, free. Aboriginal people have paid dearly for their "handouts" a million times over with the loss of their lands, resources, dignity, self-reliance, self-respect, self-confidence, and the total loss of control over their lives. Arguably, for a system which is not of their making and over which they have no control, Aboriginal youth are paying literally with *their lives*, given the grossly disproportionate suicide rate amongst Aboriginal youth.

There must be a common understanding about how this situation is harming Aboriginal people. There must be a common resolve from Aboriginal communities and leadership, and from all levels of government that it is time to do something *now*. Aboriginal people must take ownership of *their* problem. How much worse can we do than the federal government? While Aboriginal people are not likely to go physically the way of the now-depleted East coast cod stocks or West coast salmon under the federal government's watch, we have died a spiritual death and endured a massive blow to our dignity. This loss cannot be replaced by anything or anyone except our own individual and collective resolve to take action to make our own lives better. There is no question that some level of federal programs and services are required; Aboriginal people are doomed, however, to be ongoing victims of the current welfare trap if they really believe the federal government can actually solve their problems.

FROM INTERDEPENDENCE TO UTTER NONSENSE

We have seen how government policy and legislation has completely undermined the ability of Aboriginal people to be economically self-reliant. While that largely took care of their independence, transfer payments pretty much took care of their interdependence. As discussed, while Aboriginal people were largely reliant on Nature for their survival, they were also, historically, very dependent upon each other. Experience taught Aboriginal ancestors of antiquity that, to safely guide the Aboriginal canoe through 9,600 years of existence and self-reliance, a high degree of cooperation and interdependence amongst tribal members was fundamental to survival.

Introducing welfare and transfer payments to Aboriginal communities introduced an artificial system of survival—a system that would not exist without being provided by others. This scheme very unwisely replaced those critical social and cultural bonds whose time-honoured value ensured the survival of Aboriginal societies throughout the millennia. In an insightful article by Candis McLean, the situation and view of one elder were summarized:

> Nelly Sunshine, 62, is raising her 8-year-old grandson. "I pick bottles to make ends meet instead of running to the food bank," she explains. "The little guy [her grandson who lives with her] gets $81/month plus $174 in child tax; we manage. Work makes me feel I'm doing something for my family. In the old days when someone needed help, everyone pitched in; if someone killed a moose, we shared. Today people are selfish—the more [government] money they see, the more they want. It's controlling everyone."[213]

With the introduction of transfer payments and welfare, Aboriginal people no longer had to pay as much focussed attention to their families and kin. When I was a child in my community, my granny needed a house. There was an unspoken understanding that her tribal members would simply cut the timber and build her house. They did this without hesitation and with the greatest efficiency. Why? Because their elders also needed housing. At some point my family would return the tacit obligation.

This situation changed once federal government reserve housing was introduced. Now, since the federal government supplies a very basic house for a nominal cost, community attention has shifted from working together and relying on one another, to sitting on the couch and waiting for a house to fall on your lap (to paraphrase Professor Bern above). Out of this system arose the infamous Band "housing list." This list was intended to provide housing on a first-come-first-serve priority basis and would set out the order in which community members received their houses. Now there are huge waiting lists for housing in most Aboriginal communities across Canada. Often community members complain that the list order is changed and some unfair queue-jumping takes place as patronage payments take precedence for those persons or families that supported the newly-elected Chiefs and Councils.

There can be no question that providing an artificial revenue source to Aboriginal communities has hastened the disintegration of the social and cultural fabric of communities. The dignity, respect and self-satisfaction received from working together and supporting one another have been replaced by a system that has turned Aboriginal people into spectators of their own painfully slow demise. Welfare and transfer payments, have replaced the important social and cultural habits and practices that evolved from several millennia of experience. Aboriginal people need to be reminded of this and consider it carefully in seeking solutions to their current problems.

INDIAN CRABS: THE PHENOMENON OF LATERAL VIOLENCE

> O, beware, my lord, of jealousy!
> It is the green-eyed monster which doth mock
> The meat it feeds on.
> WILLIAM SHAKESPEARE (1564—1616), *Othello*, Act 3 scene 3

The late American comedian Rodney Dangerfield joked: "My wife's jealousy is getting ridiculous. The other day she looked at my calendar and wanted to know who May was." Most people think that lottery winners are lucky when they win, but few understand that they are especially envied and ridiculed when their difficulties hit the headlines.[214] A supposed French proverb states: "It is only at the tree loaded with fruit that the people throw stones." The great English novelist Henry Fielding wrote: "Some folks rail against other folks, because other folks have what some folks would be glad of."[215] While some level of envy seems to be part of human behaviour, in Aboriginal communities a legacy of the dependency mindset has been uncommonly high levels of jealousy and ill will directed towards one another (particularly at those that seek to get out of the welfare trap).

This situation is so bad that there is a familiar anecdote called the "Indian Crab" story. My uncle Art told me the story this way. He was walking down the dock one day and passed a white guy with a bucket of crabs. As soon as he set his bucket down a crab climbed out and he chased after it. By the time he got back to his bucket, two others had climbed out. He went a little further down the dock and there was an Indian that also had a bucket of crabs. He was sitting calmly having a puff on a cigarette. My uncle looked back at the white guy who was in a sweat chasing his crabs and then looked back at the Indian. "Aren't your worried your crabs are going climb out?" he asked. The Indian had a long drag on his cigarette and replied, "Nah, not these ones. They are Indian crabs; whenever one tries to climb out, the rest pull him back down."

I thought this was a pretty good original story until I read a version of it in an article on Native American economic development in *The Atlantic Monthly*. I also learned that this story is used by some East Indian politicians to illustrate lack of cooperation amongst their own people. My uncle used to joke that he had been attacked so many times by people in his own community that he wore an Arrow shirt; not one made by the famous American Arrow company, but one that had all the arrows sticking in the back! Kidding aside, with the delicate level of self-confidence that exists within communities, more than anything, Aboriginal people need to encourage and support one another and the efforts of everyone who seeks to make their life better—not criticize them. One explanation for this phenomenon is "lateral violence." Lateral violence is a product of colonization, and has been applied to describe the conditions of various oppressed ethnic and non-ethnic minority groups (such as women). When you are at the bottom of the social heap and cannot strike out "vertically" (i.e., at those above you), frustration erupts and is directed instead at your peers by your side. Ironically, it amounts to the colonized colonizing one another, a situation of the oppressed oppressing each other.

This violence can take the form of shaming, humiliating, damaging, belittling and sometimes violent behaviour directed toward a member of a group by other members of the same group. This kind of violence has been identified as being so prevalent in Aboriginal communities that workshops are offered to assist community members in dealing with the emotional fallout from it. Lateral violence impacts the whole community and has been described as "an internalized feeling of anger and rage that develops in a person as a result of being constantly put down. It also manifests itself ...[in the] community through family feuds, gossip and organizational infighting. It is responsible for dividing...communities into factions, thereby preventing... [them] from becoming a more strong and unified people."[216]

THE AMERICAN DREAM?

For in all the world there are no people so piteous and forlorn as those who are forced to eat the bitter bread of dependency in their old age, and find how steep are the stairs of another man's house. Wherever they go they know themselves unwelcome. Wherever they are, they feel themselves a burden. There is no humiliation of the spirit they are not forced to endure. Their hearts are scarred all over with the stabs from cruel and callous speeches.

DOROTHY DIX (American journalist and columnist, 1870–1951)

In the United States, where the welfare trap has even more dire implications than in Canada, the problems as deeply rooted, calling into question the concept of the American Dream. Lurking at the forefront is a growing gulf between rich and poor, magnified against a backdrop of huge military spending. According to some sources, 37 million Americans live below the official poverty line,[217] with tens of millions more struggling each month to pay for basic necessities, or running out of savings when they either lose their jobs or face health emergencies. (In Canada, although the plan is criticized, access to minimal healthcare is universal.) In 2005, the richest 1 percent of Americans held 19 percent of the nation's income—the largest share since 1929. At the same time, the poorest 20 percent of Americans held only 3.4 percent of the nation's income.[218]

Poverty often translates into time in jail. The U.S. has the world's highest incarceration rates. To some observers, this situation points to broader failures in U.S. society, particularly in regard to racial minorities and others who are economically disadvantaged. Native and African Americans, and to a lesser extent Hispanics, face the inevitable prospect of going to prison. In fact, Native Americans have the second largest state prison incarceration rate in the nation.[219]

Poverty also translates into homelessness—that is, lacking a permanent, safe, decent, or affordable place to live. Today in the U.S., between 500,000 and 600,000 people at any given time are considered homeless. Disturbingly, the fastest-growing group of homeless people are families, which currently make up one-third of the homeless population. The homeless elderly are also expected to be a growing segment in the next decades, with 80 million people set to retire—a problem likely to be further exacerbated by a social security system widely known to be in peril of going broke.

Akin to the Aboriginal people of Canada, Native and African Americans and others among the poorest of U.S. citizens need consciously to choose a more beneficial path to self-reliance. If, as Samuel Johnson has commented, poverty leads to dependency, then government policy should focus on finding ways out of poverty that do not reinforce dependency but instead encourage self-reliant attitudes. While the creation of sustainable forms of wealth is part of the solution, education, obtainable with or without wealth, is the key to long-term self-reliance. In the end, our grandparents would tell all of us that the way to feel better about ourselves is to engage in old-fashioned hard work. Their counsel suggests that we are not only social animals but social animals who have been hardwired to work in order to maintain our social balance and dignity as people.

8

ECONOMIC IMPACTS OF THE WELFARE TRAP

"SHAMAN ECONOMICS" AND ECONOMIC ISOLATION

Any priest or shaman must be presumed guilty until proved innocent.
ROBERT A. HEINLEIN, *The Notebooks of Lazarus Long*

In modern economic parlance, the term "voodoo economics" is often used. The term refers to the notion of using supply-side economic stimulation to create economic growth. In this discussion I have coined the similar term, "shaman economics," to describe the economic impacts of the welfare trap—which includes amongst other attributes, the general structural defects by which tribes have been economically isolated and initially force-fed welfare.

The word "shaman" has emerged in popular usage. It was originally used by anthropologists and ethnographers to describe indigenous holy men or women. They were of the mistaken view that all "primitive" religions were the same. As a result, they pigeon-holed all of the various kinds of healers under one umbrella term, much to the annoyance of some indigenous healers. Notwithstanding this misconception, the term is used here because of its popular usage.

No disrespect is intended to the valuable cultural role played historically by shaman whose role involved solemn tribal responsibilities akin to psychologist-priests. While they served a valuable function, both practically and culturally, the modern misconception about ancient shaman is that they mostly practiced a form of witchcraft, a misconception similar to those made about voodoo priests. Unfortunately, modern "neo-shamans," of the self-anointed crystal packing variety (those who might typically be found leading New Age drumming groups), have done little to rehabilitate the association of shaman with black magic and vaudeville-like trickery.

It is in the latter negative sense that I use the term shaman economics. Specifically, the term refers to the government's "black magic" belief that waving the fiscal magic wand over tribes, without addressing the fundamental structural flaws of the system, will create a sound economic base. And, tongue-in-cheek, Aboriginals/Native Americans would also likely suggest "shame on" those governments and government officials that have perpetrated such a system leading to so much misery.

Creating sustainable economies for a system that is, at its roots, deeply defective, will take much more strategic thinking and basic re-engineering. Throwing government money at poorly-designed schemes and band-aid solutions without a well thought-out game plan will not stimulate economic development, but instead, waste precious resources. As discussed throughout this book, the welfare trap will never be overcome until Aboriginal people take ownership of their problem. As well, government efforts to create positive economic results will never be realized until there is recognition of the existing governance and structural impediments.

So what, exactly, is it about the mechanics of shaman economics that has led to the almost total economic collapse of tribal economies? There are two overriding factors that have resulted in shaman economics: (1) the enforced economic isolation of indigenous communities, and (2) the evolution of government as the sole-source of wealth creation in tribal communities. An unfortunate consequence of the manner in which Aboriginal people were historically isolated, usually on remote reserves for assimilation purposes, is that modern Aboriginal communities have also been largely economically isolated. Transfer payments as the sole source of wealth for most Aboriginal communities is actually, as suggested, another form of welfare dependency with a distorting impact on the mindset of indigenous people and their governments.

A clue as to why and how the shaman economics system is flawed can be found by examining how economic opportunity is created in the mainstream. In major Western countries, wealth is largely created by the business sector. In the United States, the private sector typically accounts for around 90 percent of the gross national product (GNP)[220] or approximately 80+ percent of the gross domestic product (GDP[221]).[222] The private sector seems to be the most efficient environment for the creation of wealth. Certainly efforts by governments to create wealth, such as in the former Soviet Union and the poorly-run, state-owned companies in what is currently a booming Chinese economy, are examples of the state's comparative ineffectiveness.

A review of the reform process in various post-communist countries of Eastern Europe reveals further the significant extent of the contribution by the private sector to the wealth and subsequent health of these nations. In these economies, at a time when they were still in early transition from

SPIRIT BEAR MAGIC

On the Nass River, in a northern westcoast Indian village, a magical light show illuminates the evening sky and silhouettes six very ancient totem poles. Within the cascades of colours tossed towards the earth by the Creator, a story unfolds of the great white raven and the spirit bear (both very rare in Nature). These mythological spirits, along with those of the animal totems atop the poles, are the sentinels that keep watch over the sleeping village below. Original was painted with acrylics on canvas in 2004 and reproduced in a small limited edition by the giclee method.

communism to market economies, the contribution of the private sector to GDP already exceeded 50 percent in 19 of the 26 states of the former Soviet Union.[223] This information is a good starting point for analysing the economic problems experienced by Aboriginal people.

A look at the current circumstances of Aboriginal communities reveals that typically 100 percent of the wealth flowing into Aboriginal communities comes in the form of transfer payments from the Federal government. Since there are few businesses in most Aboriginal communities, the monies flowing in are not recycled through the community economies (as occurs with most non-Aboriginal small town communities), but flow right back out. This has caused some Aboriginal pundits to observe that "a buck only stays in the community for a day" (no pun intended).

Vicious Cycle of Transfer Payment Dependency

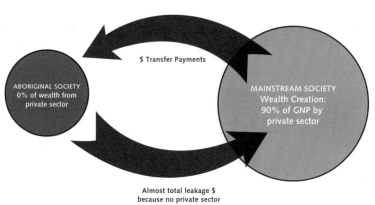

While Aboriginal communities cannot be directly compared to full-blown national economies, having virtually no private business sector cannot be good for either the day-to-day health or long-term self-reliance of those communities. Communities, no matter what their ethnic make up, simply cannot survive in the real world without a sound economic base.

For their own self-preservation, Aboriginal governments must focus on sustainable ways in which they can encourage economic development in their communities. Like every other government, they must be vigilant about creating an environment conducive to attracting entrepreneurs and investment. They must also look to the long-term for the means to sustain their government operations from activities within their own territories. Shaman economics has had its day; it is time to leave it where it rightfully belongs—as a sad interlude in the long history of a proud people. The bottom line is that Aboriginal communities need, more than anything else, to begin creating their own wealth outside of the barriers created by shaman economics.

FEDERAL TUNNEL VISION

> It is dishonest for a man deliberately to shut his eyes to facts which he would prefer not to know. If he does so, he is taken to have actual knowledge of the facts to which he shut his eyes. Such knowledge has been described as "Nelsonian knowledge," meaning knowledge which is attributed to a person as a consequence of his "willful blindness" [conjures up an image of the Admiral holding a telescope to his blind eye and claiming to see no ships] or (as American lawyers describe it) "contrived ignorance."
>
> LORD MILLET, House of Lords Judgement 2002, *Twinsectra Limited v Yardley and Others*[224]

With federal transfer payments the sole source of Aboriginal wealth over the past 100 years, it follows naturally that the attention of Aboriginal leaders would be focused almost exclusively on the "hand that feeds"—the federal government. With neither a tax base nor other revenue source, Aboriginal leaders have, over time, been conditioned reflexively to simply ask for more money.

Unfortunately, this has evolved further into what might best be described as a form of willful blindness on the part of indigenous leaders, and which has become their total formula for governing. If there is a community problem, it is simply the fault of the federal government. While some federal blame may be justified, this ploy does little to deal with the overarching issues and does not advance a real long-term solution. In addition, some community leaders may feel that, individually, they can do nothing locally to make differences that require national change. This form of response has also arisen because it is easy to simply blame the federal government for the myriad of community problems—a political tactic used to a lesser extent by municipal and provincial politicians.

Regrettably, at the national level this pathetic approach is the creative thinking predominant among Aboriginal leaders regarding just about any problem that arises. There appears to be a complete lack of ideas or innovation on how to move Aboriginal people more effectively and constructively forward. Certainly, begging the federal government for more interim financial resources will never provide a long-term solution.

Indigenous leaders' willful blindness to the economic reality of their circumstances has resulted in a situation where Aboriginal governments are completely reliant and at the total mercy of federal transfer payments for their operation. Furthermore, it has sadly retarded the advancement of Aboriginal people and blinded leaders to the real economic action taking place in the mainstream all around them. The key to solving Aboriginal problems must come from within. No matter how attractive the prospect seems, the necessity and obligation to pay attention to your own business simply cannot be off-loaded to some remote bureaucracy without serious negative consequences. Without self-generated wealth, there will never be real *self*-government. The federal powers that control the purse strings will continue to control Aboriginal leaders and their communities no matter how much "smoke is shoveled" by politicians to argue otherwise.

The focus on federal government differentiates indigenous leaders markedly from non-Aboriginals. Non-Aboriginals must be more obsessed with the business sector which is the very lifeblood of their existence. While it is true that some non-Aboriginal governments also receive federal transfer payments, beside the business sector, the primary form of their revenue comes from personal, corporate, property, commodities and related forms of taxation (revenues are also generated from resource royalties and the provision of services on a fee basis). Unless they are prepared to levy their own taxes, Aboriginal governments must focus on ways they can generate their own source revenues by developing a business sector and attracting investment to their communities.

Difference in Government Focus

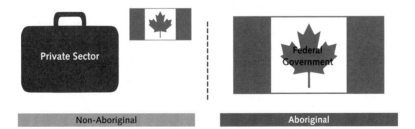

The only hope for Aboriginal communities to move forward, then, is to begin creating their own wealth. And the private sector is the most efficient forum for the creation of that wealth.

One of the most alarming results of being entirely focussed on the federal government for such a long period of time is that Aboriginal people tend to mould their behaviour, activities, and community institutions on the model of the federal bureaucracies with which they are intimately engaged—the Department of Indian Affairs and Northern Development Canada. While imitation may be the sincerest form of flattery, in this case it may be the sincerest form of folly—what a bad precedent! The documented history of the INAC bureaucracy has proven it to be possibly one of the most incompetent government departments in Western experience.

An observation sometimes heard from within and without Aboriginal communities is that there is simply too much bureaucracy. In this case, the available data bears out this criticism. A recent labor study showed that Aboriginal people were noticeably absent from management services, finance and insurance, and professional, scientific and technical services, but hugely over-represented in public administration—which includes local government and Band administration.[225] The chart below is reproduced from this study

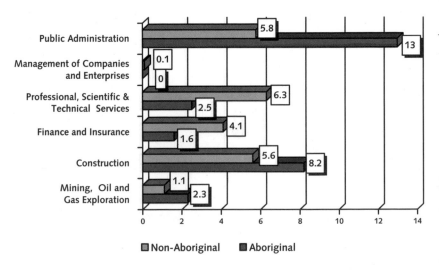

Proportion of Aboriginal Workforce in Selected Sectors vs Total Workforce

Source of data: Canadian Labour and Business Centre Report

and shows Aboriginal employment in government bureaucracy at more than twice the rate of the non-Aboriginal population.

This is arguably in large part the result of mimicking inefficient and wasteful federal bureaucracy.[226] As well, this over-representation is due to the fact that the only way to create employment without a business sector and independent form of wealth creation is the continual seeking to expand the bureaucracy and government transfer payments in tandem.

The over-bureaucratization of communities impacts tribes' abilities to develop their own economic base. Firstly, the top-heavy bureaucracy simply adds too much expense to the cost of doing business. As well, bureaucratic indecision and the lengthy timelines in making decisions creates further cost and uncertainty. Investors always seek to minimize uncertainty. Furthermore, they react strongly against over-politicization of what should be rational business decisions motivated by self-interest. The tribal political system is based on a patronage award system, and making administrative appointments entirely on political criteria without reference to merit or individual ability further entrenches the notion that uncertainty prevails. Chinese leaders figured out thousands of years ago how counterproductive such a system was when they introduced a merit-based exam system.

To survive, tribes need to create their own wealth by attracting investment and creating their own community entrepreneurs. To attract investment, tribes must create an environment conducive to investment. To create their own community entrepreneurs, tribes must create an environment to support and nurture those of their members who are prepared to take risks to create wealth. To do this, tribes must adopt a more beneficial model upon which to base community development. Likely the worst model upon which they should move forward is the example of the Indian Affairs bureaucracy.

NO MARKET, NO RISK, NO ATTENTION

A running joke amongst Russians under the communist regime of the Soviet Union was "We pretend to work and they pretend to pay us." This underscores the view that tends to naturally arise when there is no personal stake in an outcome. Since any action taken will not impact me, who cares what happens? Therefore in Russia, the workers pretended to work, and the government (that was often broke) pretended to pay them.

As under a communist regime, no one in a reserve community has worked directly to create the wealth generated via transfer payments or welfare. The result is that no one has risked anything, and no one's neck is on the line for anything. In such a situation, no matter what you do, the same situation will continue. So goes the logic: why do anything? For something to happen, somebody must have something on the line; there must be something at stake! Back in the days of our ancestors, they had their very existence on the line. Remember the detailed attention paid by the Tsimshian trapper to the bargain he got for the fox furs he had worked hard to trap (Chapter 3)? Though it may sound like hyperbole, this is true today. Aboriginal people will not starve as a result of welfare and transfer payments, but the real long-term health and spiritual well-being of Aboriginal people is definitely at stake.

Unlike the Soviet Union though, in the current welfare trap system, the federal government pays Aboriginal people who might be said to have long ago dropped any pretence to work for the welfare and transfer payments received.

A similar kind of lackadaisical mindset relates to communal ownership of property. When property is communally-, rather than individually-owned, no one pays much heed to it or tends to be responsible for it. This kind of ownership is a disincentive to preserving collective property and has an impact on minimizing economic returns from assets. Such a disincentive supposedly existed as a result of communal ownership of land in the first American colonies:

> When they arrived in the New World in 1620, The Pilgrims of Plymouth Colony tried communal ownership of the land. It didn't work: crops were not well cared for and the result was a severe food shortage. So in 1623 each family was given a private lot of land along with responsibility for maintaining it. This worked much better… people worked harder when they had private lots, and crop yields were much higher. The moral of the story…is simple: people take better care of things they own individually than the things that they hold in common.[227]

In this example, private ownership created a stake, and therefore an incentive, in the outcome of growing a crop. It shouldn't take a rocket scientist to realize that an even worse form of ownership applies to tribal lands. In their case, generally the lands are actually owned by the federal government in trust for the use and benefit of indigenous people.

We must look carefully to creating a practical new reality that provides Aboriginal people a real stake in their futures. When an outcome has a

SPIRIT OF THE FOREST

Our ancestors believed that you need to see through the eyes of the creatures of the forest to be one with them. This is an important lesson for survival and teaches children how to respect all of creation. This also helps to maintain a balance on earth and gives thanks to the Creator. The Chief of the wolf is ghosted in the trees as he runs through the forest with his lifecrest creature. He is *Laxgibuu* (of the wolf clan), jumping over the ancient fallen wolf totem. Acrylic on canvas.

potential to reward efforts made, it is simply human nature to pay much closer attention.

There are four ways in which you can spend money. You can spend your own money on yourself. When you do that, why then you really watch out what you're doing, and you try to get the most for your money.

Then you can spend your own money on somebody else. For example, I buy a birthday present for someone. Well, then I'm not so careful about the content of the present, but I'm very careful about the cost.

Then, I can spend somebody else's money on myself. And if I spend somebody else's money on myself, then I'm sure going to have a good lunch!

Finally, I can spend somebody else's money on somebody else. And if I spend somebody else's money on somebody else, I'm not concerned about how much it is, and I'm not concerned about what I get. And that's government. And that's close to 40% of our national income.[228]

As economist Milton Freedman opined, the best economic decisions are made by people spending their own money. The corollary of this is that people never spend someone else's money as carefully as their own. In the context of a discussion about the Aboriginal welfare trap, it might seem out of place to be talking about the views of Warren Buffet, the world's second wealthiest man, but there is an interesting parallel to be made to the government decision-making environment created within the welfare trap.

Consider Mr. Buffet's views about abuses relating to the stock option-fuelled salaries of America's CEO's (where apparently the take-home pay of the average U.S. chief executive is now about $9.43 million annually). The role of the directors and executive compensation committees in large public corporations is supposedly to protect the interests of shareholders. Conversely, Mr Buffet says:

"Chief executives talk about 'diversity' but they don't care whether they've got men or women on the board, any of that kind of stuff. They just care about their comp [compensation]. It's a very uneven balance. Usually in any negotiation people on both sides are dealing with something very real to them. On executive compensation, [for] the CEO, the compensation is very real to him, **but to the comp committee, to the directors, it's play**

money. There never has been such a transfer of wealth in our history. And it's obscene [Emphasis added]."[229]

In Aboriginal communities, transfer payment monies are simply provided, not self-generated. While the same observation and criticism can be made about any government, many grassroots community members charge that a similar lack of *gravitas* sometimes applies to band council decision-making in relation to such transfer payment monies. As with the compensation committee and directors in relation to shareholders' money, there are no direct consequences to band councillors for ill-considered decisions. In the sense used by Warren Buffet, transfer payments are "play money" to some if they did nothing personally or collectively to acquire the money in the first place. This circumstance has led to equally "obscene" wastage of federal monies. The situation is one without a normal baseline since it operates outside the parameters of a market system and the normal institutional rules of accountability that might otherwise impose some level of reality on decision-making.

This is all the more reason why such expenditures should be totally transparent, and a high level of accountability should apply. Where negligent decisions are made, outcomes should be tied to compensation received by the decision-maker. Where corruption or criminal wrong doing may be involved, the full force of criminal law should be brought to bear on the perpetrators of the deceit.

9

THE WELFARE TRAP AND POLITICAL PATHOLOGIES

> Poverty and powerlessness are bound up with each other. Poverty leads to powerlessness, and powerlessness leads to poverty.
>
> MARTIN WYATT, *Gifts and Discoveries* (1988)

THE STATE OF ABORIGINAL DEMOCRACY

> When in doubt, tell the truth.
>
> MARK TWAIN

The questions surrounding Aboriginal political institutions and their defects are not without controversy. Notwithstanding the often polarized views, the effective reform of Aboriginal political institutions is absolutely critical for advancing the immediate and long-term interests of Aboriginal peoples. These issues must be discussed openly, in a respectful environment in order to begin the process of effecting well-considered reform. It is important to reiterate that the development of good governance for Aboriginal communities is a matter that should also be in the self-interest of Canada as a nation. Modernizing tribal governance structures may after all help to unleash the massive economic potential trapped by the current archaic governance structure.

Self-generated wealth is critical to Aboriginal aspirations of self-government. Without a revenue source independent of the federal government, Aboriginal communities will continue to be trapped in the cycle of poverty, remaining dependent on transfer payments and the agendas of those interests providing this revenue. As Martin Wyatt suggests above, poverty leads to powerlessness. The corollary of Wyatt's statement is that wealth leads to power. If Aboriginal people want the power to control their own destinies, they must generate their own wealth. A 10-year study released in 2005 by Harvard University's Project on American Indian Economic Development titled "Sovereignty and Nation Building: The Development Challenge in

Indian Country Today," determined that stable and reliable governance was the single most critical factor in developing tribal economies' wealth.[230]

Strategically, tribes should focus on the low-hanging fruit, given the immediate impending opportunity to capitalize on a booming resource economy and other areas of economic expansion. In tandem, the longer-term governance question absolutely needs to be addressed. One of the keys to moving Aboriginal people forward in Canada is to immediately look at realistic ways of correcting the fundamental flaws in the current governance system.

There are over 700 Aboriginal communities in Canada.[231] In addition to approximately 614 First Nations communities, there are approximately 88 tribal councils, and 50 Inuit communities.[232] Many of the Aboriginal communities are in the North, which occupies 40 percent of Canada's land mass. The three northern territories contain some 96 organized communities; most of them home to small, mainly First Nations, Métis or Inuit populations.[233] The 614 First Nations communities comprise 52 nations or cultural groups and more than 50 languages. About 60 percent of First Nations communities have fewer than 500 residents—only 7 percent have more than 2,000.[234]

The 614 First Nations communities are governed under the *Indian Act*. As cited earlier, Chief Joe Mathias has pointed out that under the *Indian Act*, "...any [Band Council] decisions made [are] subject to the ultimate approval of the Minister of Indian Affairs." This is one of the biggest defects of the system of governance set out under the *Indian Act*. Even though elected Chiefs and Councils are voted in through community elections, they are not ultimately accountable to the very community members that elected them in the first place. According to Aboriginal academic and Director of the Indigenous Governance Programs at the University of Victoria, Taiaiake Alfred, the result is that "there is almost complete lack of accountability under the system of government established by the *Indian Act*, and the system makes the band governments answerable to Ottawa—where they are answerable at all—rather than to their own people. That's the inherent corruption." Alfred argues that most Chiefs try their best. But, he says, the system is ripe to be taken advantage of by "people who are corrupt and greedy and selfish because of lack of accountability."[235]

Imagine a situation where ordinary Canadians voted for their Member of Parliament, but rather than be accountable to the electorate that gave them their office, these politicians were instead accountable to a Member of the British Parliament. This would be an absurd situation for the Canadian state, yet it is one which the government sanctions for Aboriginal people under the current *Indian Act*.

'NEEXT HUNTS

'Neext (orca) are the wolves of the sea. Similar to wolves, they are

extraordinarily intelligent and sensitive. They have sophisticated forms

of communication and cooperate in hunting to an astonishingly sophis-

ticated degree.

The further problem with the manner in which governance is exercised in First Nations is that the system that has arisen is effectively a closed loop that concentrates all political power in the hands of Chiefs at the same time politically disempowering the great masses of community members. To again paraphrase Martin Wyatt, this powerlessness directly contributes to the existing status quo of Aboriginal poverty. Don Sandberg, a full-blooded Cree and an Aboriginal Policy Fellow of the Frontier Centre for Public Policy describes further the system for selecting a regional Grand Chief:

> Once powerful and respected, this office is no longer either in today's context of money and power. The rules for accountability, developed with the help of the Indian industry in cities, make leaders a power unto themselves. Candidates for Grand Chief are selected from their ranks, and the average band member is not consulted at all.
>
> Band chiefs are currently the only ones allowed to vote in a Grand Chief, placing the office at the mercy of the few that elect them. The average person on any reserve will tell you that, if you are having leadership problems, the last place you would seek help is from the Grand Chief. In northern Manitoba, with 32 first Nations representing 50,000 people, only 32 of them get the privilege of voting for the Grand Chief.
>
> Many First Nations people therefore have little interest in these elections and do not believe that the Grand Chief represents them. If that individual were directly elected, not only would respect and support be restored to the office, the incumbent would be empowered with the independence to evaluate band performance objectively and to act effectively to address chronic leadership problems.[236]

Many community voices have expressed a similar view in relation to the Assembly of First Nations (AFN). Critics contend that AFN is itself in a democratic deficit since the National Chief is elected by the Chiefs across the nation and not from the individuals in the communities it professes to represent. In other words, the AFN National Chief who purports to speak for the over 600,000 First Nations people in Canada, is elected by approximately 400 Chiefs (since, typically, fewer than-two thirds of the 600 Chiefs show up to vote), rather than directly by the First Nations people. Community members ask how such a process can be considered democratic. The way that the electoral system operates for choosing the National Chief is akin to having some of the mayors across Canada select the prime minister, rather than the citizens. I acknowledge that position of prime minister is chosen by party delegates at a national convention, however, mainstream citizens have a right that Aboriginal people do not: they have the opportunity to cast a vote for a member of parliament during a national election which indirectly determines who becomes prime minister (in fact, the leader of the party is often the reason they vote for the local MP). If such a scenario were proposed for the general population, it would likely receive virtually no public support. Again, however, such an absurd elitist election system exists for the Aboriginal population.

Former National Chief, Matthew Coon Come, acknowledged the democratic shortcoming of the AFN and made a bid to have his office chosen by direct election. Though there were many Chiefs that supported this idea, it was fought fiercely by many leaders who argued that "most native people aren't informed enough to vote for national chief."[237] Presumably, however, these uninformed local people were informed enough to vote for those Chiefs themselves in local elections. The people were also informed enough to vote in provincial and federal elections. Many Chiefs contended that the move was actually a plan by the National Chief to boost his power. More cynical observers have speculated that the real issue is "whether chiefs at the local level...[are] willing to give up some of their authority to a Canada-wide native government."[238] In 2005, the Assembly of First Nations struck the AFN Renewal Commission[239] which has carried out hearings across the country and will produce a report expected to address these criticisms. Once again the question of reform will be put to Chiefs who succeeded earlier in blocking any effective efforts at progressing forward to a fairer, more democratic and accountable system.

So First Nations democracy amounts to a situation where Chiefs are not directly accountable to their community members who elect them, but instead to the Minister of Indian Affairs. Furthermore, the Chiefs, rather than the Aboriginal citizens, generally elect all other regional and national leaders. As a result, you have a political circumstance where almost all of the political power is concentrated in the hands of a few individuals—a situation not unlike many banana republics. Community members contend that it is no surprise that what gets advanced on these political agendas are those issues that serve the dictates and interests of the Chiefs, rather than the will of the people. Impoverished community members grumble further that since the Chiefs also control transfer payment monies, it is virtually impossible for their political voice to be heard. They ask in what sense this system can be considered a democracy? Many suggest that, while Aboriginal people received the federal franchise to vote in mainstream elections in 1960, they question when they will receive the Aboriginal franchise. They say further that it is an odd situation when Aboriginal votes are good enough for premiers and prime ministers, but not, apparently, for Chiefs.

A 2003 study,[240] purporting to be among the first of its kind in Canada, found that 37 percent of those reserve members surveyed rated the performance of their band government as good.[241] Some Aboriginal people have observed cynically that, given the small population base of most First Nation communities (93 percent of First Nations communities having fewer than 2000 residents), this level of approval rating accords roughly with the number of family members that Chiefs and Councils are likely to have in a community. The study also noted that 32 percent of those surveyed rated the performance of the government as poor. This segment of those surveyed was composed of three key demographic groups—the young (aged 25–34), the more educated (those with a university education), and the employed.[242] In general, given the demographic characteristics of these three groups, it is clear that the more informed and ambitious community members viewed the performance of their Band governments poorly.

The same study found that overall, a majority of 51 percent of First Nations people surveyed supported the failed Bill C-7, First Nations Governance Act (proposed by the Government of Canada)[243]. The intent of the act was to: (1) ensure that Band Councils were more transparent and accountable to their members; (2) address the legal status of First Nation governments; and (3) develop a more equitable system for conducting band elections. It is also interesting to note that the survey found the legislation was supported by 72 percent of the general population.[244]

Aboriginal Chiefs across the country were angered and opposed to the legislation which they claimed was developed without *their* consultation, would strip them of their inherent rights and would continue to perpetuate a colonial relationship. In point of fact, it would be difficult to imagine a more colonial relationship than that which currently exists under this archaic *Indian Act* system of governance—one in which Chiefs are accountable to Ottawa rather than their electorate. Furthermore, the effective colonization under this system has been said to be further exacerbated by the Chiefs and Councils as colonizers of their own disempowered people. Notwithstanding the response of the Chiefs to Bill C-7, INAC officials countered that between the spring and fall of 2001, 10,000 First Nations people across Canada were directly consulted and had an opportunity to provide their opinions and ideas. The Chiefs and the national organization representing off-reserve members, the Congress of Aboriginal Peoples, raised many objections to the Bill. In November of 2003, it died on the order paper while waiting to proceed for third reading.

At the time the Bill was proposed, then-Minister of Indian Affairs, Robert Nault, commented that Aboriginal leaders who have allowed life on Canadian reserves to resemble that of a welfare state—with mass unemployment and poverty—based on government handouts, must be forced to rethink their priorities. "[R]ight now the chiefs really are only answerable to the Department of Indian Affairs and directly to the Minister," Nault said, adding that some of the Chiefs may have legitimate reasons for demanding a different set of priorities, but many are motivated by self-preservation.[245]

Bill C-7, though not perfect, was also seen by many Aboriginal people as an improvement and opportunity to right some of the defects of the colonial era *Indian Act*. It is interesting to note that if the above survey were accurate, the Bill would have passed had it been put to a direct vote of reserve members. There appears to have been a significant constituency of Aboriginal people that supported the Bill echoing the views of former Minister Nault that the efforts of the Chiefs to kill the legislation were mere self-preservation.

A RISING CALL FOR GOVERNANCE REFORM

You can straighten a worm, but the crook is in him and only waiting.
MARK TWAIN, *More Maxims of Mark*, Johnson, 1927

In relation to Aboriginal communities, there has been considerable public debate on whether Aboriginal people have been getting good government. On one side of the issue, conservative organizations and think tanks such as the Canadian Taxpayers Federation and the Fraser Institute have rallied for an end to alleged corruption, abuses of power, wasteful and extravagant spending, and mismanagement of resources. In response, the national political organization for the First Nations in Canada, the Assembly of First Nations, conversely contends that such criticisms are a collection of "myths" that are "...sowing misperceptions as to how funding to First Nations works, what the money is for, and what happens with it."[246]

Unfortunately, the din in relation to this issue has grown loudest from grassroots Aboriginal people living in the communities which the Assembly of First Nations supposedly represents—particularly from Aboriginal youth who seem to be fed up with what they perceive as systemic corruption. Complaints from community members about the state of First Nation democracy and the attendant political pathologies in Canada are escalating significantly. The widespread views of ordinary Aboriginal citizens canvassed from the extensive national hearings held by the Royal Commission (as expressed in its Report) found that:

> **There is a widespread perception in some communities that their leaders rule rather than lead their people, and that corruption and nepotism are prevalent.** Increasingly, Aboriginal people are challenging their leaders through a variety of means, including legal suits brought against leaders by individual members for alleged breaches of public duty.[247] [Emphasis added]

Not surprisingly, many of the younger and more educated Chiefs are now beginning to lend their voices to this chorus and are calling for governance reform.

Don Sandberg contends that democracy is dysfunctional on Canada's First Nations reserves because: "Nothing divides tribes more than band elections, which are almost always controversial and in many cases fundamentally anti-democratic."[248] He supports this view with actual examples citing the gross abuses of power, and mismanagement of resources. These are taking place, he suggests, in an atmosphere where there is virtually no accountability for such indiscretions.[249] Another writer suggests that: "Rank-and-file members feel vulnerable when so much power is concentrated in the hands of a few band councillors. Most bands lack an opposition party, an ombudsperson, or a locally applicable charter of rights."[250] The frustration with what has been called the lamentable status of Aboriginal democracy is being vented more and more by Aboriginal youth fed up with what they term "elitism," "corruption," and "cronyism."

Aboriginal youth bloggers[251] are flooding the Internet with their dissatisfaction:

> Democracy? Where? Freedom does not exist, only a lenient amount of restriction. …I think we need to address the challenges we face first, and be really aware of what our Chief and council are spending the funds on. I hate to say that I'm from my reserve, because I'm ashamed of it. For

example, I'm ashamed of how it's being run, how the funding is blown, and how deep corruption runs. It's the peoples' fault for voting for corruption, over and over again.[252]

In another account:

[In a letter] to other band members [on the Sturgeon Lake reserve], a group calling itself "Concerned Community Citizens" wrote: "We have all sat quietly and watched our community weaken, even crumble before us through GREED, CORRUPTION, LYING, FAVORITISM, SELFISH-NESS, and plain IGNORANCE for long enough. We need to take a strong stand against the way we are being treated as people [by their Chief and Council]. We desperately need changes in the way our housing is selected and basically toyed with, the way our Social Services department treats or ignores needy clients, the way OUR ELDERS are used, shunned, or pushed aside, and the lack of communication between our leaders and the rest of the community."

Two months later, a letter to the Auditor-General of Canada signed by 51 band members "pleads" for a forensic audit, alleging favouritism in financial assistance, as well as lack of both accountability and transparency on the part of the administration. Chief and council refuse to assist handicapped children despite the availability of funds, the letter claims. "CMHC [Canadian Mortgage and Housing Corporation] housing guidelines are not followed by chief and council; e.g.: dismantling the Housing Committee the day before housing selections, then turning around and appointing themselves the selection committee, applying for and accepting CMHC dollars for one band member and awarding the house to another band member...

"Based on the information above," the letter concludes, "membership and undersigned plead with your office to conduct the forensic audit immediately. Indian and Northern Affairs Canada (INAC) has been notified and failed to take our concerns seriously and have labelled our concerns an internal matter."

As Verna Soto, one of the letter's authors discovered to her dismay, there is no legislation concerning accountability between First Nation leaders and members. With the phasing out of the Indian Agents in the 1960s, Aboriginals moved abruptly from being governed to governing themselves without any accountability being built in: administrative and financial practices evolved without baseline standards throughout the country. ...[253]

Such views are widespread in the Aboriginal community.

Clearly, those bearing the brunt of Aboriginal leadership corruption are the disillusioned Aboriginal youth. They see a system where Chiefs play a political game for the sole purpose of keeping the gravy train of benefits and perks flowing to their families and their supporters. They perceive a system wherein Chiefs keep federal politicians at bay (who never actually take on real reform initiatives) by means of campaign contributions or threats designed to create political embarrassment. The goal of these Chiefs is to continue to deliver government funds into the hands of the chosen few and their cronies. The views of Aboriginal youth are possibly mirrored in one writer's description of Palestinian youth's views after the recent death of Yasir Arafat:

> Young Fatah cadres in the West Bank and Gaza soon found that corruption of their elders was matched by a complete lack of positive ideas— however farfetched or loony—about the form that the future Palestinian polity might take. There would be no Year Zero of the Palestinian revolution. Western-style parliamentary institutions did exist but had little power. What followed Arafat's return was a decades-long thieves' banquet at which Fatah's old guard divided up the spoils of Oslo and treated ordinary Palestinians as conquered subjects [allegedly stealing half of the approximately $7.5 billion in foreign aid contributed for the building of the new Palestinian nation] ....[254]

What many young Aboriginal people have seen too often in their own communities is more like a century-long thieves' banquet masquerading as democracy under the so-called rule of law. They see federal politicians wilfully blinded to their reality by threatened political controversy from Chiefs whose interest is in keeping the banquet going—Chiefs who also play the political party game and loudly let it be known that they expect that their political contributions and support be returned once federal MPs are elected. Aboriginal youth see a system that cannot be reformed because the only way to reform is to ask the gorging banquet participants themselves to bring it to an end. As we have already seen with Bill C-7 (the governance accountability-transparency legislation thwarted by the Chiefs), there is no rush to end the

Indian Act banquet. There is little wonder that youth are leaving such communities in droves. There is little wonder that without some hope of improvement, Aboriginal youth view their futures as bleak, which may be a serious contributing factor to the high suicide rates. Many Aboriginal youth do feel they are "conquered subjects" of a systemic and antiquated form of governance suited to the benefit of elites and paid for on the backs of the suffering of grassroots indigenous people.

An organization "…called the First Nations Accountability Coalition (FNAC), a grassroots organization claiming a membership of 5,000 from across Canada [that has arisen in frustration], has called for an independent body to hear complaints of band council improprieties. FNAC, along with the [former] Alliance Party, has called for a First Nations Ombudsman [as is found in every province in Canada with the exception of Prince Edward Island]. The ultimate purpose…is achieving good governance by monitoring First Nation and Aboriginal governments' accountability."[255]

What is quite clear is that real democracy, fair election procedures, and transparent and accountable governance are fundamental to creating a sustainable economy for moving Aboriginal peoples forward. What is equally clear is that such governance structures are available in only the most generous interpretation of the current *Indian Act* system. What is required is leadership at the federal level to see the situation largely for what it is. For the sake of ordinary Aboriginal people, it is time for leadership at all levels to institute real governance reform.

ABORIGINAL ELITES AND GOVERNMENT LATERAL VIOLENCE

> To unequal privileges among members of the same society the spirit of our nation is, with one accord, adverse.
> THOMAS JEFFERSON TO HUGH WHITE, 1801, ME 10:258

Effectively, by making Aboriginal people reliant on welfare and transfer payments, and with Band Councils as gatekeepers for the only wealth coming into communities, a natural tension has been created between those in government and their community members. This technique of colonization was employed by the British Empire throughout the world and served the brilliant purpose of distracting populations that might cause trouble externally by redirecting that aggression internally. In practice, what results is a situation in which Band Councils are often perceived by a significant portion of their membership as oppressors. This scheme has worked well for the government. They have been able to keep Indians more or less in line by having them fight amongst themselves for what is, in the larger context, a few fiscal welfare crumbs. From a business person's perspective, this infighting has consumed communities and blinded them to the real economic action that has been taking place all around them in which they might have shared handsomely. It also arguably leads to retarding the Canadian economy generally by blocking major development projects throughout the country that might otherwise proceed.

In reality, Band Councils are all-powerful. As gatekeepers to the transfer payment gold, they make all the rules. It is not wise to criticize the Band Council if you are reliant upon them for welfare, employment, economic development grants, housing, or whatever. While there are many Band Councils that temper the powers that they exercise over community members, there are some that rule by out-and-out intimidation. In some Aboriginal communities, the air of oppression and tension is so thick you can almost cut it with a knife. It is no wonder that many Aboriginal people are simply leaving these communities. Despite approximately 50 percent of the Aboriginal population in urban centres receiving only 3.5 percent of government spending, this is still perceived by many to be a better alternative than living in such negative, oppressive environments.

One Aboriginal writer expresses her view as follows:

The...First Nation is controlled and manipulated to the benefit of an elite. ... In reality...the band council serves merely as the legal front for a handful of career politicians, who early on in devolution in the department of Indian affairs were first in line to claim funds and authority. ... This small group became the beneficiaries of the Indian affairs system, while purporting to be the vanguard of self-government.

In the interest of its own political survival, the...band council has given over areas of authority to the director of tribal operations, who manages our home community in the style of a feudal lord, and the hereditary chiefs and treaty negotiation team—groups organized to benefit the old guard who claim responsibility for "everything we have today."

Meaningful community consultation doesn't exist.

...

The reality of our community is lateral violence. ... Instead of striking out at those responsible for oppression, people long rendered powerless strike out at each other. The result is feuding, gossip, blaming and constant internal battle… We carry out the oppressor's work towards societal destruction ourselves. … Lateral violence thrives because it serves the interests of those few positions in power.[256]

As we have seen, Aboriginal community governments are different from non-Aboriginal communities since the kinds of oversight and checks and balances on government excesses are largely not found there. We have already learned that there is generally no opposition party in communities, and those who dare run against the incumbent government are at an enormous disadvantage. Furthermore, there is no ombudsperson or locally applicable charter of rights to provide some kind of check on local governmental power. If there is any suspicion of wrongdoing, community members are virtually powerless in seeking the sort of accountability that ordinary Canadians take for granted. If there is a complaint or suspicion of wrongdoing, there is generally no local newspaper that will report this to bring it to the attention of the community. What exists in most communities are what have been referred to by some of the more cynical community members as "newsletter propaganda rags" sent out by some Band Councils. These are perceived by many as mostly an effort to convince off-reserve Band members (who recently won the right to vote in on-reserve elections) that they deserve to be re-elected.

You can seek some kind of court action against a Band Council, but few unemployed people can afford to take on a Band Council cashed up by federal transfer payments. You might request documentation directly, or seek to have INAC intervene, or even seek to have an RCMP investigation. The problem with all of these options is that the Band Council is in control of any documentary evidence and, as they say on the police television drama series "NYPD Blue", are usually "lawyered up" (with the help of government money of course). Band Councils respond to inquiries about fiscal questions with the line that they have prepared audited statements, and those statements reveal the Band's true state of affairs. From a community member's perspective, however, the problem with current audits is that they can bury extravagant excesses and wrongdoing under subject headings which make it impossible to tell exactly what monies were actually spent on. Bands should be compelled to provide members access to their general ledgers any time they wish to see them (in a manner similar to access to Minute books which corporate shareholders enjoy). Community members are simply placed in a system where they have no practical ability to pursue the kinds of information relating to transparency and accountability that all other Canadians take for granted.

As noted earlier, under the system of government established by the *Indian Act,* band governments are answerable only to Ottawa, rather than to their own people. Despite the massive power inequities that exist between band members and their governments, INAC rarely intervenes to assist ordinary Aboriginal people. In utter frustration, many Aboriginal groups are taking their complaints to organizations such as the Canadian Taxpayers Federation and to mainstream media outlets[257] in order to get some kind of airing of their grievances.[258] This is being done despite the fact that many Aboriginal people disagree with the solutions proposed by such conservative organizations. Clearly, democracy and the exercise of power in these communities needs to be fixed.

CORRUPTION, NEPOTISM, AND ABUSE OF POWER

> In the wake of scandals about government-funded cruises taken by native leaders [using monies earmarked for grassroots community healthcare], another regular spot [on the CBC radio program "Dead Dog Café Comedy Hour"] was launched to teach listeners conversational Cree phrases for such things as, "Is there a charge for that deckchair?" and "How long will we be in port?"[259]

According to Aboriginal historian, Olive Dickason, humour was a recognized hallmark of Aboriginal peoples from the earliest of times. To this day, one of the really endearing qualities of Aboriginal people is their wonderful sense of humour and willingness to poke fun at their own shortcomings and foibles. One well-known Aboriginal comedian tells the joke about the Minister of Indian Affairs slipping and falling on the stairs and landing on his backside. He said, "You know what happened when he landed? He broke the noses of seven Indian Chiefs!" When it comes to real discussion about problems that many grassroots members feel plague their communities, however, the hallmark humour becomes strained.

Many are uncomfortable talking publicly about corruption, nepotism and mismanagement in their communities. On the one hand, they do not wish to provoke a backlash and the often vicious retribution from their Band Councils. Don Sandberg is one of the few Aboriginal people who has had the courage to write about wrongdoing on his reserve, and he tells of the steep price he was made to pay. He was sued by the Chief he wrote about (using Band funds) with the Chief positioning himself as a victim seeking $40,000 in damages. The suit was subsequently withdrawn just prior to trial since it was without merit. Mr. Sandberg, who had to fend the frivolous suit off with his own limited finances, was made miserable for the two year period this dragged on.

Apparently, the same Chief had previously sued six elders from his community for bringing forward damaging information, but when it got to trial, a very upset judge warned the Chief about bringing such frivolous cases to his court and dismissed the case.[260] As if this weren't enough, the Chief and his cronies took further retribution (following an *Indian Act* process) and Mr. Sandberg was given 24 hours to vacate his home on the reserve. This forced him and his wife to abandon some family pets, while some of the horses used in his business had to be sold at a loss. He was then summarily turfed out of his house and could not return to his community. And, it turned out, this was only the beginning of the retribution taken against him.[261] All because he apparently had the gall to criticize the almighty Chief. Under the *Indian Act* system he was essentially powerless.

Mr. Sandberg comments further: "On many First Nations, anyone who dares question the actions of incumbent leaders runs the risk of being 'BCR'd.' That stands for "band council resolution," an edict forcing you off the reserve. If you refuse to comply, the council invokes its police powers, augmented by the ultimate sanction, the RCMP."[262] In another sordid account of a Chief and Council's gross abuse of power and process (in another community), on a flimsy pretext, a family was evicted summarily from their homes, kicked off the reserve, and their children threatened with forceful placement in child welfare care. Mr. Sandberg asks, "Is this legal? No, but redress is nearly impossible. Indian Affairs tends to ignore such problems. The courts? You may obtain legal assistance, but the council has money to hire the best lawyers available. In theory, you can ask the Grand Chief to intervene, but the chiefs elect him and he seldom criticizes them."[263]

To appreciate the full extent of the reprisal atmosphere existing on some reserves across Canada, one should read Mr. Sandberg's full account of these incidents. I have included these extensive quotations because they provide a good sense of the banana republic-like mindset existing in many communities.

If you were not aware that we were talking about Canada in the above incidents, it might lead one to believe the atrocities of displacement were currently taking place in third world African countries such as Zimbabwe. Many Aboriginal youth are voicing the opinion that might be summarized as "God save ordinary community members from the Mugabe-like dictates of some of the Chiefs." It is difficult to imagine that an ordinary Canadian must or would put up with such tyranny. One must ask, "Where is the Canadian government while these gross abuses of power and fundamental human rights are taking place?" At the very least, knowledge that such activities are allowed to exist is a scathing indictment on a supposedly advanced G-8 country! How are Aboriginal people supposed to move forward when their own federal government-sanctioned elected officials are enforcing the poverty and attendant corruption that is the causal link to most of the problems in the first place?

Aboriginal people are also reluctant to speak publicly about these issues because they do not wish to provide grist for the political right in Canada who many feel are racist, and have no real interest in actually trying to make the situation better (though often there is a sizeable, but silent contingent that support the publication of such issues in what might be considered right-of-center publications, because they are regarded as only telling the truth and trying to make things better for the ordinary Aboriginal folks). Generally, non-Aboriginal observers have been reluctant to raise this issue as well because, in the current climate of political correctness, they might automatically be labelled as racists. Even the many Chiefs and Councils that are running honest governments in the best interests of their members feel compelled to defend against such reported abuses, because they fear their activities may become tarred with a brush that does not apply in their particular circumstance. Usually when this matter is raised publicly, there are entrenched positions on both sides of the debate and little communication as to how to solve these problems.

The fact is that there are some Aboriginal communities that are run well and some that are not. Many Chiefs, particularly some of the younger, well-educated ones, have tried to break the paradigm of tyranny created by some of the old-school *Indian Act* Chiefs. If I were to hazard a guess, however, I would suspect that, on a per-community basis, the incidences of abuses of power greatly exceed the incidences in non-Aboriginal municipalities. If these problems exist, they should be discussed openly and real solutions sought. If there are problems, to paraphrase Martin Luther King's famous speech, "let transparency and openness reign from the mountains."

In 1999, the Auditor-General Report confirmed that INAC had reported receiving over 300 allegations relating to 108 First Nations during the two-year period prior to its audit. The allegations related to such matters as social assistance issues, mismanagement of funds and other concerns. The report indicated that because departmental data was incomplete, the total reported was the minimum known number of allegations. Because of the poor and inconsistent system of recording these cases, it is difficult to know exactly what the scope of complaints by First Nation community members is in regards to their governments.[264] If there were a real system of accountability in place where whistleblowers were shielded from retribution, I suspect the incidence of complaints would be much higher.

Another source required an Access to Information Request from INAC to learn that "From 2002–2004, the Department of Indian Affairs reported 984 allegations of criminal or complaints of non-criminal wrongdoing by their native government bodies or organizations."[265]

Again, what is surprising is that the kinds of abuses described above are taking place under the noses and with the knowledge of the existing government and bureaucracy. It truly is outrageous that they should be perpetrated on anyone in Canada, much less the poorest of the poor. It is time to reform this archaic, feudal, third-world system that can be called democratic only with the most generous of interpretations. We need real Aboriginal and federal level leadership now—leadership that has the best interests of Aboriginal people foremost—to take the reins in calling for and implementing an agenda of reform.

MISMANAGEMENT

> This is an indispensable aspect of ensuring democratic accountability, both within Aboriginal communities and more broadly in this country. Aboriginal Canadians need to have the same tools available to them as are available to all other Canadians to identify and constrain any excess in the use of government power, or corruption, or for that matter, mismanagement.
>
> MR. JIM PRENTICE, Calgary Centre-North, CPC[266]

"The 1999 Auditor-General's Report… revealed that Indian Affairs had to intervene in the management of 167 of 585 of the country's Indian Bands, after financial audits reveal debts totalling $139 million. Fifteen bands required third-party management. …."[267] The Indian and Northern Affairs Canada and Canadian Polar Commission Report for 2003–2004 indicated further that as of March 31, 2004, 23 percent of First Nations, Tribal Councils and political organizations were under some form of management intervention (with 5 percent being managed by a third party, 8 percent being co-managed, and 10 percent recipient managed under a remedial management plan).[268]

Another source suggests that:

Indian people are becoming increasingly vocal about band mismanagement, and have lodged hundreds of complaints about band councils and administrators. But instead of vigorously addressing these concerns, Ottawa has tip-toed around the issues, and has been slow to act. Whether this is due to a misguided sense of political correctness, stumbling self-government initiatives, or bureaucratic inertia is beside the point. Healthy communities cannot survive under banana republic rules.[269]

Former National Chief of the Assembly of First Nations, Matthew Coon Come, openly admitted that some Chiefs mismanage funds and they: "should open their books to members who have accountability questions. ..."[270]

How can such a situation exist? We have seen that the question of accountability and transparency has systemic roots. In relation to mismanagement, however, there may be other factors that might be considered causes. Don Sandberg suggests: "Part of the source of the problem, if not the main one, is that many Aboriginal leaders have only limited education and business experience themselves. As it now stands, some elected leaders have little or no high school education and in some cases little grasp of the English language. Not to put these people down, but allowing them to operate a band office that receives millions of dollars from Ottawa to run businesses is a recipe for mismanagement and waste. The people of these First Nations pay the price."[271]

There must be real accountability in the management of Aboriginal assets and resources in Canada. Many governments squander enormous amounts of resources that could otherwise be put to good use. If there is an abuse of power or corruption, Aboriginal wrongdoers should face the same criminal sanctions that anyone else in Canada faces. To argue otherwise is tantamount to contending that Aboriginal people in Canada don't deserve the transparency, accountability, and careful fiscal management that ordinary Canadians take for granted. Leaders who are abusing the system and resisting constructive reform will continue to condemn their communities to poverty and the abuses of lateral violence.

"We have to stop letting lawyers and consultants suck up all of our money."
ROBERT NAULT, former Minister of Indian and Northern Affairs[272]

The failed Governance Act, Bill C-7, was touted by former Minister of Indian Affairs, Robert Nault, as a plan "to stop putting [federal monies for Aboriginal people]…in the hands of people who have made an industry out of Aboriginal people's misery."[273] In 2003, Aboriginal Peoples Television Network held a call-in program titled "Is there a Misery Industry?" The original email promo for the program read in part: "Whether they're lawyers, prison guards, doctors, social workers or Indian Affairs bureaucrats, it seems a lot of people make a living off of Aboriginal dependency… the business of keeping Aboriginal people poor, un-educated and sick and perpetually in need of others' 'help'… [H]ow much [government money] actually makes its way down to the people? How big is the 'cut' sliced off by consultants and administrators? And does it matter if any of them are Aboriginal or not?"[274]

There is no question that, given the social conditions of Aboriginal people, a considerable amount of external support is necessary. But how much of this amounts to real support, and how much of it involves exploitation by the Indian Industry? It is difficult to know since there is apparently no specific government data published to shed light on this question.

The scale of the problem is more discernible in the treaty negotiation area. The Auditor-General of Canada, Sheila Fraser, in her first budget for fiscal year 2000 disclosed that the debts of Indian Bands negotiating treaties stood at a staggering $550 million. (These are monies that were borrowed from the federal government to negotiate these treaties.) The Auditor-General indicated that "For a few First Nations, the amount of their negotiation loans now approach 50 percent of the expected settlement amounts and has become another impediment to settlement."[275]

This situation is nothing short of astonishing. Who is monitoring this? Surely Aboriginal community members would not sanction seeing the future trust of their nations, half of their treaty settlements, wasted on negotiations alone? Community members rightfully ask whether they have given up the birthright and land rights of their ancestors to see over 50 percent of the compensation given to the Indian Industry before a settlement is even reached? According to British Columbia Aboriginal leader Bill Wilson (representing the First Nations Summit) the only groups benefiting from the negotiations were lawyers and consultants.[276] Community members complain that many

Aboriginal negotiators have latched onto the sinecure as well and have made profitable careers largely through negotiating one treaty. Youth view many of these negotiators as elitists not wishing to bring an end to the "ongoing banquet" but instead are sucking the assets out of a treaty settlement before it is even made. Ordinary Aboriginal folk wonder where the incentive for their negotiators to settle their treaties is, when they are profiting handsomely from the process. Many also ask where this debt stands in 2006.

In New Zealand, Maori negotiators, when they are paid, receive only modest *per diems* for negotiations; lawyers and consultants largely "spec" (work for no charge on) the negotiation work until a settlement is actually reached. In addition to not squandering the resources of community members in the negotiation phase, this process has the built-in "adverse clock" which ensures that settlements are concluded on a timely basis. Finally, Maoris do not receive transfer payments as in Canada. Once the settlement is made, it is critical that competent trustees are selected to ensure that tribal members receive an adequate return on their assets. Resources in such a small country must be managed carefully. For the Maoris, other than their treaty settlements, there are no other resources. As a result, there is simply no room for the types of mismanagement, nepotism and related shenanigans without severe long-term fallout for the tribes and their members.

Even though it is difficult to quantify what the Indian Industry is "skimming" off the financial resources intended for Aboriginal peoples, there seems to be no question that this amount is substantial. Where possible, these entrenched interests should be shuffled aside (since their real interest is in keeping the system that is rewarding them handsomely just as it is). Once this is done, the real business of moving forward can take place.

{ 4 }

**THE FOURTH WAVE:
A WAY OUT OF THE STORM**

IO

FROM GRIEVANCE TO DEVELOPMENT MODE: AN AGENDA FOR ACTION

The only cure for grief is action.
GEORGE HENRY LEWES, *The Spanish Drama—Life of Lope De Vega*

ASKING THE RIGHT QUESTION

Some men see things as they are and say, "Why?" I dream of things that never were and say, "Why not?"
GEORGE BERNARD SHAW

We have seen how the mythical indigenous canoe has been swamped in the high seas stirred up by the colonial storm. We have also examined the legacy of this tumultuous period, the welfare trap. This era of chaos has resulted in dependency and has reduced once-proud peoples to the status of an impoverished underclass. While Aboriginals may have been the *first* peoples in Canada historically, the statistics clearly reveal that they are actually the last peoples by most social and economic measurements.

In response to the tribulations of this time, a prolonged period of grieving has set in while Aboriginals have mourned the loss of their cultures, languages, self-reliance, and the precious societies from which they emerged. There is no question that the Aboriginal canoe has been visited by massive trauma and there is substantial justification for grieving. The basic purpose of grieving is to allow for a period of adjustment to a psychological trauma. Grieving and bereavement rituals are said to have the common theme of serving a tremendous therapeutic value in transitioning, or assisting in moving forward with, one's life.[277] Unfortunately, the current Aboriginal response has not changed much from those ancient Chiefs in whose time the trauma of colonization was a fresh experience and their grief very much justified.

Typical historical grieving is clearly articulated by Red Jacket, a Seneca Chief of the Iroquois Confederacy and perhaps the most outstanding Aboriginal orator of the eighteenth century. In rejecting the efforts of land promoters seeking through the U.S. federal government to take a portion of Seneca land received not long before under a treaty with the United States, Red Jacket said:

> "I have told you of the treaty we made with the United States. Here is the belt of wampum that confirmed that treaty. Here, too is the parchment. You know its contents [pledging never again to disturb the Seneca in the possession of their lands]. I will not open it. Now the tree of friendship is decaying; its limbs are fast falling off. You [pointing at the government agent] are at fault."[278]

The current problem is that many indigenous leaders still seem to be stuck in grieving mode when the time to move on has already come and gone. The tendency is to look only inward at the wreckage from the storm—at the horrendous social pathologies, and the dysfunction that has resulted. Many leaders have made a subtle shift from "grieving" to "grievance." Seemingly mesmerized by the carnage, they continue to ask only one question: "Who are we going to blame for this mess?" This has been a useful question while in a grieving phase. It has allowed indigenous people to clearly pinpoint the causal agents of their trauma, and provided for a considerable period of emotional readjustment to the new, more dismal circumstances.

It is true that in Canada and the United States, the respective federal governments are largely the culprits in the well-known historical drama of deceit, cultural villainy, and genocide. At the end of the day, however, the only practical and useful question that should be asked is: "*What are we going to do about the mess?*" We would be much better off at this stage heeding the ancient words of wisdom from the eloquent Omaha tribal orator, Big Elk. Upon being asked to deliver a speech befitting the occasion of the burial of Black Buffalo, a deceased Teton Sioux Chief, Big Elk sagely advised:

> Do not grieve—misfortunes will happen to the wisest and best of men. Death will come, and always comes out of season; it is the command of the Great Spirit, and all nations and people must obey.
>
> What is passed, and cannot be prevented should not be grieved for…[279]

The problem with always looking back is that there is nothing we can do about what has already happened. How can the constructive future of indigenous nations be founded on festering grievances of the past? Should we not be focussing on positive, forward-looking solutions to a new polity, a new economy, a fresh outlook, rather than being anchored entirely in rancorous injustices of the past (no matter how justified such views are)? How is dwelling on historical injustices going to lift indigenous people out of the morass of social and political pathologies? Memories of government duplicity from Red Jacket's time are distant history to today's youth who see only a systemic treadmill of misery with little hope of reform.

We should be asking, "What pragmatic steps can we take now to make the lives of ordinary indigenous people better?" It should be obvious that we must begin moving forward and start looking for real solutions. To paraphrase Bill Wilson, the result of simply continuing to seek blame is that we continue to "wallow in the puke of our own suffering."

As the Maori in New Zealand say, the time is ripe to switch gears from *grievance* to *development mode*.[280] There is no substitute for a practical development programme for a better future—one with a clear strategy, timeline, and measurable goals. While wealth creation is something that can take place immediately (and there is no question that it can have constructive dramatic impacts on the indigenous populations affected), a more carefully considered, longer-term strategic plan must be designed in parallel.

THE ABORIGINAL STARTING POINT: MOVING FORWARD FROM A REALISTIC POSITION

> If everyone keeps moving forward together, then success takes care of itself.
> HENRY FORD

As maintained throughout this book, the responsibility for getting out of the welfare trap rests, first and foremost, squarely on the shoulders of indigenous people themselves. In order to move forward, certain fundamental principles must be recognized, understood and accepted as the basis for developing a strategic plan. At this point it may be useful to summarize these principles:

1 Indigenous people must want to change the course of their history and pledge total commitment to constructive change.

2 Indigenous people must take ownership of the welfare trap as their problem even though it was not caused by them. The truth is that no third party

(such as the federal government) could ever really provide a solution to a deeply-embedded crisis of another group.

3 Before moving forward, indigenous people must admit their real condition, no matter how unflattering or brutal the conclusions. This should include acknowledgement that:

    a most indigenous governments and individuals are almost completely dependent on welfare and transfer payments for their survival;

    b this circumstance has lead to the welfare trap and a host of damaging social and political pathologies; and

    c simply asking the government for more money without addressing the fundamental causal issues will never lead to a solution.

4 The welfare trap has created self-erected attitudinal barriers in the indigenous mindset that prevents moving forward (the culture of expectancy, lateral violence, learned helplessness, etc.)

5 In going forward, Aboriginal people must understand the realities of their ancestors' success and self-reliance over millennia (a foundation of independence, interdependence, self-discipline, ethical leadership, and cultural cooperation.)

6 As long as Aboriginal people do not control their own purse strings, those who do will control Aboriginal peoples' destiny.

7 Aboriginal problems can never be solved by money alone. The future of Aboriginal nations does not depend on how much monies Chiefs are successful in extracting from the government; real success will be measured by the well-being, health and happiness of community members. In fact, simply pouring government monies down the current welfare black hole may not only exacerbate existing conditions, but may actually contribute directly to prolonging the suffering of Aboriginal people.

8 All parties must acknowledge the uncompromising reality of the demographic tsunami. Neither Aboriginals nor ordinary Canadians have the choice of doing nothing—the current system relating to Aboriginal people must be reformed to achieve practical, progressive outcomes for everyone.

Indigenous people must engage in the process of creating their own wealth, and use this to create meaningful work and further opportunities. In the same manner as we take ownership of our problems, we must also take ownership of our future.

SPIRIT BEAR (MOOKSGM'OL)

The spirit bear is a sub-species of black kermode bear, not an albino. It is considered a rare protected species found in the ancestral Tsimshian territory on Princess Royal Island. The bears' habitat is now jeopardized by aggressive logging practices. Many salmon streams have been logged to the point where salmon, a primary food source for the bears, no longer return. This painting shows the Spirit Bear waiting for the salmon to return. Real conservation measures have to be taken to protect this species now. A percentage of the proceeds of the Spirit Bear limited edition giclée prints go towards educating and warning people about these concerns .

> Economic independence is the foundation of the only sort of freedom
> worth a damn.
>
> H.L. MENCKEN

In the final analysis, a key component of a solution is "the economy, Stupid." If indigenous people ever want to be truly self-reliant, they have to develop their own source of wealth creation—in exactly the same fashion as our ancestors did throughout their 9,600 year canoe journey. Everyone in the world needs an economy to survive. We are only fooling ourselves and prolonging the conditions of the welfare trap if we think we can do otherwise. Without self-generated revenue, all the political talk about self-government is just talk. It is tantamount to arguing that you are personally independent, but still live (rent free) with, and receive an allowance from, your parents. In a column titled "Tell the truth & then leave the room," Aboriginal writer, Arnie Louie, asks:

> How can we have sovereignty when we are heavily dependent on DIA funding? We don't have control over our own education and social programs; we can't do anything without permission from DIA. That's sovereignty? Any logical person would say that's dependency.[281]

Some indigenous people contend that engaging in business compromises our cultures and "indigenousness." Mr. Louie's response:

> There's no culture in an unemployment line. There's no pride or heritage in a welfare cheque. Culture, pride and heritage are enhanced when people are supporting themselves and their families.[282]

For communities, it is important that the social impact of business development be gauged carefully; poorly conceived development can exacerbate existing problems. At the same time, while it is possible that business development may negatively impact indigenous culture, the same question might be asked as to whether Chinese, Japanese, or Jewish people are less Chinese, Japanese, or Jewish because they engage in business? The answer should be fairly clear. These groups still continue to be culturally Chinese, Japanese, and Jewish and actually use the wealth created from business to bolster their cultures. Even if there were significant negative impacts resulting from economic integration, it would be difficult to imagine how these could be worse than what is being delivered under the welfare trap.

Indigenous cultures cannot remain frozen in time while the rest of the world progresses. All societies must evolve and adapt to the ever-changing dynamic conditions of everyday life—just as our ancestors adapted to and profited from the fur trade upon the arrival of Europeans. In fact, this evolution is what makes life challenging and interesting. At a recent conference, an Aboriginal speaker talked about how he was tired of hearing some indigenous people speculate about how bad economic integration was when the alternative—poverty—is delivering so much misery and hardship. He sarcastically commented that he would "prefer economic integration to starvation."

AN AGENDA FOR ACTION

Wai Wah—Tsimshian expression for *"just do it"*

If you want to know your past—look into your present conditions. If you want to know your future—look into your present actions.
CHINESE PROVERB

Thousands of years before Nike coined its advertising slogan, "Just do it!" the Sma'lgyax (coastal Tsimshian language) phrase "*Wai Wah*" was commonly used. What more need be said? We need to stop talking and "Just do it!" We do not need more studies into problems already well-known. We do not need more expensive Royal Commissions, or political puffery. We need to have a clear strategy for development, and a timeline for specific actions with measurable outcomes. *Wai Wah.*

The only thing we have to lose is the welfare dependency mindset, the colonial grip of a patronizing bureaucracy, and the plague of social and political pathologies. What we have to gain is control over our lives, and the satisfaction of being able to provide educational and other opportunities for our families. We need to act now to return the dignity, self-respect, self-reliance, and pride vital to the survival of our ancestors. It is time to quit belly-aching and start developing. The new discourse of indigenous people should not be about assigning blame with most effort concentrated on extracting welfare from the government. **The new discourse should be about action, moving forward with a real strategy, about creating a polity that is fair and widely-accepted to the indigenous grassroots, and the development of an economy that leads to self-reliance.** *Wai Wah.*

SPIRIT BEAR TRADITIONAL DESIGN

This painting represents a stylistically more traditional design depicting

the *mooksgm'ol* (spirit bear). Tsimshian people have a special respect

for the spirit bear because of its great rarity.

It is critical for Aboriginal people to commit to not only getting themselves out of the mess, but demographic trends have revealed that it is also essential for the future health and prosperity of Canada as a nation. *Neither Aboriginals nor mainstream Canadians have a choice*—to survive in the style to which we have become accustomed as a nation, the system must be reformed. The situation and the many obstacles may look insurmountable. The reality now, however, is that Aboriginal people are likely in the best position since the arrival of the colonial storm to move themselves forward in partnership with business, industry, government, and labor—and this couldn't have occurred at a better time in the economic history of Canada. *Wai Wah.*

There is no one simple solution for such a complex problem. There are short-term measures that can have a major impact if addressed immediately while the longer term strategic goals are being mapped. While economic opportunities must be pursued to begin creating revenue, building capacity, and understanding business and industry, a longer-term solution requiring a carefully crafted strategic policy framework is also required.

DUAL STRATEGIES: COMMUNITIES VS. URBAN POPULATIONS

A strategy for moving Aboriginal peoples forward must recognize the new reality of circumstances and conditions between rural communities and the larger and rapidly-growing urban-based Aboriginal population. While most solutions have focussed solely on the development of communities, this focus ignores the fact that over 50% of Canada's Aboriginal population live in urban centres. What then might be suggested to help out the largest part of the population? We have already learned that almost 90% of federal government transfer payments go to rural communities while the larger off-reserve population receives only 3.5% of this assistance when, arguably, they have equivalent needs. There must be a better accounting to Aboriginal stakeholders and taxpayers for how, strategically and effectively, these monies are spent.

In effect, to move Aboriginal peoples forward, there must be two strategies: one for rural communities and one for urban-based Aboriginals.

WAI WAH, AMERICA

> Our England is a garden, and such gardens are not made
> By singing:—"Oh, how beautiful!" and sitting in the shade.
> RUDYARD KIPLING

Mark Twain purportedly quipped: "There are basically two types of people. People who accomplish things, and people who claim to have accomplished things. The first group is less crowded." For mainstream American society, an important moment of truth is emerging that requires the nation to be in the first group.

The financial and social problems facing Americans are substantial. Regarding diabetes, a writer discussing the city of New York points out, "Within a generation or so, doctors fear, a huge wave of new cases could overwhelm the public health system and engulf growing numbers of the young, creating a city where hospitals are swamped by the disease's handiwork, schools scramble for resources as they accommodate diabetic children, and the workforce abounds with the blind and the halt."[283]

Another financial problem linking the staggering cost of health care and the nation's poor is reflected in statistics on overweight and obesity. By 2015, 75 percent of the American population (approximately 250 million people based on current projections) is expected to be overweight and 41 percent obese (over 20 percent of their ideal weight).[284] In other words, 135 million Americans will be obese in 2015—approximately four times the projected population of Canada at the time. As is now the case in many indigenous communities, obesity is fast becoming America's number one health threat.

A recent study suggests that obesity is in fact an economic issue and more prevalent in zip codes representing poor neighborhoods with low property values.[285] Across the Seattle metropolitan area where the study was conducted, obesity rates reached 30 percent in the most deprived areas but were only about 5 percent in the most affluent areas. For each additional $100,000 in the median price of homes, researchers found, obesity rates in a given zip code dropped by 2 percent.

By tackling the deeper issues of poverty, America can also address the long-term financial burden threatened by the oncoming demographic tsunami. As has been suggested for the indigenous population of Canada, what is required is an honest, open, and respectful dialogue beyond partisan politics that leads to a plan of action. Ralph Waldo Emerson commented that "good thoughts are no better than good dreams, unless they be executed." Once such a plan is wrought, America must call on the character trait for which it has become renowned—buckling down—to carry out such a plan of action. *Wai Wah*, America.

II

THE OPPORTUNITY

THE BOOMING AND GROWING ABORIGINAL BUSINESS SECTOR

We have discussed the substantial, negative fiscal and labor force consequences of failing to address the Aboriginal situation. The flip side is that it has the potential to be an enormous and largely untapped opportunity. There is no question that the Aboriginal impact on the economy can greatly exceed the raw population numbers. Charlie Coffey, Executive Vice-President of Government Affairs with the Royal Bank of Canada, has summarized the global opportunity:

> I am well aware that in many businesses, people don't always grasp the business benefits of relations with Aboriginal people and communities. For the Bank, the business benefits are clear. We see a significant and expanding market opportunity. The rapid increases in the Aboriginal population represent new customers. Land claims represent increased economic and financial clout of Aboriginal peoples and communities. The Aboriginal business sector—which has grown at a dramatic rate in recent years and is steadily moving the Aboriginal population towards economic self-sufficiency—is generating wealth and creating jobs.[286]

A 2002 report noted that there were over 27,000 self-employed individuals of Indian, Métis and Inuit heritage creating economic opportunities for their peoples—and making an important contribution to Canada's economy.[287] The Aboriginal business sector is expanding dramatically with the number of self-employed Aboriginal people in Canada increasing by 30.7% since 1996—*a rate nine times higher than for self-employed Canadians overall* (3.3%).

With the appropriate environment, Aboriginal business is poised to be a major contributor to the Canadian economy.

Although Canada's economy is becoming more "knowledge based," it is still primarily natural resource extraction driven. Unbeknownst to many, natural resources influence a significant portion of the world economy and are the largest "non-financial" market in the world.[288]

Resource development is currently growing at an astonishing rate. For Canada, expansion of resource growth is largely driven by huge, unremitting commodities-demand in the world markets. While, up until 2002, natural resources had been in a bear market for a quarter-century, commodities and raw materials are now experiencing a strong bull market—one projected to continue until at least 2015.

In what analysts are calling the China effect, "'Chinese demand for commodities is revolutionising global commodity markets,' say Merrill Lynch Investment Managers. 'China has already overtaken the United States as the largest consumer of iron ore, steel and copper.'"[289] In 2003, China overtook Japan as the world's second largest oil consumer and may outstrip the consumption of the United States by 2020.[290] This increase in demand has helped to send global oil prices skyrocketing. Although China still uses 17 times less wood per person than the United States, it is on course to become the world's top overall consumer within a few years. China imported about 1.5 billion cubic feet of timber in 2003, and expects to triple this to 4.4 billion cubic feet a year by 2010.[291]

While China is leading the international charge of Asian countries whose natural resource consumption is seeking to keep pace with their rapidly-expanding economies, India is also becoming a major factor. "'As China and India grow their economies and working families begin earning middle-class incomes, the demand for energy expands,' said Floyd J. McKay, Journalism Professor Emeritus at Western Washington University. ... '[With a total population of nearly 2.5 billion people,] one of the implications of a shift of wealth to these nations is a frightening increase in demand for the world's natural resources, particularly oil and natural gas,' he adds."[292] While this is occurring, Canada has the added luxury of circumstance– located as we are on the doorstep of the United States, still the largest single market in the world and the largest consumer of energy and natural resources in the world.

It so happens that the bulk of the Aboriginal population is found in Western and Northern Canada. This is exactly where most of the natural resource development is taking place—within the traditional territories of most Aboriginal nations. A 2005 newspaper article, reporting on the regional

RAVEN STEALS THE SUN

The story of the Raven stealing the sun is shared by many Northwest coast tribes. According to the legend, at the beginning of time there were no moon or stars at night. Raven was the most powerful being. He had made all living creatures. But they were all living in darkness because he had not made the sun. Raven learned that there was a chief living on the banks of the Nass River whose beautiful daughter possessed the sun, the moon, and the stars in a *gal'üünx* (a carved bentwood cedar box). To steal the sun, Raven decided to turn himself into a grandchild of the great chief. He flew into a large tree above the long house and turned himself into a hemlock needle. The needle fell into the daughter's drinking cup while she drank and was consumed. Raven was then born as a son to the Chief's daughter. Raven was dearly loved as child and would not stop crying unless he was allowed to play with the contents of the *gal'üünx*. As soon as he had the stars and moon, Raven threw them up through the smoke hole and they scattered across the sky. His grandfather, the Chief, was not happy with what he had done, but his soft heart could not take his crying and he gave him the *gal'üünx* again. Raven played with the box for a while, and when he thought the time was right, he turned himself back into a bird and flew up through the smoke hole with the sun, releasing it into the sky, which is how we came to have light today.

economic outlook of the TD bank, suggests that although there may be some cooling of the resource sector, the "Surging commodity prices and the soaring dollar have shifted the Canadian economic growth to the North and West. ..."[293]

Currently the economies of western and northern Canada are flying. Alberta, as of March 31, 2005, has generated so much revenue from the oil patch that it is now the first province in Canada to become fully debt free (by comparison Ontario has total a debt of $126 billion).[294] As of 2006, $87 billion dollars worth of investment is proposed, underway or committed in Alberta's oil sands. The oil sands alone purportedly contain more than 3 trillion barrels of oil (more than all of the oil in the Middle East) with proven reserves close to 180 billion barrels. This represents the world's second-largest proven reserves of oil, after Saudi Arabia (a country with one-quarter of the world's proven reserves).[295] U.S. Senator Orrin Hatch recently observed that Canada is set to be the "world's oil giant" and will inevitably overtake Saudi Arabia as the world's number one producer of oil.[296] Shell Canada Ltd. and its partners may spend as much as $17 billion in the next decade to double its oil production.[297] Two oil transportation giants, Enbridge Inc. and Terasen Pipelines, are teeing up competing multi-billion dollar plans to satisfy demand for crude oil in California and the Far East by proposing pipeline expansion from the rich oil sands of Alberta to the British Columbia coast.[298]

The economy of the Northwest Territories is booming. This area is home to 43,000 people living in 33 small communities with some fifty percent of the population of Aboriginal descent. Ekati and Diavik diamond mines are in production and the De Beers Snap Lake project is expected to begin production in 2006 (with the Jericho Diamond project in Nunavut also coming onstream in 2006).[299] Combined, these three mines will contribute an estimated $26 billion to the GDP over their lifetimes, with over $7.5 billion going into government revenues and the creation of almost 126,000 person-years of work. Diamonds from the Northwest Territories have made Canada the third largest producer of rough diamonds in the world by value. Promising possible mineable deposits have been discovered across almost every northern Province in Canada from Saskatchewan to Quebec.

Oil and gas activity in the Northwest Territories has increased markedly and the $8 billion dollar Mackenzie Valley Pipeline Project is expected to proceed once treaty issues there are settled. According to the Northwest Territories' premier, the Honourable Joe Handley, if it is developed properly the project has "the potential to trigger a level of economic growth unprecedented in the history of the Northwest Territories."[300] He comments further that "The scope and magnitude of this project for the Northwest Territories and Canada is a little overwhelming. Investment for this project and the associated long-term development of the Beaufort Mackenzie Delta reserves is expected to be almost $8 billion dollars, while total project revenues could be in excess of $50 billion dollars and the project is expected to create some 157,000 person-years of direct and indirect employment."[301]

The Yukon is supporting the Alaska Highway Pipeline Project, intended to bring natural gas from Alaska through Canada to hungry markets south of the 49th. This project will traverse the southwest corner of the Yukon, the northeast corner of British Columbia, and the western edge of Alberta. The construction cost of the project is estimated to be close to $12 billion and could boost Canada's GDP by a cumulative $26 billion to $31 billion including $18.6 billion for British Columbia and Yukon.[302] Premier of the Yukon, the Honourable Dennis Fentie, supports the vision of two northern pipelines (including the Mackenzie Valley), both with substantial Aboriginal participation.[303] The Alaska Highway Pipeline is expected to generate up to 375,000 person-years of employment within Canada over a 24-year period. Recently, the U.S. Senate passed bills with several key provisions for the pipeline, one of which includes loan guarantees of up to $18 billion.[304] There is also renewed industry interest in exploration and drilling for potential Yukon energy reserves. The Yukon currently has several advanced projects in the minerals sector which could result in as much as $400 million in new capital investment in the next few years. Forestry activity is also on the upswing in the territory.

Across northern Saskatchewan, Manitoba, Ontario, and Quebec, enormous hydro and related infrastructure and forestry projects are planned. In Northern Quebec, the massive Voisey's Bay Project is underway and a mine and mill/concentrator processing facility will be constructed over three years to process the over 32 million tonnes of proven ore reserves containing mostly nickel, copper and cobalt deposits. The construction cost is approximately $710 million and the construction of these facilities is expected to generate 1,700 person-years of employment (550 jobs at peak). Annual employment during the operations phase will be approximately 400 people.[305] The Quebec Cree have signed numerous multi-billion dollar agreements relating to huge hydro, forestry and similar projects. Across Canada generally, the residential construction boom totalled $70 billion in 2004, up 14 percent from $62 billion in 2003.[306]

The prospect of the 2010 Olympics and related infrastructure developments in British Columbia are fuelling close to $80 billion in infrastructure projects in the province.[307] There is $8.5 billion slated for development in BC's north[308] with two competing proposals for a liquefied natural gas plant (ranging in estimated cost from $300 to $500 million) for Prince Rupert or Kitimat.[309] In BC's Thompson-Okanagan region there is $7 billion in development projects under construction or on the books.[310]

Gas revenue royalties in BC hit record levels in 2004: exploration, development, distribution and production netted close to $2 billion in provincial payments with a record of 1,269 wells drilled representing an increase of 21 percent over 2003. The industry currently is providing 11,400 direct jobs and continues to accelerate at a torrid pace. Several BC coal mines have also reopened with the resurgence of interest in coal. As well, the offshore oil and gas potential likely will be on hold for a year or so according to recent announcements.[311] British Columbia government statistics suggest there is 10 billion barrels of oil, and 42 trillion cubic feet of gas in place offshore. Most activity is taking place in the northeastern portion of the province; while the rest of the province is estimated to contain 7.6 billion barrels of oil, 146 trillion cubic feet of natural gas, and 29 trillion cubic feet of coal bed methane gas.[312] Exploration interest in the mining and minerals industry is surging, and the forestry industry is experiencing banner years.

Furthermore, BC's proximity to Southeast Asia has all container ports running at over capacity with expansion planned for virtually every port along with attendant upgrades for rail and transportation infrastructure. Value of goods shipped through the Port of Vancouver rocketed in 2004 to $43 billion, a 48% increase from 2000—representing a $4 billion or 19% jump in the contribution to the economy.[313] Vancouver's port is expected to expand to a total capacity of 5 million TEUS (a standard container is two TEUS, or the size of the average truck trailer). The Deltaport at Point Roberts is set to begin a $1 billion expansion, tripling its capacity to more than 3 million TEUS.[314] Prince Rupert is about to become a container "superport" with capacity just slightly smaller than the Port of Vancouver of 4 million TEUS.[315] The reason for such expansion is that container traffic from Asia, particularly China, is simply exploding.

Prior to discussing the specific nature of opportunities available, we should look at the enormous asset base of the Aboriginal sector, and other leverage that they bring to the table as emerging players that will unquestionably grow rapidly in importance in the Canadian economy.

Land

In general in the past, Aboriginal people have been asset-rich and cash-poor. With reserve lands and only a handful of modern treaties concluded, Aboriginal people currently own—lock, stock and barrel—over 600,000 square kilometres of land (including reserve lands and settled treaty areas). Such a land mass covers an area over eight times the size of Ireland, twice the size of New Zealand or England, and larger by a substantial margin than either France, Germany or Spain. And there are still many, many more settlements to come. Some estimates suggest Aboriginal people will own or control one-third of the entire Canadian land mass—an area equivalent to a third of the total land area of Europe!

While some of the Aboriginal land base may be "moose pasture," it is moose pasture where more and more oil, gas, diamonds, base metals, valuable forests, and flowing rivers are located.

Cash

Current settlements have resulted in approximately $2.5 to $5 billion in cash payments. Some estimate that there may be between $10 to $20 billion paid in future settlements. As outlined in the following Chapter, many Aboriginal communities and entrepreneurs are also generating significant revenues from a variety of business and related projects.

Labor Force [316]

We have seen that the existing demographics trends heighten the importance of the Aboriginal participation in the labor force. Failure to address the issue of employing the rapidly growing Aboriginal population could have enormous impacts on the continuing health, prosperity and competitiveness of Canada as a nation. In many areas, particularly in northern and western Canada, Aboriginal people are the only population. Out of sheer necessity, corporations will have to incorporate the Aboriginal work force into those business projects (particularly since Aboriginals will likely have ownership or control over the land). This reality and its advantages were summarized by Francois Fleury, a Director General of Inmet Mining, when he observed:

Most of the deposits we are discovering today are in the north, in Aboriginal territory. One major advantage of having them as partners is that it makes it easier to gain acceptance for the project from community and government stakeholders, and we make friends instead of enemies. In some cases, they are even ready to invest in the project. They bring an available workforce since they already live there and are proud to develop their region. As well, personally I believe that we give hope to them and their young people, who are too often not given the chance to demonstrate that they are also able to develop their community.[317]

It thus behooves private enterprise to become better apprised of the work force upon which they may ultimately depend. Former President and CEO of Syncrude Canada Limited, Eric Newell has commented:

As the largest employer of Aboriginal people in Canada we feel great responsibility to help educate other companies and Canadians in general about Aboriginal culture—and to replace negative stereotypes with positive realities. ... The payoff of our Aboriginal employment strategy runs both ways. The benefits in employment to the Aboriginal community are matched by the benefits to Syncrude of capable and committed employees.[318]

Many stereotypes exist in relation to the Aboriginal workers. Views of Aboriginal people as being intrinsically lazy, unreliable or unwilling to compete are not borne out by the information available. In her solidly-documented book, *Lost Harvests*, historian Sarah Carter largely debunks the myth of the feckless anti-farming prairie Indian.[319] Ms. Carter suggests that the alternative of starvation was a compelling impetus for prairie Aboriginal groups to undertake farming. Unfortunately, their efforts were met by a ponderously slow bureaucracy and Ms. Carter discovered, "Aboriginal people face horrifying ineptitude from their supposed guides at Indian Affairs."[320]

Federal bureaucrats in many cases provided seed too late to be planted, faulty grist mills and, rather than sending plough-trained oxen, "the Indians got freight animals or unbroken range cattle from Montana."[321] Additionally, Aboriginal people had to contend with pathetically incompetent patronage appointees as farm instructors, and a situation where "small but vocal pockets of whites pressured politicians to end competition from Indian farmers" (who at that time could not vote federally).

The result? "Inescapable dependency encouraged the shiftless, violent behaviour that still flourishes alongside healthier habits on reserves. They [Indian Affairs] fostered dependency in every available way," reports Wilton Littlechild, a Cree Lawyer from Hobbema and conservative MP for the riding of Wetaskiwin, AB. His own father cultivated wheat. "Thanks to the department from the earliest period to the present, the psychological damage to our peoples' work ethic has been enormous. Nevertheless, the will to work survives in most families that I know."[322]

This view is supported by projects such as Syncrude's operation employing a sizable Aboriginal work force: "Statistically, there's no significant difference in employee stability or absenteeism."[323] More impressive, in a sense, are the past hiring successes of Saskatoon-based Cameco Corp. and Amok Ltd., whose mining work forces are respectively, 35% and 50% Aboriginal. "We intend to push our share up to 50% by 1995," says senior vice-president Bill Allan. His company employs 584 workers in three isolated northern mines (two uranium and one gold). Mr. Allan clocks employee turnover at about 14% annually for southerners and 12% for Aboriginals. Absenteeism is virtually a non-issue at both firms.[324]

Development Leverage Over Traditional Territories: Consultation and Accommodation Requirements

As the result of legal decisions requiring genuine *consultation* and *accommodation* (where warranted), Aboriginal Canadians for the first time also have real legal leverage over substantial areas of development that may impact the Canadian economy enormously. The recent Haida[325] and Taku[326] cases are important decisions that set out the scope and nature of the duties of consultation and accommodation of the Crown and, in limited procedural circumstances, by industry. These duties are owed to Aboriginal peoples whose Aboriginal rights are affected by development on their traditional territories.[327] In the Haida decision, the Supreme Court of Canada found that industry is not directly responsible for consultation with Aboriginal people and the Crown alone is responsible for the consequences of the Crown's interactions and those of third parties, that affect Aboriginal interests.[328]

These findings were a relief to industry, and considered a victory by Aboriginal people because the Supreme Court of Canada confirmed the Crown has a duty to consult with Aboriginal people and that "consultation must be meaningful and the content of the duty must be proportionate to the strength of the case supporting the existence of Aboriginal rights or title as well as to the seriousness of the potentially adverse effect upon the right or title claimed."[329] While the duties of consultation and accomodation are to be determined on a case by case basis, and although the consultation process is not a veto for Aboriginal groups, one source comments that "it doesn't mean that government desires automatically trump Aboriginal concerns, either. It means that both sides bring some authority to the discussion and that competing interests should be reconciled to the best ability of both parties."[330]

In British Columbia, Aboriginal groups have been successful in obtaining interim injunctions for developments in their traditional territories where there has been inadequate consultation. In one case, it was successfully argued that the pattern of conduct by the province in approving an amendment to an existing fish farm permit allowing the farming of Atlantic salmon at the ancestral village site of the Homalco First Nation, near the mouth of Bute Inlet (200 kilometres northwest of Vancouver) demonstrated a *prima facie* case for the Homalco argument that they were not properly consulted.[331] The implications of the decisions were summarized:

> First, I think it signals that the Haida decision is going to have real consequences for the way in which government conducts itself. Consultations with first nations will have to be genuine, they will have to be undertaken in good faith; they can't simply be dispensed with or circumvented by procedural end-runs in order to "cut the red tape" that frustrates some development agenda.
>
> Second, [the] Attorney General…is going to have to find a way to persuade his cabinet colleagues to really change the corporate culture within some of the government's resource ministries. Front line managers must get the message: as far as relations with First Nations are concerned, the playing field is now much more level than it has been and Aboriginal concerns will increasingly have weight similar to industry's in reaching decisions—perhaps more, in some cases.
>
> Third, it is now becoming clear that while the obligation to consult resides with government, not private business, it will be in the best interests of industry for corporate leaders to get with the agenda.[332]

In another case, the British Columbia Court of Appeal quashed a 2003 agreement by which the provincial government sold the University of British Columbia Golf Course to the University of BC over the objections of the

Musqueam Indian Band. Three Appeal Court judges unanimously agreed that the provincial government breached its duty to consult and accommodate the band's interest before transferring title to the property. In another interesting case, the BC Supreme Court ordered the provincial government to work out compensation with the Musqueam Band for allowing a casino to be built on the band's traditional lands without properly consulting the First Nation in advance.[333]

The law in relation to this matter is complex and evolving. One respected law firm provides the following good advice to its industry and business clients:

> As a practical matter, industry strategies for consultation should continue unchanged. Industry needs to build goodwill with Aboriginal peoples affected by a given project or activity on traditional lands of Aboriginal people. This is absolutely vital. Every month of personal and business relationship-building may save one year of effort after the fact. Aboriginal peoples routinely have expressed the view that industry simply does not take the time to foster strong ties and linkages and to attempt to absorb and understand, in a *bona fide* manner, the culture, history and unique qualities of Aboriginal peoples. The more a company can articulate a desire to want to build ties with an Aboriginal people, and the less it shows it needs to build ties, can be critical. This is a subtle point; however it is perhaps the most crucial one we can offer as guidance in conducting activities on the traditional territories of Aboriginal peoples. For example, consider residing in the affected Aboriginal villages or traditional territories to build goodwill, and be prepared before your project or activity begins in earnest to contribute financially or provide in-kind support to the affected Aboriginal community in relation to education, training, cultural awareness and the like.
>
> Send to meetings with Aboriginal peoples your highest ranking officer, or chair or vice-chair of your board of directors. This sends a message that your company is taking the consultation and relationship building process seriously. If the Crown or the Aboriginal peoples concerned do not, at least you have attempted to set a high standard and have attached the requisite importance to your project or activity.[334]

As the saying goes, at the end of the day "trust is the coin of the realm." An investment in good relations with Aboriginal people is simply an investment in good business practices. While Aboriginal groups do not have an out-and-out veto over development, they can make a project time-consuming and costly—matters which surely concern corporate directors and shareholders. An investment in good relations with Aboriginal people is an investment that is a win/win for all concerned.

BUILDING CAPACITY THROUGH GOVERNMENT, PROCUREMENT AND PRIVATE SECTOR SET-ASIDES AND PREFERENCE BUYING

Government

Both in Canada and United States, federal governments have introduced preference contracting buying strategies in an effort to encourage economic self-reliance for their respective Aboriginal Canadian and Native American populations. In the United States:

- The Indian Incentive Program, which originates from the *Buy Indian Act,* provides a unique opportunity for prime contractors to receive a 5% bonus payment on work subcontracted to an Indian organization for Indian-owned economic enterprise, when authorized under the terms of the contract.
- The Small Business Administration's 8(a) program is designed to benefit the client as well as the contractor by assisting small disadvantaged businesses and by providing:
  - The ability to pursue sole-source procurements.
  - Limited-competition opportunities in the government arena.
  - The assurance to the client that bonding, insurance and other legal requirements will be met.
- Public Law 93-638 provides a contracting process by which an Indian tribe or Native Corporation can obtain government contracting opportunities without the necessity of a competitive bid process. The result of the Amended Act is to create a "partnering" relationship between the agency (BIA) and the Indian tribe.

The United States Congress, as well as the Courts have given the Act's provisions broad interpretation. This has enabled the agencies and tribes to identify and engage in creative and innovative methods of expanding Native contracting opportunities.

The effort of the U.S. federal government in building Native American businesses through preference contracting and set-asides appears to have been quite effective. In Canada, however, the federal Procurement Strategy for Aboriginal Business (PSAB) has been a source of widespread criticism. PSAB is a strategy supposedly designed to increase the number of Aboriginal suppliers receiving federal contracts, since they are under-represented amongst firms seeking and winning federal contracts. Typical complaints from Aboriginal entrepreneurs relate to the slowness of the process, including excessive foot-dragging and inertia of federal bureaucrats in implementing the strategy. There has been some modest success with this program, but by all clientele accounts it is far from reaching its real potential. In spite of much public lip service relating to PSAB there appears to be little high-level governmental leadership to translate what has been political and bureaucratic blather into reality on the ground.

Private Sector Minority Supplier Diversity Programs

In Chicago in the 1960s, African-American civil rights leaders challenged corporate America to do more for minorities. Corporations responded with a contracting preference for minority-owned corporations through what ultimately became the National Minority Supplier Development Council (NMSDC). While this was originally conceived by corporations as a form of corporate altruism, it is now considered a fundamental part of good business practice.

Minority markets are now crucial to the sustainability and bottom lines of major corporations. Providing preference contracting opportunities to minority companies has proven to be an effective means of nurturing, building capacity, and growing minority-owned businesses—one with the bonus of costing tax payers not a cent. There was approximately $100 billion in goods and services purchased from minority companies last year by NMSDC members. The NMSDC now has over 3,600 of the largest American corporations with "diversity" divisions setting specific annual percentage-buying targets from minority suppliers.

In Canada, the Canadian Aboriginal Minority Supplier Development Council (CAMSC) was formed with the support of NMSDC. While CAMSC has only begun to develop its corporate membership base, it also has a reciprocity agreement with the NMSDC so that Canadian Aboriginal and minority-owned corporations can now go into the United States and receive preference in contracting with the 3,600 members of the NMSDC and vice versa.

12

BARRIERS TO ABORIGINAL ECONOMIC
DEVELOPMENT ... AND THE WAY FORWARD

> Obstacles are those frightful things you see when you take your
> eyes off your goal.
> HENRY FORD

Barriers to indigenous development can be broken down into two different
categories: (a) systemic; and (b) inherent.

INHERENT BARRIERS

> As long as a man stands in his own way, everything seems to be in his way.
> RALPH WALDO EMERSON

A theme throughout this book has been the way in which the dependency
mindset has been socialized internally into generations of the indigenous psyche
and is creating self-erected barriers to moving forward. This is what is meant
by the term "inherent barriers." Without clearly dealing with such inherent
barriers, indigenous people will never move forward even if the more systemic
issues are dealt with. Notwithstanding the enormous grief and misery flowing
from the welfare trap, many indigenous people have found what might be
described as a comfort zone there—choosing the familiar welfare crumbs of
poverty. The current system makes it easy to stay in this welfare trap comfort
zone. Welfare provides a minimal level of income, housing is generally provided at no or minimal cost, and reserve houses cannot be seized in execution
of debts.

Welfare payments definitely ease the burden of survival for many caught
in dire social and economic conditions, and in such circumstances serve a justifiable purpose. For others, what might be described as a welfare syndrome
of survival has arisen; as long as welfare payments are an option, they continue

to build their activities around receipt of those payments. This happens even when such persons are healthy and capable of taking on employment that might provide them with a better material living and better alternatives to getting ahead. In such circumstances, individuals are effectively frozen with fear or apathy and choose not to venture into what is perceived as uncharted waters and its attendant dangers.

This condition is also observable in many indigenous governments whose entire *raison d'être* has become receipt and management of transfer payments which are actually another form of welfare. In effect, the view internalized by such governments is that their function is merely to play this role as manager of welfare payments and voluntarily restrict themselves to this highly limited capacity. They either cannot see or are willfully blind to the fact that this situation is simply a government-funded fantasy that could not exist without being entirely externally supported. Furthermore, such a situation is at odds with how the rest of the world operates. Rather than looking to build a better future through consistent application of effort in pursuit of a clear strategy, the only plan in place is the avoidance of "rocking the boat" so as not to upset federal bureaucratic masters and thereby possibly jeopardize the almighty transfer payments. Unfortunately, many do not see that this complicity is ensuring that the federal government continue to control their lives, and that the welfare trap continue to deliver the treadmill of poverty and dysfunction.

A less charitable view of what has happened is that the whole welfare trap and its impacts have made indigenous people fat, slow, lazy, and, as many youth now argue, stupid. It is not very likely that the current crop of indigenous people could compete with their own vigorous ancestors. What would our ancestors think of our current plight? If we were competition in the fur trade they would likely have been delighted that their competitors were prepared to put so little energy into their own survival, were so apparently inept, and unable to look out for their own self-interest. Looking forward from their ancient perspective of self-reliance, they would likely be not only greatly saddened, but appalled of what had become of such dynamic and proud peoples.

The results of the welfare syndrome are lateral violence and learned helplessness. These phenomena help to explain how the welfare trap has sapped our confidence and generates internal resentment and jealousies whenever indigenous individuals seek to move forward. The author does not mean to offend anyone with these observations; the true situation must be acknowledged, however, in order to develop a plan for a better future.

In chapter 10, a list of eight points was put forward as the starting point for overcoming internal barriers and proceeding forward with a strategic plan. Now we will focus specifically on how the attitudes flowing from the welfare trap syndrome create barriers to moving forward.

In the context of community development, one of the most critical issues is nurturing and promoting individual entrepreneurs. We have seen that such entrepreneurs create most of the wealth in western economies. Yet what is found in most indigenous communities is that community governments seek to set up, run, and operate most of the businesses. Tribal governments do this is spite of the fact that a government structure is very unsuited to operating businesses. A 1984 Presidential Commission study on Indian Reservation Economies noted that:

> The confusion of tribal powers extends to confusion of governmental and corporate functions as well. Businesses have different goals from governments. The failure to separate governmental and corporate functions results in confusion of goals. Using tribal enterprises as instruments of political patronage contributes to their failure. Siphoning away investment capital from tribal businesses weakens the capacity of business to expand. A major cause of tribal business failure lies in the confusion over governmental and corporate roles.[335]

The following chart (reproduced from the study) shows the differing organizational focus:

PRIVATE SECTOR	TRIBAL GOVERNMENT
Profit Driven	Social Welfare Driven
Business Planning	Big Picture Planning
Cost Control	Budget Based Planning
Entrepreneur, CEO	Tribal Bureaucracy
Reward System	Patronage System
Product Competition	Organization Competition
Focus on Needs	Focus on Rights
Independent	Dependent

In most indigenous communities, virtually no recognition, support, or encouragement is given to individual entrepreneurs that are the lifeblood of wealth creation in every other economy. The history and focus of indigenous governments on the federal government, as previously discussed, is a partial explanation for this approach. However, both fear of giving up some control and the internal jealousies generated at the thought of a fellow community member moving forward play a significant role in blinding such governments to the long-term benefits of having a strong local business community.

Instead of monopolizing tribal economic development activity, the Presidential Commission study suggests that Indian tribes need to rethink what their role should be in economic development. It is suggested that they should be:

> encouraging private sector development through tribal [i.e., individual entrepreneurial] development, investment, and implementation policies and strategies. ... Tribal leadership needs to act to improve the reservation business climate, to exercise sovereign immunity responsibly, and to link tribal public financing of infrastructure to business development activity.[336]

Another problem with indigenous communities is that they pay lip service to utilizing their own educated people, but many go out of their way to avoid this. This would make no sense to outsiders, but in the context of the dysfunctional attitudes that exist in many communities, educated community members are often viewed as a threat. Lateral violence resentment can extend to those who have worked hard and managed to get a decent education. Sometimes, ethically challenged community leaders are uneasy about having their operations exposed to (and perhaps subsequently exposed by) educated community members who may not agree with how budgets are being managed or not managed, or how resources are wasted. Many of these leaders are the first to pound the table and trumpet the virtues of self-government, but the very last to utilize the most valuable resource in making self-government a reality—their own people.

Clearly, if the lot of indigenous people is to be improved, there must be a focus on overcoming the barriers inherent in both individuals and government.

A TIME FOR TELLING TSIMSHIAN LEGENDS

The Tsimshian people , akin to most indigenous tribes, preserve their legends (*adaawx1*) and history (*maalsk1*) through a tradition of oration and storytelling. Such stories have the purpose of preserving knowledge about a tribe's history, events that have taken place, or to acknowledge important principles. Storytelling was a greatly prized ability, and when children were told a story, they listened.

The block of granite which was an obstacle in the pathway of the weak,
became a stepping-stone in the pathway of the strong.

THOMAS CARLYLE

Creating an Attractive Development Framework

We have seen that in Canada, the obstacles to development are:

1 lack of accountability at virtually all levels of indigenous government;
2 lack of transparency and accountability in the handling of monies
   and budgets;
3 poor management and allocation of existing transfer payments; and
4 in some cases, corruption or ineptitude that has resulted in monies and
   resources being wasted.

In order for an economy to prosper, there must be an appropriate development framework. Indigenous communities and tribes require more modernized forms of governments. In this regard the Presidential Commission study
concluded that:

> Indian tribal governments are hindered in their pursuit of economic and
> business development by their antiquated or inappropriate political structures.
> Moreover, the failure to adhere to a constitutional principle separating
> executive, legislative and judicial powers has had a detrimental effect on govern-
> mental functioning. For example, the failure to establish a clear separation of
> powers between the tribal council and the tribal judiciary has resulted in
> political interference in tribal courts, weakening their independence, and
> raising doubts about the fairness and the rule of law. Similarly, the pen-
> chant for tribal councils to operate by "resolution" rather than "ordinance"
> has the effect of politicizing the executive administration, particularly
> where the chairman-executive is also an elected member of the council. The
> overlap in authorities undermines stable functioning government.[337]

Interestingly, the Commission made the following observation about the
Bureau of Indian Affairs (BIA) in the mid-1980s which is still arguably applicable to the Department of Indian Affairs in Canada today:

> [T]he Bureau's organizational structure, functioning, and operational defi-
> ciencies are such that the cost of doing business on Indian reservations is

raised considerably when Indian business development is required to involve the BIA. Furthermore, business development is frequently deterred by BIA where its bureaucratic processes are required for approvals. Excessive regulation has compliance and control for its goals. A Byzantine system of overregulation actually deters investment by raising costs, creating uncertainty, and undermining local initiative. Exacerbating the development climate is the fact that the BIA consumes more than two-thirds of its budget on itself, contracting only 27% of its programs to Indian tribes; leaving very little for investment purposes. Inadequate federal funding exists as an identified obstacle to Indian economic development because the system of delivering support to Indian tribes and Native groups is not designed to provide them with the kind of support they need. **The system is designed for paternalistic control and thrives on the failure of Indian tribes.**[338] [Emphasis added]

These systemic defects must be addressed. And in the larger scheme of things, a stable governance structure, an attractive business and investment environment must be created to attract investment.

In Canada the primary barrier to development of community economies are impediments in the *Indian Act* and the glacial pace at which the Department of Indian Affairs advances forward approvals for projects. The *Indian Act* was originally intended to set up communities as rural municipalities with a view to protecting their land and property assets by placing them in trust. According to BC Aboriginal leader, Manny Jules (a dedicated advocate of Aboriginal entrepreneurship):

> The *Indian Act* was simply never designed for and never even contemplated the kinds of development possibilities we see on reserve lands today. ...
> I have spent 30 years trying to break down those barriers to getting into the economy. ... Ask yourself, what kind of economy would Canada have if it was frozen in time, locked into the way things were done in 1867?[339]

Largely, the impact of this legislation has been to deny individuals and communities access to the most common form of collateral that everyone else takes for granted—their land. It does this by not allowing development finances to be raised through mortgaging reserve real estate (although it is possible for communities to mortgage a leasehold). The question of how to innovatively allow more individual ownership of indigenous land is being proposed for the aborigines of Australia through amendments to the *Aboriginal Land Rights (Northern Territory) Act 1976.*[340] Essentially, this will put into the hands of local people the option of 99-year leases that can be mortgaged and otherwise dealt with commercially, without fear of losing the land permanently.

Importance of Local Control (Sovereignty) and Stability

According to a 2003 study[341] from the Harvard Project on American Indian Economic Development,[342] the single greatest systemic challenge to tribal development involves **using tribal sovereignty to create a stable governance structure**—one that attracts investor and business attention. The study focussed on tribes that have broken from the prevailing pattern of unemployment and poverty without depending on gaming as their primary revenue stream or source of employment: the Mississippi Choctaws, the White Mountain Apache, the Salish and Kootenai tribes of the Flathead Reservation, and the Cochiti Pueblo in New Mexico.[343]

The authors cite two approaches to economic development: the "jobs and income" and the "nation building" approaches. Under the more reactive and short-sighted jobs-and-income approach, some tribes simply try to invent a business to create more jobs and income. It is argued that it is difficult to create sustainable enterprises because the very premise of the business is not, in a sense, market-driven, and tribes often lack the stable institutions and organizational prerequisites to succeed in the long-term. Conversely, the nation-building approach is more proactive in nature and:

> argues that solving the problem will require a solution both more ambitious and more comprehensive than trying to start businesses or other projects. The solution is to build a nation in which both businesses and human beings can flourish. The nation-building approach says the solution is to put in place an environment in which people want to invest. They want to invest because they believe their investment has a good chance of paying off. It may produce monetary profits. It may produce satisfaction in a job well done. It may raise the quality of life in the community. It may reduce dependence on the federal government or bolster tribal sovereignty. ... A nation-building approach to development doesn't say, "Let's start a business." Instead, it says, "Let's build an environment that encourages investors to invest, that helps businesses last, and that allows

investments to flourish and pay off." A nation-building approach requires new ways of thinking about and pursuing economic development.[344]

The study's authors argue that their findings indicate the solution is sovereignty:

> to use the power they have to build viable nations before the opportunity slips away. This is the major challenge facing Indian country today. It also is the key to solving the seemingly intractable problem of reservation poverty. Sovereignty, nation-building, and economic development go hand in hand.[345]

While the term "sovereignty" is a loaded political term to many, the authors are simply talking about local control and returning genuine decision-making power over community development and affairs to the community level. In addition, United States tribes are sovereign in law and have broader powers than Canadian tribes. This sovereignty can be constructively exercised to create substantial opportunities.

They also point out that:

> Real self-governance is a bit of a two-edged sword for tribes and tribal leaders. Once tribes are in the driver's seat in reservation affairs, they begin to bear more responsibility for what happens in those affairs. When things go well, they are entitled to credit; when things go badly, they bear a larger share of the blame. As tribes exercise more and more real power, the argument that the federal government or some other set of outsiders alone is responsible for what's wrong becomes less convincing.[346]

Their research indicated that, in order to have practical impacts on creating employment and prosperity, tribal governments must have effective governing institutions of their own which are described as providing: (1) stable institutions and policies; (2) fair and effective mechanisms for resolving disputes; (3) separation of politics from business management; (4) a competent bureaucracy; and (5) a cultural "match" (referring to the match between governing institutions and the prevailing ideas in the community about how authority should be organized and exercised).

It is contended further that there are four building blocks of development: sovereignty, effective institutions, strategic direction, and decision or action.

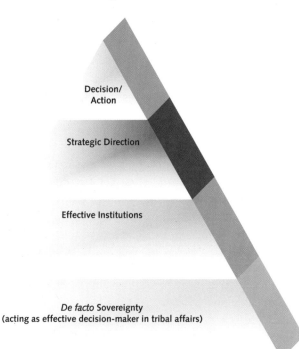

Decision/
Action

Strategic Direction

Effective Institutions

De facto Sovereignty
(acting as effective decision-maker in tribal affairs)

In summary, sovereignty (*de facto* control of the community) must be backed by effective governing institutions. The tribe must develop a strategic direction and move forward on such a course to avoid moving into reactive mode. Finally, the practical development decisions must be made and implemented.

Reform is in the Works

In Canada in recent years there have been some encouraging developments that will impact the ability of tribes to move forward.

In 1999 the *First Nations Land Management Act* was passed by the federal Parliament on the initiative of *14 Indian Act* bands wishing to escape the land management provisions of the *Indian Act*. They sought this ability in order to improve their capacities and opportunities for economic development. Each community opting to come under this Act is required to adopt a land code in accordance with the *Framework Agreement* (to replace the cumbersome land management provisions of the *Indian Act*). Validly adopted land codes have the effect of law. Essentially, this Act allows bands to establish their own regimes to manage their lands and resources, providing for more decision-making at the local level. In business terms, this could result in rapid turn-around times in relation to business development decisions.

The *First Nations Fiscal and Statistical Management Act* passed in the latter part of 2004 creates four new institutions to help communities access the bond market. These are:

- **First Nations Finance Authority** – allows First Nations collectively to issue bonds and raise long-term private debt capital for infrastructure projects.
- **First Nations Tax Commission** – administers tax bylaw approval process and helps reconcile band and ratepayer interests.
- **First Nations Financial Management Board** – establishes financial standards and assesses communities for entry into the First Nations Finance Authority.
- **First Nations Statistics** - assists communities in meeting their local data needs when making debt issues. This Act also facilitates intelligent planning options on reserves by gathering and compiling economic data that simply is not available now.

Essentially this Act provides a whole new fiscal framework for doing business on reserves. One writer comments that it "puts bands on an equal footing with other governments by creating a pool of capital and allowing qualifying bands to take on debt for things that will support development and break the dependency on the capricious hand-outs from Ottawa."[347]

To summarize, significant bureaucratic and legislative barriers exist to moving forward. Governance structures are, in many ways, simply not conducive to running businesses. Tribal leadership must create an environment that encourages and nurtures individual tribal entrepreneurs. At the same time, they need to pay careful attention to creating a stable political environment for the survival of their entrepreneurs and to attract investment. The bottom line: in order to move realistically forward beyond the barriers discussed, tribes and their members must take ownership of their problems and develop their own agendas for action.

13

THE ROLE OF EDUCATION IN BUILDING SUSTAINABLE ECONOMIES

"I have advised my people this way: When you find anything good in the white man's road, pick it up. When you find something that is bad, or it turns out bad, drop it and leave it alone."

SITTING BULL[348]

GENERAL

Throughout the ages there have been many views on education running the gamut from righteous to cynical. In the past, the pomposity of those overly impressed with their own book-learned education has attracted the scorn of some of the most famous literati. Mark Twain commented that "I never let my schooling get in the way of my education." Benjamin Franklin opined a similar theme, commenting: "He was so learned that he could name a horse in nine languages; so ignorant that he bought a cow to ride on." Philosopher Bertrand Russell commented that education is "One of the chief obstacles to intelligence and freedom of thought" and is purported to have held further that "Men are born ignorant, not stupid; they are made stupid by education." Indeed, sometimes educational systems have taught irrelevant knowledge that can sometimes be destructive.

So where do these critical views place the relevance of education with respect to Aboriginal people? It is a well-known fact that the Canadian educational system has done irreparable harm to many generations of Aboriginal children. The recent Royal Commission on Aboriginal Peoples report noted that:

The destiny of a people is intricately bound to the way its children are educated. Education is the transmission of cultural DNA from one generation to the next. It shapes the language and pathways of thinking, the contours of character and values, the social skills and creative potential of the individual. It determines the productive skills and creative potential of a people.[349]

The common thread from the quotations above is that book learning is no substitute for common sense and experience. Too often book learning has been misunderstood to represent common sense and real wisdom. In his essay, "Experience," Ralph Waldo Emerson discusses how our perception of reality is invariably clouded by our own temperament:

> Dream delivers us to dream, and there is no end to illusion. Life is a train of moods like a string of beads, and, as we pass through them, they prove to be many-colored lenses which paint the world their own hue, and each shows only what lies in its focus.[350]

In a wider sense, beyond mere book learning, the stages of a real education might also be compared to Emerson's "string of beads." As we pass through each stage of education "they [should also] prove to be many-colored lenses which paint the world their own hue," and each should show something new from what lies in its focus.

The fundamentals of education definitely involve some basic book learning. In a larger sense, however, a real education should also involve real experience in the world through doing things. A real education should involve learning the enormous range of attitudes and approaches one can have when dealing with real life issues. A real education should involve an understanding of how large the world really is and, conversely, how small our individual roles are—so that we do not let the hubris of a book-learned education make us feel superior to our fellow men. A real education should impart some appreciation for how different individuals or groups of people approach life with differing attitudes and what the pros and cons of those might be—and that there is value in all perspectives. A real education should involve learning how to "read" and understand people, and how to listen carefully for the messages in what is not directly said. A real education should involve an understanding of good manners or fundamental consideration for the feelings of other people. A real education should involve learning the value of discipline. English biologist and writer, Thomas Henry Huxley (1825–95), commented that:

> Perhaps the most valuable result of all education is the ability to make yourself do the thing you have to do, when it ought to be done, whether

you like it or not; it is the first lesson that ought to be learned; and however early a man's training begins, it is probably the last lesson that he learns thoroughly.

Few of us would feel good about being able to name a horse in nine languages and then buying a cow to ride on. The bottom line is that there are indeed other essential ingredients that make up a well-rounded education. In a knowledge-based economy, however, a substantial amount of "book learning" is certainly necessary. Nonetheless, what has been perceived in the past as the excessive pontificating of ivory tower academics is quite unnecessary.

The situation for Aboriginal people is that a significant number are deficient in many of the most basic hallmarks of education such as fundamental literacy and numeracy (a term that emerged in the United Kingdom best described as "numerical literacy"). For most Aboriginal people, there is no question that education really is the only path out of poverty. The Governor of Louisiana, Kathleen Blanc, has commented that:

> Every educated person is not rich, but almost every educated person has a job and a way out of poverty. So education is a fundamental solution to poverty.

There is no doubt that education is important in enabling Aboriginal people to earn good incomes and escape poverty—just as it is for anyone else. A recent report notes that:

> The educational premium applies to Aboriginals, as much as it does to others in the labor force. ... [T]he 1996 Census…[illustrates that] as the education level of Aboriginals rises, so do their median incomes. ...
>
> Among off-reserve Aboriginals and non-Aboriginals—less so among on-reserve Aboriginals—there are effectively three educational steps.... The first step-up in terms of increased incomes takes place with completion of high school. A high school graduation certificate is now the minimum qualification for many entry-level jobs. Those aspiring to reasonably well-paying jobs must reach at least the second step, completion of a trade certificate. The third step is completion of a university degree.[351]

Furthermore, the report found education levels and median incomes are considerably higher among Aboriginals living off-reserve to those on-reserve. The report concluded that:

Currently, the price to live on-reserve is lower incomes and education prospects for children. The median on-reserve income among Indian-identity Aboriginals in the 25-to-44 year-old cohort for 2000 was $13,700. The comparable statistic for off-reserve Indians is $18,000, a third higher. ...Even if many adult Indians choose to live on-reserve and forgo more remunerative employment elsewhere, education levels remain an important determinant of whether children can realistically choose, when the time comes, between an on- or off-reserve lifestyle. The minimum education prerequisite to render off-reserve income prospects reasonable, is high school graduation.[352]

DEVELOPING A STRATEGIC ECONOMIC PLAN AND A FOCUSSED EDUCATION POLICY

The 2002 edition of the OECD/UNESCO World Indicators Programme, "Financing Education," examined both the investments and returns to education and human capital in 19 developed and developing countries throughout the world. The study found "...robust evidence that human capital is a key determinant of economic growth and emerging evidence indicates that it is also associated with a wide range of non-economic benefits, such as better health and well-being."[353] Specifically:

It has become clear that educational attainment is not only vital to the economic well-being of individuals but **also for that of nations**. Access to and completion of education is a key determinant in the accumulation of human capital and economic growth. Educational outcomes extend beyond individual and national incomes.[354] [Emphasis added]

At the macro level, the report suggests that financial capital investment is most strongly associated with growth at early stages of industrialization. As an economy matures, however, the role of human capital increases with industrial development and the overall level of educational attainment. Eventually education-driven human capital becomes the strongest driver of economic growth.

Experience has also demonstrated that better educated people are more likely to be employed, and there are substantial increases in earnings the higher the educational level. It was revealed that the earning advantage of men with tertiary (versus upper secondary) education ranges from 82 percent

EAGLE, BOOK, FEATHER

This drawing was intended to make a symbolic connection between learning and the high status occupied by the eagle in indigenous culture. Hopefully the written word of Aboriginal people today will be guided by the sagacious spirit of Xsgiik from the past.

in Indonesia to almost 300 percent in Paraguay. The study suggests further that though economic measurements cannot adequately reflect the full dimensions of a human being:

the role of economic growth in this equation should not be underestimated. Growth in economic output not only provides the resources for tackling poverty, social exclusion and poor health but also expands the range of human choice. Economic well-being – flowing from economic output – should thus be recognized as an important component of human well-being.[355]

The relationship between education and economic well-being is well understood by the nations of the world. In his 1994 book, "Looking at the Sun," James Fallows, national correspondent and former Washington editor for the *Atlantic Monthly* commented that:

Most industrial nations have economic strategies. The plans are clearest and most assertive in East Asia; they are haziest and most hesitant in the English-speaking countries, which have told themselves since World War II, and increasingly since Ronald Reagan and Margaret Thatcher, that economic strategies are doomed to fail. When the Asian and Anglo-American systems interact, **the natural result is for the system without a strategy to become the object of strategies made by the other side.** Thus, when Japan and Korea decided in the 1980s to develop their own semi-conductor industries, The American industry became an object of those strategic choices—until the United States responded at the end of the decade with a strategy of it own.[356] [Emphasis Added]

The key focus of such a strategy must involve a focused education policy. Fallows notes further that:

for such a strategy to work, in Japan or elsewhere, the nation's people must be prepared to take advantage of it. In Japan for more than a century, and in South Korea, Taiwan, and Singapore since the end of World War II, the object of educational policy has been to bring most of the nation's people up to a basic level of functioning competence, so they can take advantage of the opportunities growing economies create.[357]

In the same manner, the key element to the rise of tribes and Aboriginal peoples is education. Aboriginal people must also have a basic level of functioning competence, so they can take advantage of the opportunities growing economies create.

It is also interesting to note Fallows' observation that:

> Training workers is not, by itself, enough to attract industry. Ireland, India, the Philippines, and Russia have at various times had a far greater supply of trained talent than jobs for them to perform. But a trained work force plus an economic strategy has, on the evidence, been a formula for growth.[358]

CURRENT STATUS OF ABORIGINAL EDUCATION

As can be seen from the table below, Aboriginal peoples in Canada lag substantially behind the mainstream population in levels of educational attainment in every category (data is for over 15 years of age).[359] To date there

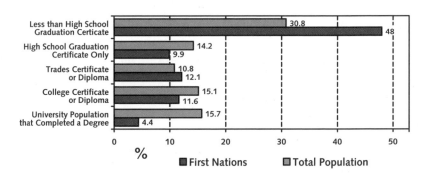

Aboriginal Educational Attainment vs Non-Aboriginal in 2001

Source of data: Caledon Institute of Social Policy Report

appears to be no national strategic plan to help improve academic outcomes for Aboriginal students. The recent United Nations Report of the Special Rapporteur on the situation of human rights and fundamental freedoms of indigenous people recently concluded that:[360]

> Aboriginal peoples in Canada are still trying to overcome the heritage of a colonial educational system, which severely disrupted Aboriginal

families, their cultures and identities. Children in particular were targeted time and again in official strategies to control and assimilate Aboriginal people. Residential schools, which for several generations Aboriginal children were compelled to attend away from their families, communities and traditional lands, did the greatest damage. They were forbidden to speak the only languages they knew and taught to reject their homes, their heritage and, by extension, themselves, thus contributing to the political, cultural and economic decline of many Aboriginal communities and people. ...

The Minister's National Working Group on Education reports that First Nation education is in a crisis. With some outstanding exceptions, there is no education system, no education accountability, no goals or objectives, and in many cases investments in Aboriginal education face comparative disparities.

Even the high hopes for the historic all-native university, the First Nations University of Canada which opened in Regina in 2003, appears to have imported the destructive political pathologies associated with Aboriginal governments. Unfortunately, the university ownership and funding scheme follows the typical federal transfer payment paradigm with most revenue provided by the federal government, and its finances exempt from public scrutiny. The board of governors is mostly represented by political appointments from the provincial Aboriginal political organization, the Federation of Saskatchewan Indian Nations. There are many allegations that many of these appointees have no experience and "do not necessarily have the expertise or even basic understanding of universities, especially if they never attended one."[361] There are apparently millions in the budget unaccounted for, and there has been a spate of unexplained firings. There are further allegations of political interference, and abuse of funds that may put the academic credentials of the institution at risk.[362]

What the United Nations report essentially states is that there is no comprehensive strategy relating to Aboriginal education. Without such a strategy, it will be difficult to determine whether progress is being made towards definable goals. At the end of the day, a well thought-out strategy towards education is still necessary for moving Aboriginal people forward. If this is the approach that Aboriginal people wish to take, they must define an economic strategy informed by a detailed educational plan with clear policy goals, to ensure the newly-educated cadres of Aboriginal youth can take advantage of the emerging opportunities.

The question as to what needs to be done to create more success in the field of education is certainly beyond the scope of this book. However, some general observations may be made.

The question of achieving broader educational success has been effectively challenged by the Maori in New Zealand. They have built educational success by developing a comprehensive strategy. A recent report on the economic well-being of Maori[363] found that part and parcel of two decades of reform involved a focus on education. There was a deliberate focus on all levels of education. By 2001, over 45 percent of all Maori children younger than five years of age were enrolled in early childhood education. Between 1983 to 2000, Maori secondary students leaving school with no qualification decreased from 62 to 35 percent. At the tertiary level, between 1991 and 2000 Maori increased participation by 148 percent. By 2002 Maori had the highest participation in tertiary education of any group aged 25 and over. Though Maori still suffer disproportionately from many social pathologies, this turning point was the beginning of a dramatic improvement in the well-being (particularly economic) of Maori generally.

Grandview/?Uuquinak'uuh Elementary School in East Vancouver furnishes a further interesting model—a story of hard-won success in achieving higher educational attainment results for impoverished Aboriginal and inner city kids. The school is located in one of the poorest neighborhoods in Vancouver; a few years ago it was a school in crisis. As the result of a violent incident where a parent threatened to kill a staff member, it was under police guard. In addition, teachers and administrators were deserting what was perceived to be a sinking ship. The school's population is about 50% Aboriginal, with many of the remainder from immigrant families from China, Vietnam, Mexico, Nicaragua and the former Yugoslavia. Overall, the kids live in poverty with many of them coming from chaotic and dysfunctional homes. A significant number are in foster care or being brought up by grandparents, while others have parents who do not speak English.

In 2001, results from the province-wide Foundation Skills Assessment found that only 22 percent of grade 4 students at the school passed the reading test, 63 percent passed writing and 42 percent passed numeracy. As a result of the persistence, hard work and innovations of former Principal Caroline Krause, her staff, and the support of the community, results from

CAROLINE KRAUSE, former Principal Grandview/ʔUuquinak'uuh Elementary School in East Vancouver

2004 indicated that 88 percent of Grade 4 students met or exceeded expectations in reading, writing and numeracy. According to Principal Krause "This school has moved from crisis mode a decade ago to a safe, highly-functioning, family-type environment."[364]

What is interesting is how this was done. Most prevailing views suggest that this should have been done through a culturally centred curriculum for the Aboriginal kids. Such an approach typically involves segregation of the Aboriginal students with a lot of vague "I'm okay, you're okay" touchy-feely support. In practice, Principal Krause found that:

> many of the middle-school Aboriginal kids had been put into a segregated program…long on cultural sensitivity, self-esteem and hugs, but very short on literacy. There were no demands on the kids, and they were out of control. Far from feeling self-esteem, they felt like failures.[365]

An article in the *Globe and Mail* on the Grandview/ʔUuquinak'uuh Elementary School educational program reported:

> "You can't fool kids," says Ms. Fouks [Wendy Fouks is the teacher that implemented the effective phonics literacy program]. "They know when they're not succeeding." The widespread failure of Aboriginal kids in the school system is probably Canada's most urgent education problem. But Ms. Krause is impatient with the fashionable notion that more cultural sensitivity is the answer. The answer, she says emphatically, is "academic success." And her teaching team has delivered. Sylvain Desbiens, the math teacher, confesses that when he started here four years ago, he thought he'd be doing mostly remedial teaching. "I never thought we'd be teaching gifted programs." He does now.[366]

In particular, what was discovered was that Aboriginal kids were keenly sensitive to being segregated from the remainder of the student population, no matter what the intentions or perceived preferential treatment. Given the right environment, it is evident that kids, whether Aboriginal or otherwise, respond to high academic expectations placed on them with results. Key elements in creating the right environment leading to school success have been summarized by Principal Krause as having:[367]

1 Common Mission and Vision
2 Commitment, Collaboration and Team Work
3 High Expectations
4 Focus on Academics;
5 Early Literacy Program
6 Regular Assessment
7 School-wide Behaviour Code
8 Student Engagement and Leadership
9 Focus on Athletics
10 Computer Technology
11 Clean and Orderly Environment
12 Greening Project and Community Garden
13 Strong Parent Support
14 Strong Community Support
15 School Pride

To achieve results, the dedicated and entrepreneurial team at Grandview/
?Uuquinak'uuh had to break many of the system's strongest unwritten rules.
Literacy instruction was based on phonics. Monies to cover necessary instruction materials were initially raised by teacher Wendy Fouks and subsequently
donated by Starbucks and other corporate donors. In fact, in their after-
school hours Mrs. Krause and her team have aggressively courted corporate
donors for funding. This was done in spite of opposition from the politically
left-leaning school board members who opposed on ideological grounds all
forms of outside fund raising sources. Since September 2000, the Royal Bank
has contributed $198,700 to fund an after-school athletics and activity pro-
gram called the Visions Athletic After School Program. The Visions program
exceeded wildest expectations and has obviously been an important element
in this success story. The staff, based upon their experience with what works,
aggressively reject a culturally-centred curriculum for the Aboriginal kids.
Instead, they create high expectations for everyone. And the kids have delivered in spades, pulling the school's academic standing from the very bottom
of the ranking charts to the top.

The results for 2006 have even been more fantastic. An article in the
Vancouver Sun titled "Inner-city school at the top of the class" summed up the
success this way:

The 2006 report card gives Grandview seven out of 10, up from 1.6 in 2001
[in the Foundation Skills Assessment or "FSA"]. Although it has the largest

ESL [English as a Second Language] population in the province at 65.8 percent last year and a special-needs group of 35.8 percent [both factors which would put it at a huge disadvantage], only 17 percent of students were excused from writing the FSA.

(*Schools are permitted to excuse beginner ESL students, children with severe special needs and any child whose parents do not want them to take the tests.*)[368]

In an interview, former principal Caroline Krause explained that this was even more remarkable given that:

> Although another inner city school that has only 18% Aboriginal students scored a perfect 10 [a first-place finish], they also excluded almost half their students [from the study]. Grandview is now ranked 7/10 with only 17% exclusion. This is well above 40 other Vancouver schools.

This model of educational success is an inspiring story about what can be done with limited resources, a dedication to innovation and results, and the leadership of Principal Krause and her staff. As well, the community must be acknowledged for pulling together in the most dire of circumstances to help create a better educational environment for one of the most underprivileged populations in the city. In an effort to expand and replicate the success at Grandview/?Uuquinak'uuh Elementary, Principal Krause is seeking to set up an independent school for inner city children free from the sometimes counter-productive restrictions imposed by public school boards and their attendant unions. This should serve as a North American pilot project regarding what can be done to achieve educational excellence for those children without the fundamental advantages that most middle class North Americans take for granted.

SUMMARY

Aboriginal parents must educate themselves regarding the value of education and its critical importance to moving their families forward. Many parents are the product of abuse and neglect from the era of residential schools. Their experience with the educational system in which they were interned was largely negative and has led to many problems that have damaged their lives and badly impacted their families. There must be some recognition that the modern educational system is not the one they were exposed to and is key to the futures of their children and grandchildren. They also must metaphorically take ownership of the educational system in which their children are immersed to ensure that they can bring out the best outcomes for their children possible, from the educational institution in which they are involved.

At the end of the day, given the demographic tsunami, the looming economic costs, and the savage toll that the welfare trap is taking on the poorest group in Canada, a real investment in education is key not only to moving Aboriginal people forward but to moving Canada forward. The relationship between education, economic development, and the well-being of people is clear. Education is the foundation of economic development. Economic development, in turn, provides opportunity for greater choices and paths to well-being. To paraphrase the OECD/UNESCO report, education not only bears on the economic well-being of a people and a nation, but provides resources for tackling poverty, social exclusion and poor health, while also expanding the range of human choice.

In concert with most developed nations, the Canadian economy is moving to a more knowledge-based economy. If Canada wishes to maintain the position of great privilege it now occupies in the world economic order, Aboriginal education must be addressed with a strategic plan similar to that developed by the Maori of New Zealand. We also need to examine innovative models developed "outside the box" of educational dogma and which have already produced definitive results—such as the experiment at Grandview/ ?Uuquinak'uuh Elementary School. These steps should be an absolute priority. While the seeds planted today will not bear fruit immediately, they should bloom in succeeding years to provide greater opportunities and more potential for fulfilment of hopes and aspirations of future indigenous generations.

14

ECONOMIC MODELS TO BUILD ON

> The most important single central fact about a free market is that no exchange takes place unless both parties benefit.
> MILTON FRIEDMAN

There are several models of indigenous development that might be examined in seeking to move tribes forward.

AN INTERNATIONAL PERSPECTIVE

New Zealand Maori

The Maori of New Zealand are an interesting population group for comparative analysis. New Zealand, like Canada and the United States, was previously colonized by Great Britain and inherited similar legal, and political structures as well as policies for dealing with tribes. It also has a comparable indigenous population facing similar demographic challenges as those in North America.

There are also some relevant differences that deserve mention. Firstly, the Maori do not get the enormous annual transfer payments that indigenous people receive in North America. For the most part, Maori receive only a one-time payment of cash and assets from treaty settlements and must make them earn revenue. Secondly, dealing with indigenous groups in the United States and Canada presents an enormous geographic barrier due to their vast sizes. By comparison, the entire country of New Zealand would fit comfortably into one-third of British Columbia. Thirdly, Canada and the United States have a great number of different indigenous groups who speak hugely different languages. In New Zealand, though there are many different tribes, they all speak the same language. Again by comparison, in British Columbia alone, there evolved approximately 30 completely different languages.

Finally, New Zealand does not have the wealth of natural resources of Canada or the United States, and is thousands of miles from most markets.

TE TARU WHITE, Kaihautū (Maori leader), national Museum of New Zealand Te Papa Tongarewa

Notwithstanding these differences, strong similarities make it a good comparative model. It might be said that necessity has forced the Maori of New Zealand further ahead in the development/economic integration curve than their North American indigenous counterparts. The straight facts of the matter are that the New Zealand economy simply could not sustain the kind of spending on their indigenous population that currently takes place in North America. In an interview with Maori corporate and cultural leader, Te Taru White (who holds the position of Kaihautū—"Maori leader"—at the national Museum of New Zealand in Wellington called Te Papa Tongarewa), several other relevant points were made:

> The fact that New Zealand is very small relative to Canada and the United States means that it is not easy to sweep social issues and problems resulting from the oppressive state under the carpet—it is too noticeable. Maori were also not placed on reserves as is often the case in Canada and the United States but were part of mainstream. It meant that we had to probably face up to the poor state we were in a lot quicker and learn to be a lot smarter in working the system.[369]

In 2003 a major research report[370] took the first look ever at Maori economic contributions to the national economy. It looked not at how the Maori fit into the New Zealand economy, but instead examined the Maori economy as a unique coherent whole comprising its own unique institutions, assets and economic transactions. Some of its findings were surprising to many:

- While Maori were often presented as a burden to the economy, this was found emphatically not to be the case. The $2.3 billion in fiscal transfers were offset by a tax contribution of $2.4 billion from the Maori economy.[371] [*This compares now to about $18 billion in estimated federal and provincial fiscal transfers to tribes in Canada in 2005 with no or very little tax returned.*]
- In 2001, the Maori commercial asset base was conservatively estimated to be worth nearly $9 billion.
- In aggregate, the Maori economy appeared to be more profitable than the national economy (while only accounting for 1.4% of the value added, the Maori economy generates a 2% operating surplus).[372]

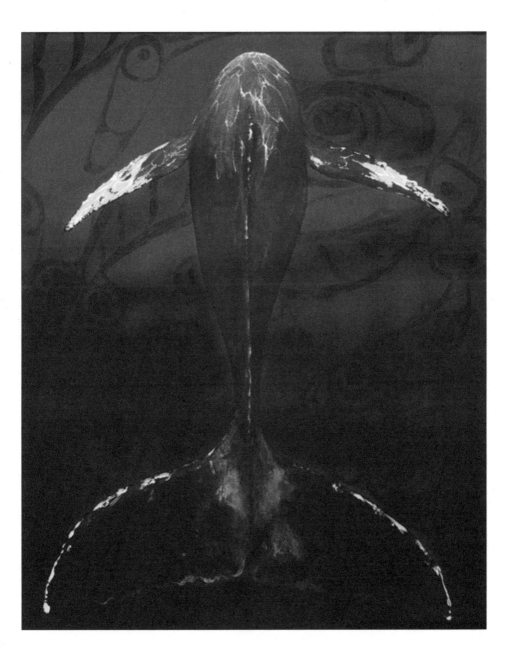

CONTENTMENT

In the depths of the ocean, suspended in a dream-like state, the hump-back whale rests in a motionless, serene "moment of solitude." Such moments are becoming less frequent with massive increases in ocean traffic. Our gentle giants are now faced with the possibility of extinction. They have no voice of their own and so must rely on us to speak up for them. The faint images in the background represent the spirits of the humpback whales of the past. The original was painted with acrylics on canvas in 2004 and reproduced in a small limited edition using the giclee method.

- The Maori economy had a higher savings rate than the national economy. This was thought to be mostly attributable to the fact that Maori corporations retained a greater proportion of the earnings than mainstream businesses (not because of higher individual Maori household savings rates). In fact, the Maori were found to be net lenders to the rest of the New Zealand economy.[373]
- The *implicit* underlying growth of the Maori economy in recent years has exceeded the rest of New Zealand. [*The report talks of implicit growth because it excludes from the analysis the increase in activity associated with the transfer of assets under various Treaty of Waitangi settlements. Such one-off adjustments tell us little about the underlying dynamics, and the authors thought it was more helpful to examine growth as if such assets had always been in Maori ownership (which is, of course, precisely what the settlements aim to replicate).*]
- The Maori unemployment rate at the time of the study stood at 12% compared to the overall unemployment rate of 5.4%, and in 2003, 10.2% versus 4% in the mainstream.[374] [*In Canada comparable unemployment rate in 2001 was 19.1% for Aboriginals versus 7.4% for the mainstream population.*[375]]

On a global basis then, compared to the collective indigenous tribes in North America, the Maori as a group have advanced further economically. In the United States, the huge revenues of the tribes with massive gaming operations distort the comparative picture because their combined revenues approached a whopping $20 billion in 2004. The enormous revenues of a few wealthy tribes, however, mask the poverty and dysfunction of those many tribes who do not have the mixed blessing of large gaming operations.

There are several reasons for the comparative advancement of the Maori. New Zealand is a small country with limited resources. It simply does not have a huge amount of financial resources to deal with Maori issues. There is basically no margin to allow for the squandering of resources, no matter how politically expedient. With economic hardships not far from the doorstep, sustainable solutions are a necessity, rather than a luxury. New Zealand must be lean and mean in order to survive—just like our indigenous North American ancestors of antiquity. As discussed previously, the amount projected to be spent annually on Canada's Aboriginal population alone could amount to half of the entire GDP of New Zealand.

So how did the Kiwis do it? In 1984, on the heels of the country's economic meltdown, New Zealand first began to focus on a new direction for Maori. At the time, reduced state dependency, devolution, and privatisation were seen as preconditions to greater Maori independence, tribal re-development and service delivery to Maori by Maori.[376] Government policy was subsequently redesigned to guide Maori towards greater self-sufficiency and reduced state dependency. Though there were some differences of opinion as to how this should be done, the new direction also suited Maori aspirations for greater autonomy and responsibility. With these actions, the pendulum was swung in a new direction toward greater self-reliance, development, and Maori economic integration.

In addition, Te Taru White notes:

> One of the great Maori statesman and leaders of the early 1900's, Sir Apirana Ngata, once said "e tipu e rea"... What this literally means is "Use the tools of the Pakeha for your bodily sustenance and the treasures of your ancestors to adorn your head" [Pakeha is the Maori word for Europeans of non-Maori, non-Polynesian ancestry]. In other words, hold fast to your cultural heritage and identity and develop the skills and capability of the Pakeha to sustain yourself and claim what is rightfully yours. Maori are currently doing both; for example there has been a huge resurgence over the past 20 years to develop the language and to develop pride in traditional culture and identity. There have been tribal universities (wananga) established which incorporate traditional ideologies and thinking to work alongside and within mainstream systems. Total language immersion schools have been developed to teach all subjects in both English and Maori. While these institutions have had their trials and tribulations, there is no doubt that they have contributed enormously to a shift in attitude from grievance to development and self-esteem. Developing systems by Maori for Maori is probably another way of putting it. Coupled with what I would term "capability building" is the increased political awareness and participation of Maori in New Zealand's parliament. Currently there are some 22 members of parliament in New Zealand who are Maori (a few may be "closet" Maori) which amounts to almost 20% of Government – this is very significant. A new Maori party has emerged with four members in parliament and with a mixed member proportional voting system in place; they have a significant influence in a number of areas.[377]

A key component of the two decades of reform was a conscious focus on education, Maori language, and cultural development. Though Maori still suffer many social pathologies disproportionate to the mainstream, the

TSIMSHIAN EAGLE

Around my home village of Lax Kw'alaams there are many eagles. Their dignified demeanor and grace in flight inspired me to try to artistically capture these regal qualities.

calculated decision to move forward with a coherent strategy was a turning point resulting in the dramatic improvement in the well-being of Maori generally. While challenges remain, today it might be fair to describe the Maori as much less state-dependent, more self-reliant, dynamic, and outward looking compared to the welfare dollar-chasing leadership of most North American tribes. As a general comment they might also be said to be much more future-oriented, and forward thinking. Te Taru White's final comments:

> Maori as Polynesians have, through the centuries, always looked out into the wider Pacific—they are traditional navigators, an ocean-going peoples. Always having to look outward for new opportunities has possibly shaped a more aggressive approach to the world as we see it. When you couple this up with the other factors, you have an indigenous population in a small country with a growing sense and resurgence of cultural pride, seizing on opportunities, and using the tools of the system as adeptly and probably even more so than our Pakeha countrymen. This is resulting in a generation that walks with pride in their culture, that also has the intellect, understanding, and tools of the mainstream system—a realisation of the quote from Sir Apirana mentioned previously. ... All this has led to a positive economic development position, and the pleasing thing I believe is that there is no going back. As is the case in Canada, there is a growing Maori population—we are growing our capability, and are cognizant that to realise our full potential will take a few generations. The important thing is that we started the shift to self-reliance, and we are on the right track. The fact that Maori are net positive contributors to the country's economy with potential to add a lot more gives me real hope for the future. I guess the Tsunami we face presents us with a simple choice – sink into the black hole of welfare helplessness of the past or swim to the future of our own choosing. Right now Maori have chosen, hands down, to swim.[378]

There is no question that a similar trajectory would benefit the tribes of North America. The results of the Maori efforts speak volumes for what can be done with limited resources. As described in Chapter 2, the demographic tsunami should provide a similar impetus for reform in Canada and the United States. Like the Maori of New Zealand, North American indigenous tribes must wholeheartedly agree that change is necessary. Parallel short-term and longer-term strategic plans should be mapped out. There must be a focus on quantifiable outcomes relating to employment, education, governance and leadership, community capacity, and economic and social goals.

Alaska's Native Americans

In 1971 the Alaska Native Claim Settlement Act ("ANCSA") was passed by Congressional Act settling outstanding Native American claims to the state of Alaska. This resulted in the formation of 220 village corporations (some have merged), 13 regional corporations, and 12 land-owning regional corporations. ANCSA established Native Corporations as *profit* corporations. However, it also envisioned, and in fact, mandated, that corporations provide for the social and cultural well-being of their tribal shareholders. While the ANCSA regional corporations are very similar to other corporations, they are different in that that their stock is inalienable (shareholders can vote to lift these restrictions, but so far none have done so). Also, section 7(i) of ANCSA requires a regional corporation to share 70 percent of its resource revenues with other regional and village corporations.

In addition, in 1971 approximately $1 billion was distributed under ANCSA and divided between Village and Regional Corporations. As well, tribes were also given 44 million acres of land. The villages received surface estate and the regions received surface and subsurface estates. In the more than three decades since their treaty settlement there have been many challenges, and some noted failures. Over time, however, the tribes of Alaska have grown into successfully integrating their lives and cultures to constructively co-exist and contribute to the Alaskan mainstream economy.

While the Presidents and CEOs of the regional corporations run their own respective businesses, they formalized the Association of Regional Corporation Presidents and CEOs in 1998 to collectively realize shared goals. Through this organization they have focused on government legislative and regulatory issues that impact their corporations, promote joint business ventures, and maximize shareholder hire. As reported in their 2003 annual economic impact report,[379] Alaska Native corporations had combined revenue and assets of $2.4 billion, and $2.7 billion, respectively. A total dividend payout of $45.6 million was also made in 2002.

Furthermore, the corporations had a combined workforce of 12,123 (with over 3,100 Alaskan Native Americans employed), and a total payroll of $408 million. According to one economic model, the multiplier effect of the payroll and dividends generated a further 3,630 jobs with an additional $100 million in payroll benefits. In that year, the Alaska Department of Labor and Workforce Development recognized further that 18 Alaska Native American non-profit organizations or corporations made the top 100 employers list in Alaska (a significant increase from the past). In fact, of the 43 corporations chosen for the report, 13 were recognized by *Alaska Business Monthly* in the October 2003 issue as ranking among the state's top 49 Alaskan businesses. They not only led the list of Alaska-owned businesses, they comprised 43 percent of the list.

The ANCSA tribes have also been rising giants in the world of federal contracting. The Olgoonik Corporation has, since 2002, won more than $225 million in contracts for construction work on U.S. military bases and embassies from Alaska to Kosovo. Halliburton corporation is Olgoonik's non-Native partner in those contracts. In another case, rather than partner, Native corporations have simply taken over services the federal government wanted to privatize. In one $2.2 billion project to run part of the military's mapmaking division, two Alaska Native corporations brought in their own managers to rehire and oversee hundreds of federal employees.

Canadian and American tribes south of the 49th could learn much from this model. Importantly, they could learn to possibly avoid many of the costly mistakes and emulate the successes of ANCSA tribes.

Mississipi Choctaws

One writer comments:[380]

> Two generations ago, the Choctaws were the poorest tribe in the poorest state in the nation. Fergus Bordewich, author of *Killing the White Man's Indian*, spent time on the Choctaw reservation in the 1960s, when it was "a forgotten community; just a scattered collection of cabins and shacks in a depressing corner of the Mississippi backcountry." Bordewich recalls that the reservation's roads were unpaved, kids were unclothed, and most of the tribe was far removed from the world of money and jobs.
>
> John Hendrix, a non-Indian who works in the tribe's economic development office, says that at that time only seven percent of the tribe had high school educations; 86 percent earned less than $2,000 a year. "To see where we are today," says Hendrix, "really paints the picture of what has been done in a short amount of time."

In 25 years, the Mississippi Choctaw tribe has emerged from dire poverty. This scale of their accomplishment is significant considering the tribe was almost totally bereft of natural resources and other assets from which to build a tribal economy. The Choctaws were living on the poorest reservation in one of the poorest counties of the nation's poorest state. Now it is ranked by the Harvard Project on American Indian Economic Development among the most successful of the nation's 559 federally-recognized tribes. This is quite an accomplishment considering the wealth created by some U.S. tribes through casinos. The Choctaws now have their own casino, but generated their initial development and wealth through a host of inventive and diverse industries.

The Choctaw organization has gone from owning little more than dirt and trees to holding $1 billion in assets in both the United States and Mexico. Choctaw Chief Phillip Martin has provided the vision and ethical leadership which has helped create 14,000 new jobs and provided free college education to more than a thousand young people. But by 2001, tribal median household income was $25,000 and more than 400 were enrolled in college. Most of the tribe's civilian labor force work for tribally-owned enterprises or government services—such as the tribe's health care center. The Choctaws are one of the largest employers in the state of Mississippi. Several thousand non-Indians migrate onto the reservation every day to work in the Choctaws' manufacturing, service, and public sector enterprises. The Choctaws import labor because there aren't enough Choctaws to fill all the jobs they've created. The Choctaw reservation—mostly in Neshoba County about 70 miles northeast of Jackson—has nearly doubled in size to 35,000 acres. In addition, tribal members drawn by better living conditions and jobs, began returning to the reservation, tripling tribal membership to 9,000.

So how did the 9,000-member tribe emerge from poverty to generate $450 million in revenues a year—and do it within one generation?

Chief Phillip Martin, the 77-year-old democratically-elected head of the Choctaw Tribal Council since 1979, says simply, but proudly: "We developed an economy." There was nothing magical about the Choctaw's success, Martin said. Business was attracted to the remote reservation by low labor costs, a favourable tax structure and a tribal court system trusted by outside business.[381] The development began with:

> manufacturing...[as] the foundation for the Choctaws' almost miraculous good fortune.

What started with a contract to make automotive wire harnesses for

General Motors in 1979—the same year Martin was first elected chief—has evolved into a portfolio of businesses worth hundreds of millions of dollars. The tribe's customer list includes companies such as Ford Motor Co., PepsiCo Inc. and McDonald's. Annual sales now top $375 million. Tribal unemployment—which hovered around 75 percent in the 1970s—is less than 4 percent today. Jobs are so plentiful that 60 percent of the 7,000 people on the tribe's payroll are non-Indian.[382]

More specifically, what the tribe did was make it an easy decision for investors to invest in tribal businesses by creating a stable governance environment—one that separated politics from business, ensured fair treatment for non-Indian investors, provided competent and professional decision-making, provided attractive incentives to locate on their lands, and dealt with many of the common misconceptions and actual problems with locating businesses on tribal lands. They also developed more savvy for attracting federal aid and then used the money from both sources to improve their lot and to gain a political voice. Leadership was unquestionably a critical factor:

[Chief] Martin enlisted in the military in 1945 and was sent overseas to help rebuild post-war Germany. Amidst the destruction of Germany, the young Choctaw soldier began developing a vision for rebuilding his own nation.

"Germans had nothing, but they salvaged every brick and rebuilt," he said during an interview Wednesday. "That was an inspiration to me: You can do something with almost nothing."[383]

Chief Martin's attitude and accomplishments should be a lesson to the many Chiefs whose only solution to helping their people move forward is to ask the government for more transfer payments. You can do a lot with ethical leadership, clear goals, a strategic plan, commitment, and a lot of hard work.

COMMUNITY AND CORPORATE MODELS IN CANADA: A WIN/WIN STANDARD

The area of Aboriginal entrepreneurship and corporate partnerships has raged and grown like an out-of-control wildfire in the past few years. This has resulted in an unprecedented opportunity to forge a new era of self-reliance. In Canada we can learn from several outstanding examples.

The combined Aboriginal businesses in Fort McMurray are represented by the Northeastern Alberta Aboriginal Business Association (NAABA). In 2004, its members generated over $400 million in revenues, and sights are set on cracking the $.5 billion mark for 2006. NAABA consists of 86 Aboriginal majority-owned businesses and 103 associate members mostly comprised of non-Aboriginal corporations. The Aboriginal businesses are involved in the massive energy developments relating to the Alberta oil sands. NAABA is a part of the Regional Economic Development Link, an innovative business-to-industry communication process designed to facilitate opportunities to enhance the Region's business sectors through information, communications, promotions, research, networking, and sales. The NAABA Aboriginal entrepreneurs have been Canadian leaders in building constructive win/win relationships with business, industry and government.

Corporations such as Syncrude Canada Ltd. and Suncor Energy Inc. have set new standards in their Aboriginal relations programs, their extensive consultations with tribes, employment of huge Aboriginal work forces, and proactive development of win/win partnerships.

Since its inception Syncrude recognized that local Aboriginal people have a significant stake in the responsible and successful development of the oil sands resources. Through the corporate leadership of former Syncrude Chairman Eric Newell and President and COO Jim Carter, there was recognition that Aboriginal people had a natural stake in their corporate success, and were also an indigenous source of talent that could help Syncrude to achieve its corporate goals. To participate meaningfully in oil sands development, Syncrude realized that they had to help Aboriginal locals transcend the challenges of living and working in a modern industrial society. This was done in a way that respected Aboriginal customs and culture while meeting their corporate objectives. Similarly, Suncor's Aboriginal employees account for a substantial 10% of their workforce. Suncor has also supported several Aboriginal businesses by sharing business knowledge and, in many cases, committing to purchase agreements as the businesses get started.

The bottom line in this success story is both Aboriginal and corporate leadership. Dave Tuccaro is former President of NAABA and a hugely successful entrepreneur in his own right. Dave provided inspiring leadership and strategic direction at critical times. What has emerged is an atmosphere of cooperation and expectations of win/win deals. Taking the reins from the

DAVE TUCCARO, former President, NAABA, President & CEO of Tuccaro Inc. Group of Companies

community perspective were leaders like Archie Cyprien, Chief of the Athabasca Chipewyan First Nation, and Chief Jim Boucher of the Fort McKay First Nation. These leaders have recognized that it takes more than holding your hand out to the government to make lives of ordinary community people better. Once they were committed to the direction of economic integration, there was no question that the new economic activities have provided new innovative opportunities for education, employment, and have allowed many community members to lead more stable and fulfilling lives.

Membertou First Nation

BERND CHRISTMAS, former Band CEO, Membertou First Nation

In 1996 the Membertou First Nation had a $1 million dollar deficit and a budget of $4.5 million. According to lawyer and former band CEO Bernd Christmas, the rate of unemployment was 95%, health and social pathologies rampant. As the result of hard work and community strategic planning, current revenues generated are $65 million, and they have 450 employees. Membertou also contributes approximately $165 million annually to the maritime economy.[384] Between 1996 to 2005, community reliance on government support decreased from 100% to 10%, with their operations making them the largest employer in the region. Mr. Christmas notes that of the approximately $9 billion in federal transfer payments to First Nations in 2005, most of the monies are earmarked as social "handouts" with only approximately $640 million available for economic development. Given the number of First Nations in Canada, this amounts to a paltry $1 million dollars a year for the most critical area of development for First Nations.

Membertou clearly acknowledged that rather than chase welfare dollars, their efforts would be better spent pursuing the enormous business opportunities available. In 2001, Membertou achieved official International Organization for Standardization (ISO) 9001:2000 certification, making it the first indigenous government in Canada, and likely the world, to meet internationally recognized business standards. Membertou, as far as the writer is aware, is the only First Nation in Canada that posts its community audited financial statements on its website for the world to see.

Membertou has been actively developing a series of contracts with international corporations. They have built a fine band office, wellness centre, Veterans Memorial Building, and an elementary school from their own-source revenues. The school apparently would have taken until 2060 to build, had they waited for government monies. From 1980 to 2003 their on-reserve population has grown from 333 to 1067, the land base has increased from 65 acres to 350, and the number of houses increased from 56 to 218.

The reason for the metamorphosis from economic basket case to Atlantic Canada tiger has to do with leadership, vision, action, and innovation.

"Membertou is a leader in the new wave of economic thinking that is emerging in native communities across the country," says Chief Terrance Paul. "We realized two decades ago that fiscal accountability made good business sense, that it would be the foundation, not only of our indigenous economies, but also of self-determination for our community. It has been hard work but we are now realizing the fruits of our efforts."[385]

Membertou leadership also realized that impending government cutbacks would alter the system of Indian Affairs support and welfare that native communities had come to depend on all too much. It was decided that permanent changes in the ways of doing things had to take place; in a sense, a new vision had to be reinvented for the community. This translated into what members of the community now refer to as "the Membertou vision." The first step in this vision was to seek out skilled young people who had left Membertou to work elsewhere and persuade them to return to work for their own people. One of these people was Bernd Christmas.

At a recent public speech, Mr. Christmas described changing the direction of the First Nation from the dependency mindset to a market/customer-focussed direction to being comparable to "trying to change the direction of a supertanker." But how does an Aboriginal community get their "house in order," as one community member noted, overcoming a $1 million debt and five years later being recognized as a prosperous community? The success of Membertou has been attributed to incorporating a corporate mindset into their leaders, their institutions and community. Early on, the consensus in the community was that in order to attract business, band administration must be run like a business, and politics separated from economic development. The leadership also developed a human resource strategy which sought to attract the more educated community members who had left the community and had valuable experience in the private sector and government.

In November 2000, the Corporate Division opened, mandated to execute the business vision of the Chief and Council. The First Nation opened a corporate office in the Purdy's Wharf Towers in Halifax. This brought the community closer to the government agencies with which it does business, and with Atlantic Canada's private sector companies, most of which have Halifax offices. Since then, Membertou's Corporate Division has participated in the establishment of several key business alliances with companies such as Clearwater Fine Foods, SNC Lavalin, Sodexho Canada, Grant Thornton, and Lockheed Martin.

In summary, Membertou now provides a stable government founded on the principles of transparency, accountability and ethical leadership. Leadership is provided in close communication with its membership—leaders lead by informed consensus rather than rule as many Aboriginal leaders do. Its success is further built on the most valuable asset of any community—its skilled members who have been away from the reserve and have vital real world education and experience to bring to the community's benefit.

Osoyoos Indian Band

According to the Chief of the Osoyoos Indian Band, Chief Clarence Louie, "The band does not owe its membership dependency. It owes them opportunity and a chance to become independent." Under his leadership, the Osoyoos Indian Band in BC's south-central interior, and with just over 400 members, has produced some early economic successes as pointed out in a 2005 article:

> Ten years ago, the Osoyoos Indian Band in the south Okanagan received more federal transfer dollars than its self-generated revenue.
>
> Today it produces seven times the revenue it receives from the federal government [with business revenue now totalling $15 million]. Anxious to assert its independence, the band administers its own health, social, educational and...[governance] services.
>
> "Aboriginal people should be able to design their own future," says Chief Clarence Louie.
>
> "It's about time for First Nations to manage their affairs. Let us learn, let us take risks. How do any people learn? They learn through trial and error."[386]

CHIEF CLARENCE LOUIE, Osoyoos
Indian Band

There are eight band-owned businesses ranging from their own very upscale winery, a golf-hotel-residential complex, campground, RV park, construction company, ready-mix concrete plant, and a gas bar and convenience store. In 2002, the band opened Canada's first Aboriginal-owned winery, and now possesses one of Canada's largest privately-owned vineyards—over 1,200 acres of leased vineyard lands or approximately 25% of BC's VQA (Vintner's Quality Alliance is a sign of quality and requires that wines be made from British Columbia grapes) grape production is grown on their lands. In 2006 the Band opened a state-of-the-art $8 million "Desert Heritage Interpretive Centre," and a four-star hotel.

Once again, as the following excerpt points out, some of the key ingredients to success are leadership, commitment, and proceeding with a strategic plan. In this case, leadership was provided by Chief Louie through the Osoyoos Indian Band's Development Corporation:

> But with the Osoyoos Band now running…[eight] business enterprises…Chief Louie has made good on his mantra that the **band should be biased towards action.**
>
> Things were different not long ago…[according to Chief Louie]. … "In 1994, our band was in the same situation as most bands in Canada. Federal transfer dollars exceeded the Band's self-generated revenue. Today, the Osoyoos Indian Band's self-generated revenue is seven times more."[387] [Emphasis added]

Chief Louie has the following recommendations connecting election results with business/employment generation performance:

> "It's about time that 'jobs' (or lack of them) determine who gets elected for Chief and Council. Off the reserve (federal/provincial and even municipal elections), the strength or weaknesses of the economy gets people elected or fired – as it should. Every Chief and Council election should be tied to the number of jobs created each year and the increase or decrease of Band revenues. If a Chief and Council do not create more jobs every year – and not just for their own family – or bring in more revenue, that Chief and Council should be fired (unless your First Nation is isolated). Most Band

members don't want to listen to your promises or your feelings. Show me your numbers, that's where the proof is – your numbers don't lie."

The motto of the Osoyoos Indian Band Development Corporation is: "Working with Business to Preserve our Past by Strengthening our Future." At a 2005 Assembly of First Nations Economic Development Forum, Chief Louie made the following comments:

> "Today, as a wise Chief in BC said to me a few months ago, 'Economic Development is how we hunt today.' If you call yourself a leader, give all your people a chance at the dignity of a job, equal opportunity and the individual responsibility to earn a living. Practice being a student (homework is not only for kids), go to school on [studying] others—no one is a know-it-all —go to school on success and failure. ..."[388]

Corporate Leadership: Examples of ATCO Group and Akita Drilling Ltd.

The ATCO Group is an Alberta-based corporation with more than 7,000 employees. ATCO Group now controls more than 11 wholly-owned subsidiaries including ATCO Electric and ATCO Frontec. The company was started by the Southern family and is engaged in a range of businesses. The innovation that ATCO has shown through its Aboriginal partnerships is exemplary. The Southern family has shown great inspiration and leadership in recruiting senior managers prepared to commit to understanding indigenous interests, concerns, and opportunities.

Recently, ATCO Electric, winner of the 2005 International Edison Award for leadership and innovation, completed the Dover-Whitefish Transmission Project. This was a 350-kilometre transmission line project that traversed the traditional territories of several Aboriginal groups. At a recent conference,[389] Sett Policicchio, President of ATCO Electric, explained how they demonstrated respect for:

- Elders and their traditional knowledge;
- Aboriginal leaders by ensuring their senior management sat "chief-to-chief," and "face-to-face";
- The Aboriginal desire to share in economic benefits of the project;
- The capabilities of Aboriginal contractors; and
- The environment and its creatures.

The project was a model for successfully managed Aboriginal partnerships. It was completed on time and on budget, ensured local Aboriginal people benefited financially, and left the traditional way of life undisturbed.

Similarly, ATCO Frontec is another trailblazer in the development of win/win Aboriginal relations in the far north of Canada and Alaska. ATCO Frontec provides site support services, and facilities management to the resource, telecommunications and defence sectors. It has established long-term relationships based on respect and sensitivity for Aboriginal concerns and interests. By taking a long-term view, they have developed six phenomenal Aboriginal partnerships and brought opportunities that might otherwise not exist for their indigenous partners (involving, for example, managing the North Warning System for the Canadian Department of Defence, the Alaska Radar System for the United States Military, and the Solid State Radar System for the United States Air Force radar protection system—with installations throughout North America, Europe, and Greenland).

Speaking to Parliament in relation to Bill C-14 (the Tlicho Land Claims and Self-Government Act) Mr. Mario Silva (Liberal Member of Parliament for Davenport, ON) described the ATCO Frontec business model:

> Several years ago the Tlicho began an association with ATCO Frontec, a logistics firm that follows a unique and successful **business model based on collaboration with Aboriginal groups**.
>
> Beginning in the late 1980s, ATCO established a series of partnerships with Aboriginal groups across the north. As an example, the Uqsuq Corporation, which stores and distributes fuel, is jointly owned with the Inuit Development Corporation of Nunavut.
>
> The Inuit of Labrador are partners with ATCO in Torngait, a company that provides support services to a range of industries. In BC, the Northwest Territories and Yukon, Northwest Tel operates and maintains microwave towers thanks to agreements ATCO has made with several Aboriginal development corporations.
>
> Each one of these partnerships with ATCO is based on a similar business model, one that **stresses the building of capacity within Aboriginal communities**. While contacts may come and go, industrial and business capacity has an enduring market value that can be adapted to suit new opportunities.
>
> This capacity-based business model appealed to the Dogrib Treaty 11 Council which then partnered with ATCO Frontec to create Tli Cho

Logistics. The business model is pretty simple. The **Tlicho own 51%** of Tli Cho Logistics and ATCO Frontec controls 49%. The company provides a range of services to the Diavik diamond mine and to the remediation project underway at the Colomac gold mine. Today more than 130 people work for Tli Cho Logistics, 50 of whom are members of the Dogrib Rae band.

When the company was founded five years ago, ATCO handled nearly all the company's administrative and managerial work while the unskilled jobs went to the Tlicho people. During the past few years, however, ATCO has helped the Tlicho acquire the skills needed to manage and to administer that company.

This **incremental transfer of technical skills** is why the Tlicho were, and continue to be, keen to partner with companies like ATCO Frontec. Tlicho leaders recognize that management skills acquired on mining projects can be readily applied to other ventures as well. In other words, the Tlicho will be better able to initiate, to manage and to operate other projects as a result of experience gained from these diamond mines. This, my honourable colleagues, represents community capacity building in its purest form, and all Canadians stand to benefit from it and should be proud of it.[390] [Emphasis added]

In 2004, ATCO Frontec was selected by the United States Air Force to manage and maintain the Alaska Radar System for up to 10 years. The approximately $400M contract (over 10 years) was won in partnership between ATCO Frontec and Arctic Slope World Services (their indigenous partner). President of ATCO Frontec, Harry Wilmot, commented:

> "For 10 years we have been recognized repeatedly for exceeding contract requirements and delivering exceptional performance. ... It is critical that every radar functions at optimum capacity so that space surveillance, attack warning, intercept control and navigational assistance is available to military and civilian aircraft."[391]

Another public company spun out of ATCO in 1993, Akita Drilling Ltd., has also set major milestones for mutually profitable partnerships with Aboriginal groups. Rob Hunt, Senior Vice President for Akita, in some real sense has set the standard by pioneering the right way to approach and manage Aboriginal partnerships. In an article in the *Far North Oil & Gas Review*, Mr Hunt commented:

ROB HUNT, former Senior Vice President for Akita Drilling, Inc.

"The wrong way to do business in the North…is to fly …in by corporate jet, spend a day then…[fly right] out." The right way, he says, **is grassroots commitment — over the long term**. Hunt says successful northern partnerships happen when southern companies cooperate fully with Aboriginal people and show respect for their land. To do that, he stresses, company representatives need to get involved. "Stay in the communities," he advises. "Get to know the people, go to their schools and talk to the kids."[392] [Emphasis added]

When such sentiments are backed by a real rank-and-file commitment, they are music to the ears of community leadership who, in the past, have become accustomed to corporations simply ignoring indigenous interests and concerns. The personal commitment of Mr. Hunt has percolated its way through the Akita organization to ensure that employees at all levels buy into the program—one that has resulted in numerous socially and economically profitable relationships throughout the North.

SUMMARY

What the models examined tell us is that where the greatest successes have been achieved, strong, ethical leadership has been critical in gaining community consensus to move forward toward economic self-reliance. As well, clear decisions have been made to develop strategic plans, build capacity and repatriate those critical tribal members with education and experience in government and industry. While capacity is being built, strategic alliances can be made with forward-looking mainstream corporations to create win/win partnerships. Another element common to all successful models is tribes having consciously sought to build a future based upon hope and opportunity rather than remaining entrenched in grievance and blame about injustices of the past. Rather than talk about change, the rubber has already hit the road for the groups profiled in this chapter; they have begun economically to integrate and to move forward. *Wai Wah.*

15

THE WAY FORWARD FOR URBAN ABORIGINALS

> They always say time changes things, but you actually have to change
> them yourself.
> ANDY WARHOL (1928–1987), *The Philosophy of Andy Warhol*

OVERVIEW

The past few decades have seen the migration of Aboriginals from rural communities to cities. Ordinary folk are attracted by better employment prospects, educational opportunities, and often the seductive lure of the bright lights. They leave their communities not only to escape conditions of poverty and unemployment, but also to escape the phenomenon of lateral violence, vicious reserve politics, miscellaneous kinds of abuse, and sometimes to avoid the otherwise negative social environments that exist in many communities. In Canada over half the population is now very mobile and urban-based.

The urban Aboriginal demographic tsunami is also impacting metropolitan areas and governments with an explosive force. In the province of British Columbia it is estimated that 70 percent of the Aboriginal population lives off-reserve, and one in five lives within the Greater Vancouver Regional District (GVRD).[393] Although there are 28 Indian reserves within the GVRD, the 2001 census data reveals that only 1,920 people live in these communities, with the remaining 36,855 living in Vancouver and its satellite cities (representing a population almost 20 times larger than the total reserve population for the region).[394] Local governments must take the urban Aboriginal population seriously because of their disproportionate dependency on costly social programs and services.

The indigenous urban populations are far from homogeneous. They are neither entirely ghettoized nor uniformly disadvantaged. Many are university-educated and there is a growing middle class developing. As well, most large cities have dozens of Aboriginally-run organizations providing a wide range of services.

While statistics reveal that the urban Aboriginal population fares better in just about every social and economic category than their reserve counterparts, that same population still regrettably forms one of the most impoverished groups found largely in the slums and ghettoes of most inner cities. Instead of the excitement of bright lights, many urban Aboriginals find themselves on the bottom rung of the community social and economic ladder—with lives revolving around homelessness, skid row alcoholism, the drug trade and prostitution. Dreams of big city life often turn into gruelling disappointments as the unyielding struggle for survival in a large impersonal city emerges into everyday reality.

Refuge is frequently sought in various forms of substance abuse. The regrettable outcome from frustrated expectations is that innocent children must bear the often harsh reality of their parental disappointments and subsequent decisions. Many go hungry, and have virtually no parental supervision or structure in their lives. Vulnerable youth become easy prey for pimps, gangs, drug dealers, and the more insidious elements of big city life. Average middle class people could simply not comprehend the vagaries and uncertainty that characterize the daily lives of many Aboriginal people living in big cities.

The general economic plight of off-reserve people is usually much better than those on-reserve: welfare rates are much lower at 22.1% versus 41.5%, while median incomes and employment rates are much higher. What is concerning about the statistics for off-reserve people is the significantly disproportionate number of single parent Aboriginal families.[395]

Percentage of Families with Two Parents

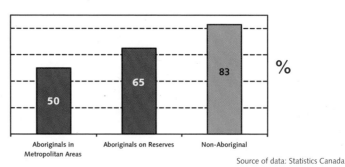

Aboriginals in Metropolitan Areas	Aboriginals on Reserves	Non-Aboriginal
50	65	83

Source of data: Statistics Canada

Forty-one percent of off-reserve Aboriginal children in Canada are living in poverty. Furthermore, fully 80% of the 4,300 children aged 0–6 studied living in the Vancouver area were found to be living in dire poverty. Yet in spite of the precarious situation of the indigenous urban population, *they likely hold the long-term key to the successful economic integration of Aboriginal people in rural communities into mainstream society.* They hold such a key because they are comparatively more advanced in education, as a group they have much more experience in the larger world, and are more familiar with how an ordinary functioning economy works. As well, the fact that many have struck out into what for many rural folks is an unknown urban world, has demonstrated that they are prepared to accept some risk to make their lives better. Probably more than most community governments are prepared to admit, they need to rely on the education and experience gained by their urban Aboriginal brothers and sisters if they wish to move forward. This reliance was demonstrated by the Membertou First Nation in recruiting their former urban members to help create the success that community now enjoys.

Limited Financial Resources

What is incredible about this situation is that while less than half the Aboriginal population now lives on reserves in Canada, they receive almost 90% of federal transfer payment spending. By comparison the massive population in cities receive a paltry 3.5% of this amount. The federal government has launched an Urban Aboriginal Strategy supposedly in response to the shifting demographic reality. This $50 million, four-year initiative developed by the Government of Canada was intended to help respond to the needs of Aboriginal people living in key urban centres. In comparison to the monies spent on the reserve population, this sum is ludicrously inadequate. The program is meant to embody a collaborative approach to bring together various federal, provincial and municipal partners, along with more than 50 community groups and Aboriginal organizations to develop and implement projects.

Many question how such an imbalance in revenue distribution can exist. The disparity is easier to understand in light of the previous discussion relating to the *Indian Act*. Essentially, the federal approach to dealing with tribes has focussed only on setting up communities as a form of rural municipality with limited powers and authority. The archaic governance structure introduced under the *Indian Act* over 130 years ago is virtually unchanged from its early inception. Federal governments in succession have simply gone along with the ponderous INAC bureaucracy ignoring the demographic reality shaping the urban Aboriginal landscape. This has been to the considerable detriment of those in the cities and to the more progressive development of Canada as a nation.

The existing political structure is centred on the rural Chiefs, and effectively denies the larger Aboriginal urban population a political voice in how fiscal allocations should be made. It is not surprising that all resources flow to the communities for expenditure only at that community level when you have over 600 Chiefs clamouring for revenues and only a few comparatively disenfranchised urban organizations advocating for resources to move urban Aboriginal populations forward.

The reality for those leaving their communities is that they are literally cut off completely without any formal connection to the local government structure and resources. This is an odd situation in light of the fact that reserve lands and their assets are supposedly held in trust for the use and benefit of all members no matter where they live.

Until the 1999 landmark Supreme Court of Canada case, *Corbiere v. Canada (Minister of Indian and Northern Affairs) (Corbiere)*,[396] off-reserve band members were legally barred from voting in reserve elections and as a result were almost completely ignored by the Chiefs, their Councils, and the INAC bureaucracy. The decision established that off-reserve band members had the right to vote in on-reserve elections, and has resulted in a little more lip-service being directed toward off-reserve members before elections (a flurry of public relations materials sent out in hopes of securing urban votes in community elections) but virtually no substantive change in terms of resources flowing from rural to urban community members.

STRANGERS IN A STRANGE LAND

As reviewed previously, many urban Aboriginal people come to large cities with no conception of how they operate, what is needed to survive, or of the pitfalls and dangers. Largely, they come from small, isolated communities where the only reality they know and have been socialized into is the "culture of expectancy" and the "welfare trap." In many cases, their views of how life works in large cities are gleaned from television; a significant number are completely unprepared for the vagaries of city life.

Notwithstanding the fact that many may be seeking refuge, in part, from oppressive community environments, they find that they have also unwittingly lost the only support system they are familiar with. At least in small communities they have access to family networks, country foods, and the social environment and "emotional community" that have defined them and with which they have identified from childhood. It is not until arriving in a large city that the realization dawns as to the importance of the social fabric they have left behind. They also learn that, without a reasonable income, surviving in large cities is very difficult. Unlike reserves where housing is usually provided without cost, city landlords demand that rent be paid on time. Also, welfare cheques don't go nearly as far when everything must be paid for.

It is not surprising then, that many Aboriginal people tend to congregate in areas where little is demanded of them and they can still feel some sense of community—on city streets, and in skid row bars. Though such gathering spots are not the most savoury, they are the most familiar and still fulfill the tribal yearning to feel connected to some community. Urban Aboriginal Friendship Centres provide some "connection" for those in the city, but are still a poor substitute for deeply-felt ancestral links to a home community.

The question as to how to rectify such a range of significant problems is far from simple. There may, however, be some simple measures that would improve quality of life, and the transition process for Aboriginals moving into the city from remote communities. **Firstly, the exploration of how it might be possible to create some link so that such community members still feel "connected," supported, and a part of their home community. Secondly, the exploration of how such persons might be better prepared for city living. Thirdly, the question as to how they can be efficiently and effectively supported throughout the transition to their new life. Finally, the question as to what resources can be transferred to support these initiatives must be addressed.**

If these issues are not approached proactively, mainstream society will be on the hook for costly social service programs dealing with a seemingly never-ending social malaise. Instead, we should focus on how to create self-sustaining, healthy, productive, tax-paying citizens. Rather than a revolving door of misery, we need to create an escalator that keeps moving urban Aboriginal people forward and upward to better, more fulfilling lives.

Retaining the Connection to Home Communities

One of the most fundamental aspects of an Aboriginal person raised in a small, tight-knit community is their strong emotional connection to that community—even when that community might be perceived by that person to be the major source of abuse and aggravation in their lives. Unfortunately, urban Aboriginal people are often discriminated against by their own Chief and Council. Once they leave, they are made to feel unwelcome by community administration and governments who see their obligations to community members as extending only to the reserve's geographical boundaries. This attitude is encouraged by the fact that transfer payments by INAC are made directly, and only, to communities. It is a hugely counter-productive situation because it unnecessarily makes urban indigenous people feel alienated from their home community. As well, it aids in severing the most precious link that communities have to their most educated and experienced human capital.

Indigenous people indeed have deep community connections and tribal relationships that are largely invisible to non-Aboriginals. Such a connection has been described by Professor Tennant as follows:

> In the Indian view, contemporary communities and tribal groups have the same essential connection with the land as did those same communities and tribal groups at contact. In most cases, indeed, **present-day Indians do retain powerful emotional attachment to ancestral community, tribal group, and territory. This attachment, which is itself regarded by Indians as fundamental to their identity, is largely invisible to non-Indians, whose immigrant-derived society and culture are based upon exodus from established communities and upon individual rather than collective values.** The fact that much social and lifestyle change has occurred among Indians is not seen by Indians themselves as having impaired historic continuity or Indian identity or as having removed the obligation of contemporary leaders to continue pursuit of land claim settlements.[397] [Emphasis added]

In this respect, the relationship between individuals and their communities remains a "powerful emotional attachment" and is something akin to the bond between a child and its parents. At their core, Aboriginal people are

CITY OF EAGLES

Bald eagles build their nests in large trees near rivers or coasts. A typical nest is around 5 feet in diameter, and used year after year, some nests can become enormous. Apparently, the shape of the eagle nest or aerie is determined mainly by the branch point on which it is built. Disk-shaped nests are built on the ground or a tree branch which is nearly level. When you look at their nests from the ground, they look a bit like little universes or self-contained cities of eagles.

tribal with a family/community focus. Largely, their entire understanding and view of the cosmos is anchored in their tribal/community ties.

Yet when they decide to move to a big city, this connection is virtually severed with no reflection as to what harm this may cause. The importance of the connection is simply not seen or is undervalued by non-Aboriginals. This is unfortunate since maintaining that connection, at least initially, could be important to facilitating a smoother transition to a better way of life in the city. It would be much wiser to marshal the strength of tribal community connections to support the migration to urban centres. There are several suggestions that may make this a painless and more productive transition.

Firstly, perhaps there should be some federal transfer payment monies in the line item budgets of rural communities specifically earmarked to provide information and support services to urban-based community members. The details of how such monies are used, whether pooled with other communities to rationalize service delivery or provided individually, should depend upon the size of the communities and the raw population numbers in particular urban centres. The spending of such monies should not be left to Chiefs and Councils to hand out as patronage perks; instead the monies should flow directly to independent non-profit societies composed of urban folks. The members and board of directors of these organizations can collectively make spending decisions.

Alternatively, such monies might be flowed directly to community-focussed, urban non-profit societies. These monies might be used to:
1 Provide information and services to those community members wishing to move to an urban centre before they actually leave the rural community. The cardinal rule for organizing anything is "preparation, preparation, and preparation." Yet most Aboriginals leave their home communities without any understanding of the complex living environment to which they are moving. Furthermore, they have no clear strategy for coping with many unfamiliar stresses and crises. Those seeking to make such a move should be provided a simple orientation on what life is like in a large city and relevant information such as:
   a Background on city neighborhoods and their characteristics;
   b Locations of schools and post-secondary institutions, programs offered, etc.;
   c Employment opportunities, training requirements, etc.;
   d Available social services (e.g., healthcare, childcare, legal, welfare), and their location in the city;

e Dangers found in large cities from gangs, pimps, drug dealers, and the like (typical recruitment techniques, etc.);

f Sexually transmitted diseases, prevention, and their prevalence in some sectors of the Aboriginal population (particularly HIV and AIDS);

g Public transportation;

h Housing, rentals rates, and availability;

i Other community members living in the city who might be contacted and who might provide useful advice, a useful perspective, and a friendly face in the city.

2 Establish an information and services office in cities (where the population base warrants it) to provide:

a The information in point 1 above on an ongoing basis;

b A website that contains the above information, and publishes newsworthy information about the urban and rural communities to assist in ensuring that a connection is maintained with members within the community;

c An office with a liaison worker whose role is to:

i run the urban office;

ii provide information to community members or to various agencies from schools or social services entities relating to community members; and

iii possibly perform a monitoring function relating to the well-being of members and their families.

3 The urban community office should have computers available with Internet connections that can be used by community members who cannot afford their own computers.

4 Provide for tri-annual gatherings of community members (possibly built around Christmas, Easter, and just before summer holidays) that would allow members to get together and reinforce tribal and community connections.

5 Might provide basic life-skills training, emphasizing:

a Parenting skills and issues to assist young families in an alien environment;

b Employers' workplace expectations. Many Aboriginal folks from small communities have never had "9 to 5" jobs and are not acculturated to what is typically expected of them in the typical work environment;

c Personal budgeting and financial planning. Most Aboriginals from small communities are completely unfamiliar with basic budgeting and financial planning since it is largely not required as part of reservation living.

d The value of education; and

e Business training.

To ensure attendance, the possibility might be examined of making this kind of training conditional to receiving welfare, employment insurance payments, or housing subsidies.

EDUCATION AND TRAINING

The key to full-blown indigenous renaissance is education. More resources must be earmarked for education based on a long-term national, strategic education plan with focus on specific areas.

Elementary and Secondary

It might also be said that the solution for moving Aboriginal children out of the welfare trap is "education, education, and education." Yet the problems experienced by children and youth are legion—they have few role models, they often have little home support, and are sometimes targets of gangs, pimps, and drug dealers.

In seeking global solutions to indigenous education, the experience of the Maori of New Zealand and the Grandview/?Uuquinak'uuh Elementary School reviewed previously are instructive. On the one hand, there must be a long-term focus on education—an unambiguous long-term strategic plan backed by clear education policy. There must also be a specific emphasis on education from early childhood to tertiary levels.

For Aboriginal inner-city school children, an after-school athletic and social interest component to schooling is required that keeps students focussed on the importance of education and a nurturing educational environment. The more time spent in such constructive endeavours, the less they will be within reach of meaner elements of the streets that might send them on less productive courses. While cultural sensitivity and reinforcement may have some role in the education process, it should not displace an emphasis on academic success, as demonstrated in the Grandview/?Uuquinak'uuh Elementary School experience.

As well, the proposed inner city independent school proposed by Principal Krause of the Grandview/?Uuquinak'uuh Elementary School should be examined seriously. In business, if you do not produce results, you are out of business. Principal Krause has already demonstrated an effective program that has produced results for inner-city children.

Partnerships between inner-city schools and local Chambers of Commerce or Boards of Trade might also be explored so that children might be mentored and exposed to other mainstream career paths and training opportunities from an early age. Perhaps such business organizations may also assist in providing speakers to schools, career fairs, and sponsoring career days-at-work. Similar opportunities might be explored with local post-secondary educational institutions. As well, Aboriginal professionals, entrepreneurs, tradesmen and those from a range of occupations might be asked to complete annual speaking circuits of inner city schools to present to children on the career opportunities available to them. Where employers commit to sponsoring the time of their employees who participate in such a program, there should be some recognition system to acknowledge their contribution.

As well, for each status Indian student that attends a public school, the School Boards typically receive approximately $9,000.00 in transfer payments from the federal government to cover the cost of that child's education. These monies are available only to public schools and not generally for independent or private school tuition. This election should clearly be at the discretion of a child's parents. If they decide their child may be provided with a better education in a private school, then this option should not be barred by a mere bureaucratic agreement between provincial education ministries and INAC. Giving Aboriginal parents this alternative is not likely to cost the taxpayer any more and will likely result in more careful educational choices being made by parents.

The city-based Aboriginal community liaison worker suggested above might also provide an important link and source of feedback for inner-school staff and Aboriginal families.

Post-secondary

Urban Aboriginals should be focussing on certain educational opportunities. Firstly, the trades are currently, and will likely continue to be, in huge demand. Trades, though they have not had the glamour of some professions in the past, are now ascending in importance to society. In fact, most trades people are becoming more significant earners than those who have taken more academic career paths. Indeed, more training dollars are now available for Aboriginals wishing to undertake training in this area. Given the trajectory of construction and trade opportunities available, trades represent a secure future of potential earnings and opportunities for Aboriginal families.

In addition, statistics indicate that the Aboriginal business sector increased at a rate nine times that of self-employed Canadians overall from 1996 to 2002. This is obviously an area of significant interest and a focus that will pay huge dividends for a burgeoning Aboriginal (and ultimately Canadian) economy. Indeed, the entire theme of this book has been to emphasize the importance of self-generated business revenues to the long-term self-reliance and health of Aboriginal communities and individuals. Entrepreneurs, business managers and administrators should be in huge demand in the Aboriginal community.

Housing

Urban housing is generally very expensive. Most efforts at assisting Aboriginal people are in the areas of subsidizing rents for low-income housing. While such assistance is necessary, it provides no incentive or bridge to actual property ownership. In fact, it likely provides an incentive to remain in subsidized housing tenements. Aboriginal people living in large cities usually have a very difficult time saving a down payment to buy their own properties. A carrot to provide impetus to this greater level of responsibility might be to provide assistance with down payments on real estate properties for qualifying candidates. Candidates might receive such assistance providing they meet specific financing criteria and assistance may take the form of low- or no-interest loans and possibly be part grant. Such an initiative would encourage:
1 development of a regular income;
2 more organization and stability;
3 familial ownership stake in property;
4 development of small businesses (since equity in an off-reserve real estate asset could be used for financing);
5 economic integration; and
6 individuals becoming more economically ambitious.
Perhaps such a program might be coordinated by the Central Mortgage and Housing Corporation.

Political Voice

Although Aboriginal people in the cities are able to vote in all elections relating to the mainstream Canadian political scene, they are largely disenfranchised when it comes to meaningful participation in Aboriginal decision-making on matters that impact them directly. The assets on their reserves are held in trust for their "use and benefit" along with those community members who physically live in the reserve communities. While they can vote in reserve elections now, urban members pretty much cannot hold elected positions in the community governments.

We have already seen how community politicians, once elected, are not answerable to their electorate, but rather to the Minister of Indian Affairs. Decisions are made by Chiefs and Councils that hugely impact the collective assets of all band members, but band members have virtually no real say in any of those decisions. In British Columbia, treaties will have far reaching implications for all Aboriginal people, yet many are being negotiated without any ongoing input from urban grassroots community members. While off-reserve members may vote in referendums on treaties once agreements-in-principle are negotiated, there is often very little reporting to urban community members and virtually no ongoing input into the substantive content of deals reached behind closed doors.

Off-reserve community members must be politically empowered. Consideration of how this is done must be part-and-parcel of reforming the archaic *Indian Act* system of governance. Exactly how this can be done is beyond the scope of this book, but should be the subject of much more detailed analysis. Such reform should involve transferring real political power into the hands of the largest Aboriginal population in the country, and out of the sole (and often self-interested) hands of the political elites.

CONCLUSION

16

MAKING UP FOR LOST TIME

The battered canoe pitches
On the murky moonlit night
Tears reflecting gently
 In the evening's muted light.
An aged Chief's heart aches
With dreams of days of yore
A time of cosmic harmony
On a welcoming, distant shore.
He knows the map is out there
In skies darkened by the storm
Evoking distant memories,
Of an ancient reckoning form.
CALVIN HELIN, *The Storm*

And so after years of reflection on my grandmother's challenge as to how to make the lives of ordinary indigenous people better, I have come to some conclusions unexpected at the beginning of this quest. It has been useful to take the metaphorical canoe journey back through the ages to examine strategies and characteristics that ensured the long survival of indigenous ancestors. We have traced the first wave of development to antiquity when North America was inhabited by vigorous tribes whose sophisticated cultures and traditions flourished in a bountiful environment. Though there were always uncertainties as a result of the vagaries of Nature, the first wave was a time when indigenous people and the environment were in much greater harmony. In many respects, the first wave was a golden era when indigenous people were fiercely self-reliant, profoundly spiritual, interdependent and self-disciplined, and guided by deeply ethical leaders.

The second wave of development involved the supposed "discovery" of North America by Europeans. Upon contact, the indigenous canoe would eventually sail directly into the "colonial storm." It turned out that indigenous customs and traditions were seen as a cumbersome impediment by an ethno-centric European culture—one more focussed on material acquisition, power consolidation, and empire building. To such colonial nations, the notions of living in harmony with Nature and in tune with the cosmos were but quaint ideas of forlorn cultures.

Initially, North America's indigenous population enabled the survival of the first Europeans by providing sustenance and protection. Tribes were later assiduously courted by competing European nations seeking to advance their trade interests and cultivate valuable military alliances. Tribal populations were subsequently ravaged and their numbers decimated enormously by introduced European diseases for which they had no natural immunity. Communities and cultures were further disoriented by the introduction of alcohol as a staple trade commodity. As the number of colonists grew, atten-tion eventually shifted from trade to the aggressive displacement and acquisi-tion of traditional tribal territories.

The third wave involved the continuation of the colonial storm from about 100 years ago until the present day. The European solution to the "indigenous problem" was to initiate a series of legal and political develop-ments aimed specifically at dismantling traditional societies. The official policy goal was to assimilate Tribal populations into what became the domi-nant European mainstream culture. This was completed by outlawing tradi-tional cultural practices, and by introducing legislation intended to displace traditional forms of governance. Tribes and their populations were isolated on reserves, and largely placed in the questionable hands of various European religious denominations.

The latter stages of the third wave involved the government's wide-spread promotion of indigenous people from self-sustaining occupations onto wel-fare roles. Out of this period arose the "welfare trap," which has resulted in economic isolation and the destructive political and social pathologies described throughout this book. This era was further witness to massive dys-function and social chaos, from which has emerged the unrealistic and unsus-tainable culture of expectancy—a pathos that has become engrained in the indigenous mindset to an appallingly self-destructive degree.

If nothing else, such developments serve to underline the fragility of deeply-rooted ways of life, and highlight how easily it becomes possible to create an enormous gulf between a people and their past. Most regrettably, the colonial storm has resulted in a dependency mindset socialized internally into the psyche of generations of indigenous populations. This mindset has

VOICES IN THE WILDERNESS

Have you ever felt like you are not being heard and no one cares to listen? This painting depicts the artist's grandfather, Chief Henry Helin, Sm'ooygit Nees Nuugan Noos, Chief of the Royal House of Gitlan. Chief Helin is meditating in the forest and praying for the return of a lost way of traditional life—yearning for a time when the Tsimshian culture thrived, when art and traditions such as the potlatch were practiced. He questions the Creator as to why the dark cloud of colonial misery has settled over a once proud and vigorous Tsimshian people, and what direction there might be to happier times. Rays of sunshine breaking through the darkness of the mystical coastal temperate rain forest represent hope in the answer to this question. He is dressed in a traditional Chilkat blanket with a raven frontlet and ermine skin head dress. A limited edition of giclee method prints was made.

become so entrenched that many indigenous people now think the welfare trap is "normal," and that they are "owed" their material survival by a government that long ago perpetrated injustices on their ancestors. Such attitudes illustrate how distant the concepts of independence and self-reliance (common to our grandfathers) have become to contemporary indigenous people.

In order to take action that is likely to make a constructive difference, we must acknowledge the brutal reality regarding the place where the colonial storm has left us. We must acknowledge the welfare trap and the impact of "shaman economics"—how this has economically isolated communities and created the current complete reliance on transfer payments and welfare. We must concede the profound destruction the welfare trap has wreaked and the disturbing social and political pathologies created. We must be prepared to change the culture of expectancy and the dependency mindset preventing us from making our lives better. We must admit that the existing system requires enormous reform if indigenous people are to have any hope of moving forward.

We have seen that the introduction of the welfare trap model has not only isolated tribes economically, but focussed tribal attention exclusively on the federal government for solving virtually all problems. With some outstanding exceptions, the mantra of most contemporary indigenous leaders has simply been to beg, threaten, or seek to embarrass more monies out of the federal government. There continues to be a virtually complete lack of positive ideas or original thought on how to effectively address the deeply embedded systemic issues. Current government policy seems to consist of reacting to the latest crisis by simply responding to Chiefs' demands for more monies. There presently is no practical, long-term strategic plan or vision that will likely lead to more healthy and fulfilling lives for ordinary indigenous folk.

Many indigenous leaders also appear to be frozen with fear, preferring to do nothing rather than take positive action that might endanger their tenure in office, and jeopardize what has become their *raison d'être*—simply managing the distribution of welfare and transfer payments. There seems to be little conscious realization that this tired old approach will never lead to real self-government or any effective measure of control over our own lives and agendas—not, at least, while there is complete dependency on transfer and welfare payments.

What is clear is that government policy and legislation has remained largely unchanged over 200 years. This has left a governance structure that is unfair, often oppressive to indigenous grassroots folks, and which poses huge barriers to moving tribes forward. The current governance system is not only antiquated, but politically disempowers a substantial portion of the indigenous population, concentrates power and financial resources in the hands of a few elites, provides for painfully poor political and financial accountability and transparency, and continues to encourage a culture of dependency. Evidence of corruption, mismanagement, wastage of resources, lateral violence and other abuses abound—with, it seems, the apparent complicity of the federal government.

In order for tribes to move forward they must first turn serious attention to cleaning up the colonial impediments still lurking in their own back yards. The following democratic reforms are necessary:

- The system for electing community governments must be overhauled so that, once elected, Chiefs and Councils are answerable to their community members that elect them, rather than government officials in Ottawa.
- The electoral process should be streamlined so that it is open and fair to all parties involved in the process.
- There should be some third party oversight of the electoral process by an Ombudsperson or other party at arms-length from the federal government and its politics (with an adequate budget). This office should have powers to investigate and make decisions in relation to resolving disputes arising out of electoral matters, or relating to allegations of corruption, mismanagement, nepotism, etc.
- There should be clear rules relating to transparency and accountability at all levels of political and administrative decision-making. There should be clear criminal and civil sanctions for those persons who breach the rules. Also, the general ledger for a community government should be open for any band member to inspect.
- The electoral system should be reformed to give urban band members (who now make up over 50% of the Aboriginal population in Canada) some political representation in community decision-making.
- There should also be reform of the electoral process to provide community members with a direct vote for the positions of President or Grand Chief of regional tribal Councils, as well as for all elected positions at the Assembly of First Nations and other national bodies (rather than having these positions solely appointed by Chiefs). The decision regarding how to change the system should not be put to the vote of Chiefs alone, but to every Aboriginal person in Canada.

Unfortunately, the existing system has powerful and entrenched interests bent on retaining the privileges established under the existing status quo (such as the elites in community government and the "Indian Industry"). For those on the outside, it is difficult to imagine how any person, Aboriginal or otherwise, could wish to retain a system wreaking so much havoc and perpetrating so much misery. The great harm that the existing system is causing to indigenous youth and children particularly should be paramount in the decision to usefully reform the system.

While the administration of indigenous affairs in Canada have remained largely unchanged, the demographics of the Aboriginal and mainstream population have transformed markedly. This new era has been described as the fourth wave, resulting in the "demographic tsunami." It has been shown that the rapidly-growing indigenous population and huge "greying" baby boom population are coinciding in a manner that could literally swamp the finances of the country if corrective measures are not taken immediately.

Even if there were the political will to continue attempting to finance the current unsustainable system, Canada simply cannot afford to do so. The vast greying baby boom generation is set to put enormous demands on social (particularly health care) spending. These costs are set to accrue to the federal coffers at a time when the work force is rapidly diminishing from retirements, and there will be much less revenue available to pay for these costs. At the same time, the Aboriginal population is growing so rapidly that maintaining per capita payments at their current levels will be impossible (particularly when the economy turns downward). Study after study has illustrated further the importance of harnessing the young and rapidly-growing Aboriginal labor force if Canada wishes to retain its current prosperous and competitive status. A situation is truly emerging in which neither indigenous people nor the mainstream population has a choice—the status quo must be reformed. Now.

Even if it were possible to continue on this unproductive course, money in and of itself, without indigenous people taking ownership of their problems and a clear long-term strategic plan, will simply not improve the lives of ordinary folks. In addition, it is questionable how useful it is to continually throw good money after bad; an option that may actually be making matters worse in the long term.

We have seen that the key to self-reliance and moving tribes forward is the creation of an indigenous business sector and own-source revenue streams. The only road forward involves economic integration and the development of indigenous enterprises and entrepreneurs. In order for communities to attract the investment and outside interest to economically develop, we have learned that:

- Community governments must understand the unsustainable economic model upon which their existence currently depends
- If indigenous people ever hope to control their own destinies they must create their own revenue by nurturing their business sector, encouraging their entrepreneurs, and attracting external business investment.
- Tribes must foster a stable governance structure that provides an appropriate development framework with a modernized form of government; one that separates politics from business, and provides a good comfort level to investors and external corporations.
- Communities should clearly adopt a business approach to managing their affairs that is open and transparent to everyone.
- A long-term strategic plan should be developed with a scheme for capacity building.
- A clear personnel recruitment plan should also be generated, with recognition of the value of off-reserve members who have invaluable experience in industry, business and government.
- Current barriers in the *Indian Act* that delay the development of projects should be removed .

The current lack of private ownership under the *Indian Act* should be examined to determine how best to allow individual members to raise monies from reserve-based real and personal property (such as allowing mortgaging of individual community member-held leaseholds as has been proposed in Australia).

Given the burgeoning economy and the hot commodities market, Canada is likely in the best position ever to create constructive change for moving indigenous people forward—a rare opportunity that should not be squandered. We also have the benefit of a host of international and local models which point the way to successful development. Indigenous people have shown they have what it takes to be economically successful, socially responsible, and responsive to the needs of their own people. The current situation urgently demands action that can be fashioned on the many different models that have been proven over the long-term.

The model of Maori development from New Zealand clearly illustrates that widespread national change for the better is possible when there is acknowledgement of the dependency mindset and a clear strategic development with the real intention of making change. The example of Alaska's Native Americans provides a closer-to-home model of the kind of economic success possible (and mistakes that might be avoided) in seeking to move forward. The Membertou First Nation has exemplified the importance of leaders leading rather than ruling, open accountability and transparency, adopting a "corporate mindset," and recruiting off-reserve member talent. It also illustrates how quickly success can be achieved when there is the will to really move forward. Chief Clarence Louie of the Osoyoos Indian Band has demonstrated the value of the new wave of economic thinking with a bias towards action in enabling community members to become employable, employed and independent.

The models examined also demonstrate that tribes do not need to wait for sweeping economic reforms in order to start moving ahead. With the right leadership and attitude, huge leaps forward can be made immediately. To some extent, as the saying goes, "Your attitude determines your altitude." The indigenous/corporate partnerships from northeastern Alberta have highlighted the leadership required from all sides to create hugely beneficial win/win partnerships. The ATCO Group indigenous partnerships have provided a further state-of-the art demonstration of a win/win capacity building model from which much can be learned. Rob Hunt of Akita Drilling Ltd. has demonstrated further the corporate commitment, mutual respect, and long-term view required to succeed in such corporate joint ventures.

We have also seen how education is the key to successfully moving indigenous people forward. At present there appears to be no national strategic plan to help improve the academic outcomes for indigenous people in Canada. We need to develop a national education policy based on the kind of economic strategy articulated by James Fallows in relation to East Asia. Indigenous people have the benefit of the enormous amount of valuable research from the OECD/UNESCO World indicators Programme that illustrates the fundamental importance of education to economic well-being, and to individual and national incomes. An investment in the educational future of human capital has been shown to produce enormous non-economic benefits in areas such as health and general well-being. We must also seek to incorporate the kind of valuable on-the-ground lessons of the Grandview/?Uuquinak'uuh School which has produced astonishing real-world educational results.

In moving forward to make the lives of indigenous people better, more innovative thinking and resources should be spent on the largest segment of the Aboriginal population in Canada, the urban indigenous population. The resources being spent now on this population group are ludicrously inadequate. Monies earmarked for urban Aboriginals are likely to give the "greatest bang for the buck" (no pun intended) given that they are likely in a better position to utilize resources provided to move forward more efficiently. As well, the urban population also *likely holds the long-term key to the successful economic integration of Aboriginal people in rural communities into mainstream society* (as proven by the Membertou First Nation) .

It is time for indigenous people to start looking forward to the future. The following illuminating story of Master Business Leader, Joe Segal is retold by author Peter Legge in his book, *The Runway of Life*:

> "Many people think of life as a road or highway," Joe Segal said. "But if you think about it, a highway can go on forever, and life isn't like that. Life is more like a runway – because at some point you are going to run out of asphalt. … [After drawing a horizontal line on a napkin with zero at the beginning of the line and the number 90 at the end, he continued,] That's how old I expect to be when I meet my maker…The part of the line between zero and your current age, that's history, its done, so forget about it.… [Pointing to the line between his current age and where he expects the runway to end, he said] The distance between where I am now and the end of my runway, that's all I have got to work with," Joe Segal concluded.
>
> Peter Legge continued, "I realized in that moment that Joe was right. No matter what we have accomplished in the past, or how successful we have been, what really matters is the time we have ahead of us and what we choose to do with what is left of our runway of life."[398]

It is time for indigenous people to stop dwelling on the rancorous injustices of the past. To paraphrase Joe Segal, no matter how unfairly or badly indigenous people were treated in the past, we cannot do anything about history. Our actions now, however, can impact the future. It is time to look forward for strategic options regarding what we should do with what is left of our runway of life. What constructive, forward-looking decisions and actions can we take now to create a better future for today's indigenous children and youth?

There is reason for optimism. Awareness of the barriers and the ways forward is growing—especially amongst educated and disaffected youth. Aboriginal businesses are growing at a rate nine times faster than for all other Canadians. Aboriginal people currently own over 600,000 square kilometres of land—an area larger than most European countries. With many more settlements to come, some suggest Aboriginal people will eventually own or control one-third of the entire Canadian land mass—an area equivalent to one-third the total land area of Europe. Aboriginal people also have enormous leverage over resource development. This is important to Canada given that commodities are largely paying the economic freight for the nation. It is also clear that Canada needs a well-trained Aboriginal work force more desperately than at any time in history. Through a common vision and mutual cooperation, there is a golden opportunity to turn the demographic tsunami from a crisis into one of the greatest opportunities the nation has ever seen.

Perhaps, with persistent diligent effort, the simple question asked by my grandmother may be largely addressed within the next few generations. The staggering human and economic price that indigenous people are paying now for a few welfare dollars is simply far too high to justify continuing on this path—particularly when we know that a healthier and more fulfilling future is possible. In the face of grossly disproportionate youth suicides, child poverty, and social dysfunction, indigenous people can no longer, in good conscience, continue to simply take the easy money from government. When the Aboriginal population, representing 3.3 percent of the total population, makes up (by conservative estimates) an astonishing 30 percent of the children in welfare care in Canada (and is on the increase), we should have no other thought than immediate constructive reform. The urgency of the situation is even more pronounced when we know without question that the current system of simply throwing money at the problems will never lead to a long-term solution and actually may be exacerbating existing struggles. Aboriginal people need a new generation of ethical leadership (as was common with our ancestors) with the courage to take the real action necessary for a brighter future.

When we look back on our runway of life, maybe we can say that we made the hard decisions and took the action that truly made a difference. Hopefully, the message that will resonate across the ages to our ancestor's spirits is that we showed the fortitude and will to find the way for our canoe, out of the storm. It is time to stop the flow of tears from mothers and grandmothers who continue to mourn the destruction of the welfare trap on their families. It is time to begin working together to take the giant leap forward for the benefit of Canada as a nation. *Wai Wah.*

A WAY FORWARD FOR AMERICA

> "America was established not to create wealth but to realize a vision, to realize an ideal—to discover and maintain liberty among men."
> WOODROW T. WILSON

Although serious, the demographic tsunami created by the Aboriginal population in Canada is but a ripple compared to the massive tsunami coming to swamp the finances of America. At the heart of this ensuing wave of destruction are deeply entrenched patterns of poverty associated with government-sponsored welfare systems and social entitlement programming that encourage long-term dependency among recipients. The resulting impoverishment has not discriminated among ethnic groups; a poor white Southerner or inner-city dweller confronts nearly the same barriers and misery faced by a poor Native or African American. The tough times ahead, should this course continue, promise radically more impoverishment among various ethnic groups.

One solution is for people of all ethnicities to start thinking less about our differences and more about the fabric that binds us together as a human species. Too often we forget that we all must answer to the same laws of nature regardless of the colour of our skin or the language we speak; that we share a commonality of cultural wisdom and ancient learning. (Indeed, people of different cultures living under the same circumstances, such as enforced dependency, over a long period of time begin thinking in astonishingly similar ways.) In owning our problems and expending effort to better our lives we all feel good about ourselves. From this perspective of our shared humanity, we can start working together to stem the tide of the encroaching storm.

Another solution is for government and private sector decision-makers to realize that while there is a role for welfare among individuals truly in need, we must also be mindful of *québécois* singer Felix Leclerc's caution that "the best way to kill a man is to pay him to do nothing." To avoid replicating the experience of Canada's indigenous people for whom welfare erases the sense of self-worth, with every welfare check eating a bit of a man's soul, it is possible for America to improve the lives of its poorest folk by ensuring them, along with everyone else, a level of fundamental dignity and hope for a better future—both of which take root in the ground of self-reliance.

In conclusion, society gains immeasurably from investing in the self-reliance of its poorest folk, for this is the way of sustainability. The alternative—continuing to invest in the administration of poverty that benefits only a few, while perpetuating the never-ending cycle of debilitating dependency—has already been revealed as economically untenable. Lifting the yoke of dependency allows the poorest children, mothers, grandmothers, and men down on their luck to wake up in the morning and feel good about themselves, hopeful about their future. Such an outcome would exemplify the founding principle of America, which was, according to former president Woodrow Wilson, to realize a vision of liberty among all people. *Wai Wah.*

ENDNOTES

1   Susan Hazen-Hammond, *Timelines of American History*, Berkley Publishing Group, 1997 at p 1.

2   John F. Bryde, Ph.D., *Modern Indian Psychology*, Rev. Ed. (Vermillion, South Dakota: Institute of Indian Studies, The University of South Dakota, 1971) at p 11.

{1} INTRODUCTION
CHAPTER 1: I HAD A DREAM...

3   Wilson Duff, *The Indian History of British Columbia* (Victoria: British Columbia Provincial Museum 1980) at p 8.

4   Ibid.

5   Ibid.

6   Rain Forest Atlas Website. Online source. Page. www.inforain.org/rainforestatlas/rainforestatlas_page3.html. Accessed March 12, 2005.

7   Ibid.

8   Supra Note 3 at p 9.

9   Margaret Seguin, Editor, *The Tsimshian: Images of the Past, Views of the Present* (Vancouver: University of British Columbia Press 1994); Chapter by James A. McDonald, "Images of the Nineteenth Century Economy of the Tsimshian," at p 41.

10   Ibid. at p 42.

11   Ibid.

12   Ibid.

13   See: Dr. R. G. Large, *Drums and Scalpel: From Native Healers to Physicians in the North Pacific Coast* (Vancouver: Mitchell Press 1968) at p 108: He was to die on a trading trip to the Haida community of Skidegate on Haida Gwaii (Queen Charlotte Islands) soon after the founding of the fort. The English name of the community was changed in his honour to "Fort," then Port Simpson where he was subsequently buried. Apparently Mr. Simpson was a good officer, but quite eccentric. It was believed he brought the first apple trees to the coast as a result of a joke when a lady, at a dinner party in England, slipped some apple pips into his waistcoat pocket. These were later discovered at a formal dinner at the Fort when the same clothes were worn and were subsequently planted.

14   Dr. R. G. Large, *Skeena: River of Destiny* (Sidney, British Columbia, Gray's Publishing Ltd. 1981) at p 17.

15   Supra Note 13 at p 108.

16   There may be significant variation in social conditions from community to community depending on such variables as remoteness, population size, etc.

17   Supra Note 3 at p 102. Wilson Duff reveals that though kinship ties were defined in a number of ways, they were always recognized among distant as well as close relatives. Duff points out: "Inheritance along these lines of kinship determined how a person was to conduct his life: what social class he belonged to, what positions of rank he could attain, where he could live, whom he could marry, where he could hunt and fish, what crest he could use, and so on. Men were not all born equal: there was social stratification into classes (nobility, commoners, and slaves), and in each tribe there was a graded series of positions of rank."

18   Ibid. at p 103.

19   Grandpa Helin was also a hereditary Chief of the Royal House of Gitlan. His chief's name was Sm'ooygit Nees Nuugan Noos.

20   Alan C. Cairns, "Citizens Plus: Aboriginal Peoples and the Canadian State," Vancouver: UBC Press 2000 at p 128.

21   Uncle Arthur Helin was a sub-chief in the same tribe as my grandmother; his Chief's name was Sm'ooygit Hyemass. Historically, the holders of this Chief's name were renowned as great warriors of considerable legend, so this title is considered to be of some distinction.

22   Speech by Cochise quoted by W.C. Vanderwerth, *Indian Oratory: Famous Speeches by Noted Indian Chieftains*, Norman, Oklahoma: Oklahoma University Press, 1971 at p 153.

CHAPTER 2: THE LOOMING CRISIS NO ONE KNOWS ABOUT

23   Online Source. Page. http://community.livejournal.com/ms_anthropology/4821.html#cutid1.

24   Ibid.

25   Ibid.

26   Ibid.

27   *Encyclopedia Britannica*, article "Germany: The Reunification of Germany." Online Source. Page. http://www.britannica.com/eb/article-58219/Germany.

28   Victor H. Mair, Professor of Chinese Language and Literature, Department of East Asian Languages and Civilizations, University of Pennsylvania, with contributions from Denis Mair and Zhang Liqing. Online source. Page. "How a misunderstanding about Chinese characters has led many astray." www.pinyin.info/chinese/crisis.html. Accessed January 12, 2005.

29   Steve Maich, Cover Story: "Is America going broke?" *Maclean's* newsmagazine, March 7, 2005 at p 22. Online source. Page.www.macleans.ca/topstories/world/article.jsp?content=20050307_101541_101541. Accessed April 15, 2005.

30   Ibid. at pp 22–23.

31   Canadian Council of Social Development. Online source. Page. "Census Shows
      Increasing Diversity of Canadian Society," January 21, 2003 release of data from the
      2001 Census. www.ccsd.ca/pr/2003/diversity.html. Accessed January 18, 2005. In com-
      parison to other Western countries, Canada has the second highest percentage of
      Aboriginal citizens in the world, behind New Zealand. New Zealand's Maori popula-
      tion accounts for 14 percent of its total population, whereas Aborigines in Australia
      accounted for 2.2 percent of the population there and Native-Americans accounted
      for 1.5 percent of the population in the United States.

      All data in this chapter is taken from Statistics Canada 2001 Census unless otherwise
      indicated. Online source from Aboriginal Peoples of Canada. Page.
      www12.statcan.ca/english/census01/products/analytic/companion/abor/canada.cfm.
      Accessed January 16, 2005. The 2001 Census further revealed that the majority of
      Aboriginal people (608,850 or 62 percent) were North American Indian, while 5 per-
      cent, or 45,070, were Inuit. There were 292,310 Métis, who represented about 30 per-
      cent of the total Aboriginal population. This was up from 204,115 in 1996. The
      remaining 3 percent were either persons who identified with more than one Aboriginal
      group, or registered Indians or band members who did not identify as Aboriginal.

32   With the natural population increase declining, immigration accounted for more the
      one-half of Canada's population growth between 1996 and 2001.

33   All data in this chapter is taken from Statistics Canada 2001 Census unless otherwise
      indicated. Online source from Aboriginal Peoples of Canada. Page.
      www12.statcan.ca/english/census01/Products/Analytic/companion/a bor/canada.cfm.
      Accessed January 16, 2005.

34   Ibid. The size of the Aboriginal children segment of the population is even more pro-
      nounced in the West. The general Aboriginal share of the total population in
      Saskatchewan and Manitoba was relatively large representing about 14 percent in each
      of these provinces. However, the proportion of children was about 25 percent and 23 per-
      cent respectively, representing a much, much larger portion of those population age groups.

35   The data source for labor statistics in this paragraph is: "2001 Census: Analysis Series:
      The Changing Profile of Canada's workforce," Statistics Canada, Catalogue No.
      96003OX1E2001009. Online source. Page. www12.statcan.ca/english/census01/
      Products/Analytic/companion/paid/pdf/96F0030X1E2001009.pdf. Accessed
      January 19, 2005.

36   The decline in the number of births that occurred since 1991 is a major factor behind
      the record-low growth in population during this period to 2001. Canada has under-
      gone a substantial decline in the number of children aged four and under. In 2001, the
      census counted 1.7 million children in this age group, down 11.0 percent from 1991,
      the result mostly of Canada's declining fertility rate. By 2011, this group may decline to
      an estimated 1.6 million.

37   Between 1991 and 2001, the population aged 80 and over soared 41 percent to 932,000.
      It is expected to increase an additional 43 percent from 2001 to 2011. By then, it will
      have surpassed an estimated 1.3 million.

38   These trends started in 1966 at the end of the baby boom when fertility began to drop drastically. From 1966 to 2001, Canada's total population increased 50 percent from about 20 million to 30 million. During this 35-year period, the population aged 19 and under declined 8 percent to 7.7 million, while the population aged 65 and over more than doubled from 1.5 million to 3.9 million.

39   The proportion of people aged 65 and over will start to increase more rapidly by 2011 when the oldest baby boomers, those born in 1946, reach 65.

CHAPTER 3: IMPLICATIONS OF DEMOGRAPHIC TRENDS

40   Online Source. Page. http://www.learnmoremn.org/facts/demographic.php.

41   Tracie D. Hall, "Reading and Forecasting Demographic Trends: 21st Century Library Services to Illinois Users." Online Source. Page. http://www.librarydiversity.info/download/DriveIn2006.pdf.

42   Original Source for retiree data and chart: 2007 Social Security Trustees Report. As cited by Online Source. Page.http://72.14.253.104/search?q=cache:giP shM U tz tA J :budget. senate.gov/democratic/charts/2007/Hearings/packet_Health%2520Care_Orszag_0621 07.pdf+long-term+budget+shortfall+david+walker+2007&hl=en&ct=clnk&cd=4.

43   Social Security Online. Online Source. Page. http://www.ssa.gov/qa.htm.

44   Luiza Ch. Savage, "Rescue Operation: Can the Canada Pension Fund save the American Social Security System?" *Maclean's* newsmagazine, June 18, 2007 at pp 28–29.

45   Chart reproduced from Centre on Budget Priorities and Policies website article, "New Long-Term Budget Projections Paint Grim Picture, Show Need For Health Care Reform, Responsible Tax Policies." Online Source. Page. http://www.cbpp.org/1-29-07bud-pr.htm.

46   Ibid.

47   Editorial, "Winning the war on terror requires fiscal discipline in the United States," *Vancouver Sun*, September 11, 2007 at p A14.

48   Steve Maich, Cover Story: "Is America going broke?" *Maclean's* newsmagazine, March 7, 2005 at p 22. Online Source. Page. http://www.macleans.ca/article.jsp?content=20050307_101541_101541&source=srch.

49   David K. Foot (with Daniel Stoffman), *Boom, Bust and Echo 2000: Profiting from the Demographic Shift in the New Millennium* (Toronto: Macfarlane Walter and Ross, 1st ed. 1996), at pp 8–9.

50   Krystle Chow, "Seniors could outnumber children by 2-1 in 25 years," *Vancouver Sun*, December 16, 2005 at p A3.

51   Paul Viera, "Economic 'shock' if Boomers retire early," *National Post*, October 21, 2005 at p FP5.

52   Ibid.

53   Ibid.

54   A recent and extensive poll indicated that most Canadians do not consider improving the quality of life of Aboriginal Canadians to be a high priority for the federal govern-

ment. In fact, improving Aboriginal quality of life is in second-last place on a list of 11 items that Canadians said should be a high priority for the federal government. The only item receiving less support is giving more money to the country's big cities (18 percent). *Portraits of Canada*, annual tracking poll conducted by the Centre for Research and Information on Canada. Opinion Canada, Vol. 6, no 37 - 2004-11-2 (from 2 surveys conducted: Environics surveyed 2,202 Canadians in all jurisdictions outside of Quebec, and CROP surveyed 1,000 persons in Quebec from mid-September to early October 2004). Online source. Page. www.opinion-canada.ca/en/articles/article_125.html. Accessed January 20, 2005. "In the 2003-2004 fiscal year, 14 federal government departments and agencies provided programs and services, directly or indirectly, to Aboriginal people with total expenditures of approximately $8.2 billion." Source: Canada's Performance 2004: annual Report to Parliament, Report of the President, Reg Alcock, Treasury Board Secretariat, Results-Based Management Directorate, Catalogue No. BT1-10/2004 at p 82. Online source. Page. www.tbs- sct.gc.ca/report/govrev/04/cp-rc5_e.asp#22). Acessed January 20, 2005. The report states further that: "Most of this amount (87 percent) is spent by Indian and Northern Affairs, whose mandate is focused on Status Indians on reserve and Inuit; and Health Canada, whose programs are primarily directed to First Nations on reserve. "*Total spending on Aboriginal Programming in 2005 is estimated to amount to approximately $9B.*" Source: For FY 1999-2000 the total amount spent was approximately $7.7B. "Aboriginal Business Canada (Industry Canada) an Overview on Women Entrepreneurs," March 23, 2003. Online source. Page. www.google.ca/search?hl=en&q=Aboriginal+Business+Canada+percent28Industry +Canadapercent29+an+Overview+on+Women+Entrepreneurspercent2c +March+23pe rcent2c +2003+&btnG =Search&meta=. Accessed January 21,2005. For FY 2003-04 fourteen federal government departments and agencies provide programs and services, directly or indirectly, to Aboriginal people with total expenditures of approximately $8.2 billion. Online source "Canada's Performance 2004: Aboriginal Peoples." Page. www.tbs-sct.gc.ca/report/govrev/04/cp-rc5_e.asp. Accessed January 21, 2005. Recently, Treasury Board President Reg Alcock indicated that there are "32 different departments delivering 240 separate programs—at a cost considerably higher than the $7 billion figure usually cited as the total annual spending on First Nations [though the exact figure was still to be determined for 2005]."Source: Paul Samyn. Online source Winnipeg *Free Press* Online Edition, Monday January 24th, 2005. Page. www.google.ca/search?hl=en&q= Aboriginal+spendingpercent2Bwinnipeg&btnG=Search&meta=. Accessed January 21, 2005.

55   Mary Janigan, "Can it be Solved?: Paul Martin is determined to get better value for the $7 billion in Aboriginal spending," dated January 19, 2004. Online source at Macleans.ca. Page. www.macleans.ca/switchboard/columnists/article.jsp?content=2004 0119_73501_73501. January 21, 2005.

56   Supra Paul Samyn at Note 54.

57   A two-year study on urban Aboriginals, prepared by a Calgary-based think tank, Canada West Foundation, was released in Ottawa on February 12, 2003, to a parliamentary subcommittee on children and youth at risk. The study found that more than half—51 percent—of Canada's estimated one million Aboriginals live in cities, while 29 percent live on the country's 600 reserves. The rest live off-reserve in rural areas. Last year, 88 percent of spending was allocated to on-reserve Indians. Kim

Lunman, "Off Reserve Natives Need Help, Study Says," *The Globe and Mail*, February 12, 2003—Print Edition, Page A11 or "Funding Must be Refocused to Urban Natives, Study Says," February 12, 2003—Print Edition, Page A9. Online source. Page. www.akwesasne.ca/gmfunding0212203.html. To see full study: www.cwf.ca/abcalcwf/doc.nsf/Publications?ReadForm&Category=wc+percent3E+Urban+Social+Fabric+percent3E+Urban+Aboriginal+People. Accessed January 23, 2005.

58   "Shift some Aboriginal spending from reserves to cities, report urges." *Community Action*. Online source. Page. www.findarticles.com/p/articles/mi_m0LVZ/is_8_18/ai_99491033. Accessed January 23, 2005.

59   Between 1996 and 2001 the Métis numbers increased 43 percent. This five-year growth was almost three times as fast as the 15 percent increase in the North American Indian population, and almost four times the 12 percent increase among the Inuit. It should also be noted that not all of the growth of the Métis population can be attributed to demographic factors. Increased awareness of Métis issues coming from court cases related to Métis rights, and constitutional discussions, as well as better enumeration of Métis communities have contributed to the increase in the population identifying as Métis. Nonetheless, this large population may still qualify for similar programming and service benefits as the North American Indian and Inuit population, as will be explored.

60   Section 35(2)of the *Constitution Act, 1982* confirms that: In this Act, "Aboriginal peoples of Canada" includes the Indian, Inuit and Métis peoples of Canada. On September 19, 2003, in a unanimous decision, the Supreme Court affirmed in its decision of *R. v. Powley* that s. 35 is a substantive promise to the Métis that recognizes their distinct existence and protects their existing Aboriginal rights (full text of the decision see online source. Pages. www.lexum.umontreal.ca/csc-scc/en/com/2003/html/03-09- 19.3.html. The Supreme Court said that the appropriate way to define Métis rights in s. 35 is to modify the test used to define the Aboriginal rights of Indians (the Van der Peet test). While there is much disagreement on the implications of this decision, it clearly established for the first time in Canadian jurisprudence that Métis have Aboriginal rights that are protected by the highest law of the land. While the case itself was fact-specific to an Ontario Métis who was fined for hunting moose out of season in the Sault Ste. Marie area, the decision is a major precedent and will be used as the basis for determining the extent of other major Métis rights such as to land, self-government, and fishing. The Métis political leadership have clearly indicated that they will use this decision as the basis for negotiating land claims and health benefits. Online source. Page. www.ctv.ca/servlet/ArticleNews/story/CTVNews/1063980477665_5938 9677///?hub=TopStories# or www.Métisnation.ca/POWLEY/home.html. Accessed January 27, 2005.

61   Estimates are from The Métis National Council Website. Online source. Page. www.Métisnation.ca/ARTS/hist_who.html Accessed January 28, 2005.

62   Francois Lamontagne, "The Aboriginal Workforce: What Lies Ahead," Canadian Labor Business Centre, September 2004 at p 5. Online source. Page. www.clbc.ca/files/Reports/Aboriginal_Commentary_piece.pdf. Accessed February 1, 2005.

63   Royal Commission on Aboriginal Peoples Report, "People to People, Nation to Nation: Highlights from Report of Royal Commission on Aboriginal Peoples," 1976

Cat no. z1-1991/1-6e, at p 137. The Royal Commission Report has pointed out that two-thirds of the cost of the existing status quo comes about because Aboriginal people are more likely than other Canadians to be unemployed.

64   Michael Mendelson, "Aboriginal People in Canada's Labor Market: Work and Unemployment, Today and Tomorrow," March 2004, published by the Caledon Institute of Social Policy, isbn 1-55382-090- at p 1.8. Online source. Page. "Publications by Date, April 2004." www.caledoninst.org/. Accessed January 25, 2005.

65   Report titled "Strengthening Aboriginal Participation in the Economy," from the Working Group on Aboriginal Participation in Economy to Federal-Provincial/ Territorial Minister Responsible for Aboriginal Affairs and National Aboriginal Leaders, May 11, 2001 at p 4. Online source. Page. www.google.ca/search?hl=en&q=strengthening+Aboriginal+participa tion&btnG=Search&meta=. Accessed January 25, 2004.

66   "Closing the Gap," A Report of the British Columbia Chamber of Commerce Skills Shortage Initiative, April 2002 at p 10. Online source. Page. www.bcchamber.org/criticalskills/skills_gap.html. Accessed January 25, 2005.

67   Derrick Penner, "More Major Projects for BC: About $62 billion in construction is being built or planned for BC," January 11, 2005, *Vancouver Sun*, at p d1 and d2.

68   Speaking Notes for Honourable Murray Smith, Alberta Minister of Energy, speech titled "Competitive Markets: Unleashing the Power of Alberta's Energy Sector," October 7, 2003, World Forum on Energy Regulation, Concurrent Session 3c, Market-based Mechanisms Driving New Investment, in Infrastructure and Production Capacity in Rome, Italy Topic: Competitive Markets: Unleashing the Power of Alberta's Energy Sector. Online source. Page. www.energy.gov.ab.ca/docs/ newsroom/pdfs/Speech2003-10-7.pdf. Accessed January 25, 2005. More specific information on oil sands spending is provided by the Athabasca Issues Working Group where it is noted that between 1995 and 1997 the National Oil Sands Task Force forecast investment in the oil sands at $5.7 billion over 25 years. This forecast was revised to $21 billion over 25 years. To-date, $28 billion has been spent, $4.7 billion worth of projects are under construction, and $32 billion of projects are forecast to be completed by 2013. "Athabasca Issues Working Group Fact Sheet," June 2004. Online source. Page. www.oilsands.cc/pdfs?Junepercent202004percent20Oilpercent20Sandspercent20 Factpercent20Sheet.pdf. Accessed January 26, 2005.

69   Bruna Santarossa, "Diamonds: Adding Lustre to the Canadian Economy" comments. Online source. Page. www.statcan.ca/english/research/11-621-mie/11-621- mie2004008.html. January 26, 2005. It is commented further that: "A relative latecomer, Canada is now a major player in the international diamond scene. Not only is Canada rich in diamonds, it is rich in high quality diamonds. From 1998 to 2002 roughly 13.8 million carats have been mined, collectively worth $2.8 billion. This is roughly a 1.5- kilogram bag of ice each day for five years, with each bag worth $1.5 million.Recent production data suggest that by the end of 2003, Canada will have produced almost 15 percent of the world's supply of diamonds, the third largest producer of diamonds, behind Botswana and Russia."

70   Scott Simpson, "Contractors hiring globally: Not enough tradespeople in Canada to fill BC's growing demand, industry says," *Vancouver Sun*, March 2, 2005 at p 2005. An excerpt from the article reads:"A shortage of skilled trades in Canada is forcing con-

tractors in British Columbia to look overseas for workers to fill out their job rosters. There are so many construction booms across the country that British Columbia cannot depend on workers coming here from other regions, industry representatives said on Tuesday."

71 Such costs can be determined from earnings Aboriginal people never receive, goods and services they do not add to the economy, and taxes they cannot pay.

72 Supra Footnote 63 at pp 136–137.

73 Ibid. at p 138.

74 Ibid. Of this amount, $2.9 billion is borne by the Aboriginal people and $4.6 billion is borne by government. For the Aboriginal people, the cost is equal to the gap between their earned income and that of the rest of the population, minus the income taxes foregone and financial assistance from government. For governments, the costs consist of direct expenditures (over and above what governments spend on non- Aboriginal Canadians) plus tax revenues foregone.

75 Ibid. at p 139. Of this estimate $4.3 billion is borne by Aboriginal people and $6.7 billion is borne by the governments.

76 Ibid. at pp 138–139. All figures used in the paragraph are from the Royal Commission Report.

77 Ibid. at p 138.

78 This Fiscal Balance in Canada: The Facts, March 2004. Online source. Page. www.fin.gc.ca/facts/fbcfacts8_e.html. Accessed February 6, 2005.

79 Backgrounder: New Zealand. Online source. Page. www.state.gov/r/pa/ei/bgn/35852.html. Acessed February 6, 2005.

80 The projections for future healthcare spending in Canada and the United states are simply staggering. In Canada, public health expenditures are projected to rise from 31 percent in 2000 to 42 percent by 2020 as a share of total provincial and territorial government revenues.See article titled, "The Future Cost of Health Care in Canada," 2001 by the Conference Board of Canada. Online source. Page. www.conference-board.ca/press/documents/futurehealth.pdf. Accessed January 27, 2005. Due to similar demographic pressures, by 2013 the U.S. is predicting that health care spending would amount to $3.4 trillion—nearly one-fifth (or 20 percent) of the nation's economic output. See article titled, "Health care spending eases, but huge growth predicted," February 11, 2004. Online source. Page. www.jsonline.com/bym/news/feb04/206853. asp?format=print. Accessed January 27, 2005.

81 While Canada will have to look to immigration to partially meet skilled workforce needs, it must be acknowledged that there are significant costs associated with this process.

82 From Globeandmail.com website report, "Globe Outlook 2007." Online Source. Page. http://www.theglobeandmail.com/partners/free/outlook_07/article_06.html.

83 Richard Benson, *MoneyWeek* website article "How indebted Americans are giving up their independence." Online Source. Page. http://www.moneyweek.com/file/31666/how-indebted-americans-are-giving-up-their-independence.html.

84 Angela Balakishnan, Guardian Unlimited website "American home foreclosures leap 93% in a year," August 22, 2007. Online Source. Page.

http://business.guardian.co.uk/story/0,,2153519,00.html.

85   "Bad-Mortgage Bailout," *Time*, Vol 170, No. 12, September 17, 2007 at p 8.

86   Supra note 83.

87   Online Source. Page. http://www.hardcore-stress-management.com/stress-statistics.html. Statistics cited are those of the American Psychological Association.

{2} A FIRST AND SECOND WAVE: FROM SELF-RELIANCE TO COLONIALISM
CHAPTER 4: THE FIRST WAVE: INDIGENOUS DEVELOPMENT PRIOR TO CONTACT

88   Supra Note 1. In this book the author and scholar points out that ancestors of today's Native American's first arrived on this continent more than 20,000 years before Christ. She notes (p 1):

> For decades scholars believed that the first human beings reached North America from Asia no earlier than 10,000 BC. But archaeologists have pushed the date back. Some say chipped bones and stones prove that people lived here as early as 400,000 years ago. More modest proposals suggest 20,000 to 70,000 BC. Today many scholars agree that few humans reached the Americas by 20,000 BC.

89   The first European contact occurred longer than 400 years ago with Christopher Columbus' supposed discovery of America dating to 1492. However, many tribes were not contacted until later as colonists spread from the East to the West coast of North America. This is meant to be an average date.

90   Olive Patricia Dickason, *Canada's First Nations: A History of the Founding People* (Toronto: McClelland & Stewart Publishers 1992), p 26. Ms. Dickason is a Professor of History at the University of Alberta.

91   Ibid.

92   Ibid. at p 63.

93   Ibid.

94   Ibid.

95   Paul Tennant, *Aboriginal Peoples and Politics* (Vancouver: University of BC Press 1991) at p 4.

96   Philip Drucker, *Indians of the Northwest Coast* (New York: Natural History Press, 1963) at p 3.

97   Supra Note 90 at pp 6–7.

98   Ibid. at p 69.

99   Ibid. at pp 74–76.

100   Supra Note 3 at p 102.

101   Supra Note 95 at p 6.

102   Ibid.

103   Ibid.

104   Supra Note 20 at p 49.

105   Gerald Murphy, distributed by the Cybercasting Services Division of the National

Public Telecomputing Network (NPTN). Online source. Page. www.wsu.edu:8080/~dee/NAANTH/IRCONST.HTM. Accessed November 12, 2004.

106   Letter to James Parker, Philadelphia, March 20, 1750, the letter was a comment on a pamphlet written by Archibald Kennedy titled "The Importance of Gaining and Preserving the Friendship of the Indians to the British Interest Considered." Online source. Page. www.courses.pasleybrothers.com/texts/franklin_indians.html. Accessed November 13, 2004.

107   Professor Douglas Sanders, Faculty of Law, University of British Columbia from paper "Self-Government, Autonomy, Sovereignty," p 2 at conference sponsored by the Native Investment and Trade Association, April 23, 24, 1992 at the Robson Square Conference Centre.

108   The international law is embodied in a series of conventions and covenants to which Canada is signatory.

109   Canada was not uninhabited when the Europeans came, nor was it 'discovered' by them. It has been the homeland for Canada's First People for millennia.

110   Early in the contact period the relationship was one of peaceful co-existence and non-interference. It was mainly after confederation that Canada began to appropriate large tracts of land to house the ever- increasing influx of settlers and that process of colonization and domination of the Aboriginal population began.

111   Report of the Royal Commission on Aboriginal Peoples, *Restructuring the Relationship* (Ottawa, Ontario: Canadian Cataloguing and publication Data, Minister of Supply and Services Canada, 1996) Part One, Volume 2, p 8. Online source. Page. www.ainc-inac.gc.ca/ch/rcap/sg/ch1_e.pdf. Accessed October 17, 2004.

112   Reproduced in part from Report of the Royal Commission on Aboriginal Peoples, *Gathering Strength* (Ottawa, Ontario: Canadian Cataloguing and publication Data, Minister of Supply and Services Canada, 1996) Part One, Volume 3, p 11. Online source. Page. www.ainc-inac.gc.ca/ch/rcap/sg/si3_e.html. Accessed October 17, 2004.

113   Ibid. Volume 3, Chapter 2, The Family. Speaker is Henoch Obed, of the Labrador Inuit Alcohol and Drug Abuse Program Nain, Newfoundland and Labrador, 30 November 1992.

114   Supra Note 95 at p 7.

115   Brian Lee Cowley paper titled "Property, Culture, and Aboriginal Self- Government" as reproduced in *Market Solutions for Native Poverty: Social Policy for the Third Solitude*, John Richards eds. (Toronto: C.D. Howe Institute 1995)at pp 70–71.

116   Ibid.

117   Attributed to Chief Seattle. This was supposedly a speech made be Chief Seattle to Governor Stevens in January 1854 and is the subject of much historical debate. There is no verbatim transcript in existence and the first version of the four known second-hand texts appeared in the Seattle *Sunday Star* on October 29, 1887. Presumably, the generally accepted version of the above speech was published in the The *Irish Times* on June 4th,1976. However, many people now believe that the speech was actually written by a Hollywood screen writer in the 1970's for the movie, Four Wagons West. It is thought that the script was based on the original statement by Chief Seattle in 1854.

Notwithstanding this controversy, this excerpt has been reproduced because the writer thinks it accurately describes the indigenous worldview of their place in nature.

118   Supra Note 90 at p 80.

119   Ibid.

120   L. T. Jones in *Aboriginal American Indian Oratory: The Traditions of Eloquence among the Indians of the United States* (Los Angeles: Southland Press, Inc., 1965) at p 86.

121   Supra Note 2 at p 86.

122   These views are now being embraced by powerful environmental groups. Many non-indigenous people hold the view that modern civilization is completely out of touch with nature and many modern activities are creating irreparable harm to the environment. In short, the hubris of modern man may lead to serious potential environmental problems.

123   Supra Note 90 at p 79.

124   Ibid.

125   Supra Note 111. Online source. Page. www.ainc- inac.gc.ca/ch/rcap/sg/sh68_e.html#1.1 percent20Apercent20Briefpercent20Historypercent20ofpercent20Aboriginalpercent20 Economiespercent20andpercent20ExternalInterventions. Accessed October 25, 2004.

126   Ibid.

127   Supra Note 95 at pp 7–8.

128   Helen Meilleur, *A Pour of Rain: Stories from a West Coast Fort* (Victoria: Morris Printing Company Ltd., 1981) at pp 105–106.

129   Ibid. at p 114.

130   Ibid. at p 105.

131   Supra Note 2 at p 39.

132   Ralph Waldo Emerson (1803–1882), U.S. essayist, poet, philosopher. Essay "Power, in The Conduct of Life (1860).

133   Supra Note 2 at p 76.

CHAPTER 5: THE SECOND WAVE: AT SEA IN THE COLONIAL STORM

134   William L. Stone, *Life of Joseph Brant* (Albany: J. Munsell, 1864) II at pp 354–355 as reproduced by L. T. Jones in *Aboriginal American Indian Oratory: The Traditions of Eloquence Among the Indians of the United States* (Los Angeles: Southland Press, Inc., 1965) at p 28.

135   Ibid. at p 93.

136   Andrew Armitage, *Comparing the Policy of Aboriginal Assimilation: Australia, Canada, and New Zealand* (Vancouver: UBC Press, 1995), p 227.

137   Ibid. at pp 227–228.

138   Ibid. at p 4. Armitage cites: "Report from His Majesty's Commission for Inquiring into the Administration and Practical Operation of the Poor Laws," 1834, Vol. 27, no.

44, p 1 and British Parliamentary Papers (House of Commons), "Report of the Select Committee on Aborigines," 1837, no. 425, 7, 1.

139 Ibid.

140 Ibid.

141 Ibid. at p 4. As summarized by Armitage.

142 Ibid. at p 13.

143 For account of the history of Indian Acts in Canada see: "Historical Development of the Indian Act," Government of Canada, Treaties and Historical Research Centre, P.R.E. Group, Indian and Northern Affairs, Ottawa, August 1978, and Tomas Issac, "Pre-1868 Legislation Concerning Indians: A Selected and Indexed Collection" (1993), University of Saskatchewan Native Law Centre.

144 Supra Note 63 at p 14. Unless otherwise indicated, much of the historical legal information in this section and some of the historical information following this section has been sourced from the Royal Commission Report.

145 The term "Indians" in section 91(24) has been held to include Inuit, and Eskimo people (see: *Reference Re Eskimos* (1939) 2 D.L.R. 417 (S.C.C.), 1939) and the preponderance of scholarly opinion suggests that this term also includes so-called "non-status-Indians" and the Métis (mixed blood) people (Hogg, *Constitutional Law in Canada* (2nd ed., 1985) at p 553; Sanders, "Prior Claims: Aboriginal People in the Constitution of Canada" in Beck and Bernier (eds.), *Canada in the New Constitution of Canada* (1983), vol. 1, at pp 254–256; Chartier (1978) 43 Sask L.R.; Lysyk " The Rights and Freedoms of Aboriginal Peoples in Canada" in Tanopolosky and Beaudoin (eds.), *The Canadian Charter of Rights and Freedoms: Commentary* (1982) 467 at p 469.

146 R.S.C. 1985, c. I-5. Under this Act, however, the federal Parliament has not legislated within the full limit of its authority in relation to "Indians" under section 91(24). The *Indian Act* applies only to Aboriginal people statutorily defined in it as "Indians" 126 and does not apply to non-status, Métis, Inuit and Eskimo peoples.

147 Jack Woodward, *Native Law* (Scarborough: Carswell, 1994) at p 95. Woodward comments further(at pp 94–95): "Soon after Confederation, Parliament began exercising its jurisdiction over Indians and Indian lands. The first *Indian Act* was passed in 1876, although five enactments prior to that date had already established its outline and contents. The *Indian Act* appeared in the Revised Statutes of Canada, 1886, as chapter 43, having been revised or re-enacted seven times since 1876. The statute remained in roughly the same form (apart from the regular statute revisions of 1906 and 1927 and some 24 amendments) prior to the rewriting and re-enactment of the *Indian Act* in 1951. The present *Indian Act* is based on the 1951 Act. Since 1951 there have been three statute revisions (in 1952, 1970 and 1985) and many amendments."

148 Note 63 at p 14.

149 Ibid. at p 12.

150 Ibid. In keeping with the notion of assimilation discussed above, in 1857 the Province of Canada passed an act to "Encourage the Gradual Civilization of the Indian Tribes." This act provided a means for Indians "of good character" (as determined by a Board

of non-Aboriginal examiners) to be declared, for all practical purposes, non-Indians (only one Mohawk from Six Nations is known to have accepted this invitation). As non-Indians, they were invited to join Canadian society, bringing a portion of tribal land with them. The fundamental purpose of assimilating Aboriginal people remained constant through various incarnations of the *Indian Act* subsequently passed by the Canadian government.

151 Supra Note 90 at p 284.

152 Section 3, Land Ordinance, 1870 R.S.B.C. 1871, C. 44.

153 Section 70, *Indian Act*, S. C. 1876, C. 18, s. 70 (re Manitoba and N.W.T.).

154 Section 141, *Indian Act*, R.S.C. 1927, C. 98, s. 92.

155 Supra Note 95. To demonstrate his rank and wealth, a chief would hold potlatches by giving away substantial amounts of personal goods and useful items. As Professor Tennant notes, potlatches ensured, therefore, not only the circulation of wealth, but also that conspicuous personal poverty was virtually a requirement of chiefly office.

156 Eg., section 3, *Indian Act*, 1880, C. 20.

157 BC, R.S.C. 1927, C. 98 s.140.

158 Chief Joe Mathias and Gary R. Yabsley "Conspiracy of Legislation: The Suppression of Indian Rights in Canada" at a conference sponsored by the Asia Pacific Institute *Business Impact of Aboriginal Claims*, Vancouver, December 4, 1990 at p 129.

159 Eg., see BC, S.C. 1880, C. 28, s. 70.

160 *Canada Elections Act*, R.S.C. 1952, C. 23 section 14 reads in part:
14.(2) The following persons are disqualified from voting at an election and incapable of being registered as electors and shall not vote nor be so registered, that is to say,
(e) every Indian as defined in the BC, ordinarily resident on a reserve, unless,
(i) he was a member of His Majesty's Forces during World War I or World War II, or was a member of the Canadian Forces who served on active service subsequent to the 9th day of September, 1950, or
(ii) he executed a waiver, in a form prescribed by the Minister of Citizenship and Immigration, of exemptions under the BC from taxation on and in respect of personal property, and subsequent to the execution of such waiver a writ has issued ordering an election in any electoral district.

161 R.S.B.C. 1948, S. 4.

162 *Provincial Elections Act*, R.S.B.C. 1948, S. 4.

163 Supra Note 158 at p 1.2.10.

164 BC, S.C. 1880, C. 28, s. 99(1).

165 Supra Note 90 at p 211.

166 Ibid. at p 6. chapter 2.

167 Supra Note 63 at p 11.

168 Supra Note 90 at p 27.

169 Ibid. at p 211.

170   Supra Note 98.

171   Ibid. at p 211. Although as Dickason points out, some estimates place the pre-contact population much lower, and the nadir at 10,000. See Thomas Berger, *Fragile Freedoms. Human Rights and Dissent in Canada* (Toronto: Clarke, Irwin, 1981) at p 229.

{3} IMPACTS OF THE THIRD WAVE: CULTURES AND COMMUNITIES IN DISARRAY
CHAPTER 6: SOCIAL IMPACTS OF THE WELFARE TRAP

172   Quotation of young Chief from an isolated northern Alberta reserve. Excerpted from Harold Cardinal's, *Unjust Society* (Seattle: University of Washington Press 1999) at p 53.

173   Supra Note 136 at p 239.

174   As Reported in CBC article titled "Canada ranked low in UN native Report," April 11, 2005. Online source. Page. www.cbc.ca/story/canada/national/2005/04/11/UNNatives-050411.html Accessed May 10, 2005.

175   Supra Note 115. John Richards, *Market Solutions for Native Poverty* at p 159.

176   Brian Lee Crowley, President of the Atlantic Institute for Market Studies, editorial titled "Atlantic Canada's dole rots the soul," in the *National Post*, May 19, 2004 at p A14.

177   Ibid.

178   John Stackhouse, *The Globe and Mail*, from a 14-part series Canada's Apartheid, "First Step: End the Segregation," December 15, 2001 at p F1.

179   Lewis Caroll, *Alice in Wonderland & Through the Looking Glass* (New York: Signet Classic 2000) excerpted from Chapter 6 at p 64.

180   Helen Buckley, *From Wooden Ploughs to Welfare: Why Indian Policy Failed in the Prairie Provinces* (Montreal: McGill-Queen's University Press 1992).

181   Geoffrey York, "Ottawa's effort: No helping hand but a mortal blow," *The Globe and Mail*, Saturday, August 29, 1992 (book published by: McGill-Queen's University Press.) Online source. Page. www.bcgreen.com/~samuel/lubicon/1992/BUCKLEY.txt. Accessed May 1, 2005.

182   John Stackhouse, *The Globe and Mail*, from a 14-part series Canada's Apartheid, "A Cut of the Action," November 26, 2001 at p A8.

183   John Stackhouse, *The Globe and Mail*, from a 14-part series Canada's Apartheid, "Everyone thought we Were Stupid," December 14, 2001 at p A16.

184   Supra Note 115. John Richards, at p 161.

185   Menno Boldt, *Surviving as Indians: the Challenge of Self-Government* (Toronto: University Press 1993) at p 223.

186   "United Nations Committee on the Rights of the Child: Non Discrimination and Diversity," First Nations Child and Family Caring Society, August 29, 2005 at p 3. Online source. Page. www.fncfcs.com/docs/UnitedNationsMay2004.pdf. Accessed February 12, 2005.

187   Marilyn Bennet and Cindy Blackstock *A Literature Review and Annotated Bibliography Focussing on Aspects of Aboriginal Child Welfare in Canada*, prepared for the First

Nations Research Site of the Centre for Excellence for Child Welfare at p 56. Online source. Page. www.fncfcs.com/pubs/fncfcsPubs.html. Accessed February 10, 2005.

188   Prevention of Violence Against Indigenous Children: Proceedings from An International Gathering, Quadra Island, British Columbia, August 31–September 3, 2004 at pp 23–24. Online source. Page. web.uvic.ca/iicrd/graphics/PVAIC%20Proceedings.pdf. Accessed May 2, 2005.

189   Supra Note 187 at p 3 and p 5.

190   Ibid. at p 4.

191   Child Care Federation *Keeping Our Promises: Right from the Start*, The United Nations day of General Discussion 'Implementing Child Rights in Early Childhood', September 17, 2004, at p 4. Online source. Page. www.afn.ca/AGA-Confederacy/04-09-21percent20AGApercent20Report.pdf. Accessed May 2, 2005.

192   Ibid.

193   All suicide figures are from report by Health Canada titled *A Statistical Profile on the Health of First Nations in Canada*, November 2003 at p 34. Online source. Page. www.hc-sc.gc.ca/fnihb-dgspni/fnihb/sppa/hia/publications/statistical_profile.htm#Highlights. Accessed May 3, 2005.

194   Ibid. at p 53.

195   Ibid. at p 23. Diabetes Information from Aboriginal Diabetes Initiative, *Diabetes Among Aboriginal People in Canada: The Evidence*, March 10, 2000, ISBN H35-4/6-2001E, Catalogue No. 0-662-29976-0. at p 5.Online source. Page. www.hc-sc.gc.ca/fnihb-dgspni/fnihb/cp/adi/publications/the_evidence.htm#-Executivepercent20Summary. Accessed May 3, 2005.

196   Supra Note 111. Royal Commission Report, VOLUME 3, *Gathering Strength* Chapter 3 - Health and Healing. Online source. Page. www.ainc- inac.gc.ca/ch/rcap/sg/si17_e.html. Accessed May 4, 2005.

197   Kirk Makin, "Top court appalled as native fill Canada's jails," *The Globe and Mail*, April 24, 1999. Online source. Page. http://fact.on.ca/newpaper/gm990424.htm. Accessed May 5, 2005.

198   Information from Correctional Service Canada website. Online source. Page. www.csc- scc.gc.ca/text/prgrm/correctional/abissues/know/8_e.shtml. Accessed May 5, 2005.

199   Jenny Manzer, "Aboriginal sex abuse rates high, but under-researched" The *Medical Post*, November 27, 2001, Volume 37 Issue 40. Online source. Page. www.medical-post.com/mpcontent/article.jsp?content=/content/EXTRACT/RAWART/3740/02B.html. Accessed May 5, 2005.

200   Canada's Performance 2004, IV Aboriginal Peoples. Online source. Page. www.tbs-sct.gcca/report/govrev/04/cp-rc5_e.asp#22. Accessed May 6, 2005.

201   Article by Peter Daniels, "Diabetes in the US: a social epidemic," 30 January 2006. Online Source. Page. http://www.wsws.org/articles/2006/jan2006/diab-j30.shtml.

202   Pre-diabetes means that either the cells in the body are becoming resistant to insulin

or the pancreas is not producing as much insulin as is required. Blood glucose levels are higher than normal, but not high enough to be called diabetes. This is also known as "impaired fasting glucose" or "impaired glucose tolerance." A diagnosis of pre-diabetes is a warning sign that diabetes may develop later. Online Source. Page. http://diabetes.about.com/od/whatisdiabetes/p/whatisdiabetes.htm.

203   American Diabetes Association Website. Online source. Page. http://www.diabetes.org/about-diabetes.jsp

204   Ibid.

205   National Aboriginal Diabetes Association booklet, "Pathway to Wellness: A Handbook for People Living with Diabetes." Online Source. Page. http://www.nada.ca/resources/resources_pathways.php. The health impacts attributable to this one disease (largely invisible to the public) have been described by one journalist in a visit through the Montefiore Medical Center in the Bronx as follows:

> Begin on the sixth floor, third room from the end, swathed in fluorescence: a 60-year-old woman was having two toes sawed off. One floor up, corner room: a middle-aged man sprawled, recuperating from a kidney transplant. Next door: nerve damage. Eighth floor, first room to the left: stroke. Two doors down: more toes being removed. Next room: a flawed heart.

From article by N.R. Kleinfeld, "Diabetes and its awful toll quietly emerge as crisis," New York Times, January 9, 2006. Online Source. Page. http://query.nytimes.com/gst/fullpage.html?sec=health&res=9907E2DA1F30F93AA35752C0A9609C8B63.

CHAPTER 7: EXTERNAL EXPRESSIONS OF INTERNALIZED INDEPENDENDENCE

206   Cynthia C. Wesley-Esquimaux, Ph.D and Magdalena Smolewski, Ph.D, research paper prepared for The Aboriginal Healing Foundation Research Series, *Historic Trauma and Aboriginal Healing*, 2004 at p 66 (see: www.ahf.ca/newsite/english/publications/research_series.shtml).

207   Ibid.

208   Dennis Guest, *The Emergence of Social Security in Canada* (Vancouver: University of British Columbia Press 1986) at p 1.

208   Ibid. at p 1 and 2.

209   Supra Note 54.

210   Article from Associated Press, "Are lottery winners less happy?: People get more satisfaction out of earning their cash, study finds," May 13, 2004. Online source. Page. www.msnbc.msn.com/id/4971361/ or www.rednova.com/news/display/?id=58787.

211   Candis McLean, "Our own soap opera: Life and politics on the Sturgeon Lake Reserve amount to a struggle against futility," The *Report* newsmagazine April 30, 2001 at pp 42–46.

212   Ibid.

213   Ibid.

215   *The Works of Henry Fielding*, Edited by George Sainsbury in Twelve Volumes, "Joseph

Andrews," Vol. 2, Book IV, Chapter VI. Online source. Page. sailor.gutenberg.org/etext05/8jan21oh.htm. Accessed May 10, 2005.

216 *Legacy of Hope: An Agenda for Change*, Volume I, Final Report from the Commission on First Nations and Métis Peoples and Justice Reform, Chapter 3, "VIOLENCE AND VICTIMIZATION," June 21, 2004 at pp 3-2 & 3-3. Online source. Page. < www.justicereformcomm.sk.ca/volume1.gov. Accessed May 10, 2005.

217 From report titled "From Poverty to Prosperity: A National Strategy to Cut Poverty." Online Source. Page. http://www.americanprogress.org/issues/2007/04/poverty_report .html. All information on the discussion of poverty in this section is from this source.

218 Ibid.

219 "Behind Bars: Native Incarceration rates increase" July 13, 2001. Online Source. Page. http://www.indianz.com/News/show.asp?ID=law/7132001-1. A black male in the United States would have about a 1 in 3 chance of going to prison during his lifetime. For a Hispanic male, it's 1 in 6; for a white male, 1 in 17. Gail Russell Chaddock, The Christian Science Monitor website article "US notches the world's highest incarceration rate." Online Source. Page. http://www.csmonitor.com/2003/0818/p02s01-usju.html. According to article "US incarceration rate climbs," the incarceration rate in 2004 increased 2.3% over 2003. Online Source. Page.http://www.abc.net.au/news/newsitems/ 200504/s1352643.htm. Also see article "US incarceration rates hit record high in 2003-2004," April 25, 2005. Online Source. Page. http://jurist.law.pitt.edu/paperchase/2005/ 04/us-incarceration-rates-hit-record-high.php. The entire report can be read at the Bureau of Justice Statistics website, U.S. Department of Justice. Online Source. Page: http://www.ojp.usdoj.gov/bjs/pub/pdf/pjm04.pdf.

CHAPTER 8: ECONOMIC IMPACTS OF THE WELFARE TRAP

220 United States Department of Interior, Report of the Task Force on Indian Economic Development (July 1986) Presidential Commission on Indian Reservation Economies, Report and Recommendations to the President of the United States (November 1984) at p 37. Online source. Page. ftp://ftp.loc.gov/pub/thomas/cp106/sr149.txt.

221 Jason L. Saving, *Privatization and the Transition to the Market Economy*, Economic, Fourth Quarter 1998 at p 17. Online source. Page. www.dallasfed.org/research/er/1998/.

222 Gross national product is the total output of a nation's economy economy. Gross domestic product is the total annual output of a nation's economy, measured by its final purchase price. GNP and GDP tend to be used as synonyms. GDP is definitely the preferred measure among economists and is gaining popularity in general conversation as well. The two measures are fairly close numerically. The difference is that GDP measures all production within the nations' economy, by whoever happens to be working there. GNP measures the production of all of the nations workers, wherever they happen to be working. This explains why the GNP percentage is larger in the paragraph.

223 Supra Note 221.

224 Online source. Page. www.parliament.the-stationery-office.co.uk/pa/ld200102/ldjudgmt/jd020321/yardle-4.htm.

225 Supra Note 64 at pp 5–6.

226 The bureaucratization of Aboriginal communities also results partially from the fact
that the only wealth available to be shared comes into the community in the form of
transfer payments or welfare. The best route to sharing in this wealth is to have an
official bureaucratic job. Since the available wealth is really usually limited to this one
source of transfer payments, bureaucratic jobs are additionally the only form of
patronage appointments available for Chiefs and Councils.

227 Editorial Opinion from Column titled *The Agenda* by Robert J. Shiller, "American
Casino: The promise and perils of Bush's 'ownership society,'" The *Atlantic Monthly*
magazine, March 2005 at p 33.

228 David Farrar, "Milton Friedman on Spending Money," Blog Posted January 15, 2005.
Online source. Page. www.kiwiblog.co.nz/archives/008879.html. Accessed
May 20, 2005.

229 Article from *Vancouver Sun*, "Buffet still enjoys making money the old school way,"
Monday, May 12, 2003 at p A5.

230 Stephen Cornell and Joseph P. Kalt. Online source. Page.
www.innovations.harvard.edu/showdoc.html?id=2700. Accessed May 21, 2005.

CHAPTER 9: THE WELFARE TRAP AND POLITICAL PATHOLOGIES

231 Paper titled "Aboriginal Sports Strategy in Canada," cites as original source for numbers Indian and Northern Affairs, 1991 Census; 2001 Census, January 2005 p 5. Online
source. Page. www.sasksport.sk.ca/aboriginalsport/pdf/AboriginalSportStrategy.pdf.
Accessed May 22, 2005.

232 *Indian and Northern Affairs Canada and Canadian Polar Commission*, 1998-99
Estimates: A report on Plans and Priorities, at p 4. Online source. Page. www.ainc-
inac.gc.ca/pr/est/ or www.ainc- inac.gc.ca/pr/est/rpp98e.pdf. Accessed May 23, 2005.

233 *Indian and Northern Affairs Canada and Canadian Polar Commission Performance*
report, for the period ending March 31, 2004, Catalogue No. BT 31-4/6-2004 at p 15.
Online source. Page. www.tbs-sct.gc.ca/rma/dpr/03-04/INAC-AINC/INAC-
AINCd3401_e.asp. Accessed May 23, 2005.

234 Ibid.

235 Dianne Rinehart, "Indian women say fraud, nepotism rife on reserves," *Vancouver
Sun*, April 13, 1999 at p A1.

236 Don Sandberg, Aboriginal Policy Fellow, "Where does Eight Billion Dollars Go?:
Much Poverty Despite Spending" March 14, 2004. Online source. Page.
www.fcpp.org/main/publication_detail.php?PubID=721. Accessed May 23, 2005.

237 Alex Roslin, "Power Struggle: Native groups balk at national chief's plan to boost his
power," April 5-11, 2001, Vol. 20 No. 31. Online source. Now Online Edition, Toronto.
Page. www.nowtoronto.com/issues/2001-04-05/news_story3.html. Accessed
May 24, 2005.

238 Ibid.

239   Online source. Page. www.afn.ca/article.asp?id=120. Accessed May 24, 2005.

240   Ekos Research and Associates Inc., *Fall* 2003 *Survey of First Nations People Living On-Reserve*, Integrated Final Report, Submitted to Indian and Northern Affairs, March 30, 2004. Online source. Page. www.ainc-inac.gc.ca/pr/pub/fns/2004/srv04_e.pdf. Accessed May 25, 2005.

241   Ibid. at p 14.

242   Ibid. at pp 14–15.

243   Ibid. at p 20.

244   Ibid.

245   Justine Hunter, "End welfare state, chiefs told," *National Post*, May 30, 2001 at p A6.

246   *Federal Government Funding to First Nations: The Facts, the Myths, and the Way Forward* at p 4. Online source. Page. www.afn.ca/Federalpercent20Governmentpercent20Funding percent20topercent20Firstpercent20Nations_web2.pdf. Accessed May 25, 2005.

247   Ibid. Note 111, Vol 2, *Restructuring the Relationship*, Chapter 3 Governance. Online source. Page. www.ainc- inac.gc.ca/ch/rcap/sg/sh34_e.html. Accessed May 26, 2005.

248   Don Sandberg, Editorial, "Native Democracy Is Broken," *National Post*, August 6, 2004 at p A11. Online source. Page. www.fcpp.org/main/publication_detail.php?PubID=802. Accessed May 27, 2005.

249   Ibid.

250   John D. Weston, "A Nisga'a Chief Takes on Third Order of Government and the Nisga'a's Treaty," *Fraser Forum* at p 14. Online source. Page. www.accesslaw.ca/cmc/cmc.asp. Accessed May 30, 2005.

251   According to Web Hosting Glossary a blog is: "A frequent, chronological publication of personal thoughts and Web links." Blogs (web logs) are often a mixture of what is happening in a person's life and what is happening on the Web, a kind of hybrid diary/ guide site. Online source. Page. www.marketingterms.com/dictionary/blog/. Accessed May 31, 2005. Bloggers have become a powerful source polling peoples' views and providing a powerful guerrilla form of journalism (even impacting the U.S. election significantly). From Jefferson Flanders, "Bloggers are Busy Rewriting the Definition of 'Journalism'," March 13, 2005. Online source. Page. www.freerepublic.com/focus/f-news/1361855/posts. Accessed May 31, 2005.

252   Curtis Kayseas, Editorial "The Illusion of Democracy," Regina Saskatchewan, October 1, 2001. Online source. The Aboriginal Youth Network. Page. www.ayn.ca/ViewNews.aspx?id=194. Accessed May 31, 2005.

253   Supra Note 211, 254. David Samuels, "In a Ruined Country: How Yasir Arafat destroyed Palestine," *Atlantic Monthly*, September 2005 at p 74. 227 Paper prepared by Jo-Ann E.C. Greene for Indian and Northern Affairs Canada, Women's Issues & Gender Equality Directorate, "Towards Resolving the Division of On-Reserve Matrimonial Property Following Relationship Breakdown: A Review of Tribunal, Ombuds and Alternate Dispute Resolution Mechanisms," May 2003, Catalogue No. R2-270/2003E at p 17. Online source. Page. www.dsp-psd.pwgsc.gc.ca/Collection/R2-270-2003E.pdf. Accessed June 2, 2005.

254   David Samuels, "In a Ruined Country: How Yasir Arafat destroyed Palestine," *Atlantic Monthly*, September 2005 at p 74.

255   Paper prepared by Jo-Ann E.C. Greene for Indian and Northern Affairs Canada, Women's Issues & Gender Equality Directorate, "Towards Resolving the Division of On-Reserve Matrimonial Property Following Relationship Breakdown: A Review of Tribunal, Ombuds and Alternate Dispute Resolution Mechanisms," May 2003, Catalogue No. R2-270/2003E at p 17. Online source. Page. www.dsp-psd.pwgsc.gc.ca/Collection/R2-270-2003E.pdf>. Accessed June 2, 2005.

256   Karen Charelson in Opinion section of *Vancouver Sun*, "Finger Pointing and feuding hinder aboriginal advances," March 25, 2000 at p A3.

257   For example, see: "Indian group warns of armed rebellion over band money issues," *Vancouver Sun*, April 5, 2000 at p A13; Kathy Tait, "Where's our Money," *Vancouver Province*, November 16, 1999 at p A1; Peter Cheney, "The Money Pit: an Indian band's story," *The Globe and Mail*, October 24, 1998; "Reserve headed towards trusteeship," *The Globe and Mail*, September 1, 1997; "Expenses doubled natives' salaries," *The Globe and Mail*, September 4, 1997; Peter Cheney, " How money has cursed Alberta's Samson Cree," *The Globe and Mail*, April 24, 1999 at p A1.

258   From "Native Protestors End-Run Government and take Protest Directly to Canadian Taxpayers," July 21, 1999. Online source. Page. www.taxpayer.com/main/news.php?news_id=1618. Accessed June 3, 2005. Article describes how residents from the Lake St. Martin First Nations reserve took their grievances with allegedly corrupt band officials to the Canadian Taxpayers Federation offices in Winnipeg, following a four-day protest march.

259   As quoted by John Stackhouse, in "Comic Heroes of Red Niggers," *The Globe and Mail*, November 9, 2001 at p A18.

260   Don Sandberg, "Hefty personal price writing about Aboriginal politics: Given the consequences, would you speak up?" July 17, 2004. Online source. Page. www.fcpp.org/main/publication_detail.php?PubID=779. Accessed June 4, 2005.

261   Ibid.

262   Don Sandberg, "The tragic death of Bill C-7: Act quickly to write an adequate replacement," February 13, 2004. Online source. Page. www.fcpp.org/main/publication_detail.php?PubID=691. Accessed June 4, 2005.

263   Ibid.

264   *The Indian and Northern Affairs Canada and Canadian Polar Commission Report for* 2003-2004, March 31, 2004, DPR 2003-2004, Catalogue No.: BT31-4/6-2004. Online source. Page. www.tbs- sct.gc.ca/rma/dpr/03-04/INAC-AINC/INAC-AINCd3401_e.asp. Accessed June 6, 2005. Treasury Board of Canada Secretariat website. INAC reviews and assesses financial stability and compliance with the requirements of funding agreements. When any of the terms and conditions of the funding agreement are not being met, the department applies intervention mechanisms tailored to the cause and severity of the problem. Prescribed intervention mechanisms include a requirement to develop and implement a Remedial Management Plan (most often necessitated by financial difficulties); a requirement for the First Nation to appoint a co-manager;

and, in extreme cases, appointment of a third-party manager by INAC.

265 From Canadian Taxpayers Federation publication *Dividing Canada: Pitfalls of Native Sovereignty* at p 4. "Number of Allegations and Complaints about the conduct of Indian and Inuit government bodies and organizations were received by the department between the years 2002- 2004." Online source. Page. www.taxpayer.ca/pdf/Dividing_ Canada_(Centre_for_Aboriginal_Policy_Change).pdf. Accessed June 6, 2005.

266 Edited Hansard, Number 015 (Official Version). Online source. Page. www.parl.gc.ca/38/1/parlbus/chambus/house/debates/015_2004-10- 26/han015_1900-e.htm. Accessed June 7, 2005.

267 Gordon Laird, "The Outlaw," *Saturday Night* Magazine, June 1999 at p 70.

268 Supra Note 263. INAC reviews and assesses financial stability and compliance with the requirements of funding agreements. When any of the terms and conditions of the funding agreement are not being met, the department applies intervention mechanisms tailored to the cause and severity of the problem. Prescribed intervention mechanisms include a requirement to develop and implement a Remedial Management Plan (most often necessitated by financial difficulties); a requirement for the First Nation to appoint a co-manager; and, in extreme cases, appointment of a third-party manager by INAC.

269 Richard Truscott, Canadian Taxpayers Federation website, "Road to Bankruptcy Paved with Tax Dollars," October 28, 1999. Online source. Page. www.taxpayer.com/main/news.php?news_id=563.

270 Rick Mofina, "Native leader calls on chiefs for accountability," *Vancouver Sun*, January 7, 2001 at p A7.

271 Supra Note 247.

272 James Baxter, "Nault signals end to BC 'industry,'" *National Post*, April 19, 2002 at p A11.

273 Ibid.

274 Online source. Page. www.aptn.ca/forums/index.php?showtopic=288. Accessed June 10, 2005.

275 Jack Aubrey, Tim Naumetz, and Peter O'Neil, "Liberals can't make boondoggle go away," *Vancouver Sun*, December 5, 2001 at p A13.

276 Ibid.

{4} THE FOURTH WAVE: A WAY OUT OF THE STORM
CHAPTER 10: FROM GRIEVANCE TO DEVELOPMENT MODE

277 John D. Canine, Ed.D., Ph.D., "Bereavement Rituals," Online source. Page. www.prayfuneral.com/max_living_rituals.html. Accessed June 10, 2005.

278 William L. Stone, *Life of Joseph Brant* (Albany: J. Munsell, 1864) II at pp 354–355 as reproduced by L. T. Jones in *Aboriginal American Indian Oratory: The Traditions of Eloquence Among the Indians of the United States* (Los Angeles: Southland Press, Inc., 1965) at p 57.

279 L. T. Jones in *Aboriginal American Indian Oratory: The Traditions of Eloquence Among*

the Indians of the United States (Los Angeles: Southland Press, Inc., 1965) at p 89.

280   In a speech, Chief Judge for the Maori Land Court and Deputy Chair of the Waitangi Tribunal, Joe Williams, presented the paper, "Reparations and the Waitangi Tribunal to the Moving Forward Conference," August 15 & 16, 2001 at the University of New South Wales in Australia where he noted:

> The approach of the Waitangi Tribunal is to support packages which restore a lost economic base, bearing in mind the extent and nature of the loss and the current needs of the grieving community. This tends to make settlements more future-looking and should help to get communities out of grievance mode and into development mode sooner.

Online source. Page. www.humanrights.gov.au/movingforward/speech_williams.html. Accessed June 12, 2005.

281   Arnie Louie as cited by Chief Clarence Louie, Speaking Notes, First Nations Economic Forum, November 7–9, 2005, Calgary.

282   Ibid.

283   Supra note 205, N.R. Kleinfeld article . One might be tempted to suggest that the journalist was fear-mongering. Unfortunately, this writer has seen first-hand how diabetes is impacting his own extended family and literally cutting a swath of destruction and medical horror through the indigenous population.

284   Reuters, "75% of Americans forecast to be overweight" *Vancouver Sun*, July 19, 2007 at p A9.

285   *Science Daily* article "ZIP Codes And Property Values Predict Obesity Rates." Online Source. Page. http://www.sciencedaily.com/releases/2007/08/070829090143.htm

CHAPTER 11: THE OPPORTUNITY

286   Charles S. Coffey, "The Cost of Doing Nothing: A Call to Action," October 23, 1997. Online source Page. www.rbcroyalbank.com/aboriginal/r_speech.html. Accessed June 14, 2005. Also reproduced in report, "Strengthening Aboriginal Participation in the Economy," Supra Note 65 at p 13.

287   Report titled "Aboriginal Entrepreneurs in 2002." Online source. Page. strategis.ic.gc.ca/epic/Internet/inabc- eac.nsf/en/ab00313e.html. Accessed June 15, 2005. All statistics that follow within the section are from this report.

288   Jim Rogers (co-founder of Quantum Fund with George Soros), "Why Raw Materials?" 2002. Online source. Page. chinese- school.netfirms.com/raw-materials.html. Accessed June 14, 2005.

289   "China Effect Convulses Commodity Markets," *Financial Post*, November 15, 2003. Online source. Page. < chinese-school.netfirms.com/commodities-market-China.html. Accessed June 14, 2005.

290   Matthew Yeomans, "Crude Politics," *Atlantic Monthly* Magazine, April 2005 at p 48.

291   CNN.com International, "Group: China timber demand threatens world's forests," March 8, 2005, Online source. Page.

edition.cnn.com/2005/TECH/science/03/08/china.logging.ap/.

292 "Outsourcing leads to demand for resources," 19 August, 2004. Online source. Page. www.openoutsource.com/resource-dated9720-Outsourcing%20leads%20to%20demand%20for%20resources.phtml.

293 Michael Kane, "Greatest growth seen in Canada's North and West," *Vancouver Sun*, March 22, 2005 at p D1.

294 Jim MacDonald, "Alberta quietly becomes debt-free province," *Vancouver Sun,* March 31, 2004 at p A5.

295 "Saudi Arabia: Brief Country Analysis," Online source. Page. www.eia.doe.gov/emeu/cabs/saudi.html. Accessed June 16, 2005.

296 Sheldon Alberts, "Canada set to be 'world's oil giant,'" *Vancouver Sun*, October 18, 2005 at A11.

297 *Bloomberry News*, article titled "Oil-sand production may double," reproduced in *Vancouver Sun*, March 25, 2005 at p H4.

298 Paul Harris, "More crude set to flow BC's coast," *Business in Vancouver*, January 11–17, 2005 cover page.

299 Bruna Santarossa, "Diamonds: Adding Lustre to the Canadian Economy" comments. Online source. Page. www.statcan.ca/english/research/11-621-MIE/11-621-MIE2004008.htm. Accessed January 26, 2005. It is commented further that: "A relative latecomer, Canada is now a major player in the international diamond scene. Not only is Canada rich in diamonds, it is rich in high quality diamonds. From 1998 to 2002 roughly 13.8 million carats have been mined, collectively worth $2.8 billion. This is roughly a 1.5-kilogram bag of ice each day for five years, with each bag worth $1.5 million. Recent production data suggest that by the end of 2003 Canada will have produced almost 15 percent of the world's supply of diamonds, the third largest producer of diamonds, behind Botswana and Russia."

300 Premier Joe Handley, Presentation to conference, Resource Expo 2004, organized by the Native Investment and Trade Association, Vancouver, November 12, 2004. Online source. Page. www.exec.gov.nt.ca/minSpeech.asp. Accessed June 14, 2005.

301 Ibid.

302 Alaska Highway Pipeline Project pamphlet, produced by the Oil and Gas Branch, Department of Energy, Mines and Resources, Yukon Government. Online source. Page. httpA://www.economicdevelopment.gov.yk.ca/documents/pipe.pdf. Accessed June 16, 2005.

303 Press Release, Yukon Government, Premier Keynote Speaker at Alaska Pipeline Symposium, December 2, 2004, #04-284, Online source. Page. www.emr.gov.yk.ca/info/archive.html.

304 Honourable Archie Lang, Minister of Energy & Resource Development, Yukon Territory, presentation made at conference "Resource Expo 2004," organized by the Native Investment and Trade Association, Vancouver, November 9, 2004. Online source. Page. www.emr.gov.yk.ca/info/archive.html. Accessed June 17, 2005.

305 Labrador Inuit Association website. Online source. Page. www.nunatsiavut.com/en/voiseysbay.php. Accessed June 18, 2005.

306 "Residential construction booms in BC and Canada," *Business in Vancouver*, March 22-28, 2005 at p 12. Article cites Statistics Canada numbers for those quoted.

307 "Major projects set another record," *Business in Vancouver*, VRCA Advertising Supplement, at p c2; Derrick Penner, "More Major Projects for BC: About $62 billion in construction is being built or planned for BC," January 11, 2005, *Vancouver Sun*, at p D1 and D2. "Why are so few Aboriginals being trained for jobs?" *Vancouver Sun*, March 30, 2005 at p H3, in which Don Cayo points out that around $65 billion in projects are slated for the Lower Mainland only.

308 Derrick Penner, "$8.5 billion slated for BC's north," *Vancouver Sun*, Wednesday, April 27, 2005 at p c12.

309 Dermot Mack, "Assessing the Northwest," *Western Investor*, March 2005 at pp B7 & B8.

310 Derrick Penner, "$7 billion in projects spurs Okanagan's urban development," April 27, 2005.

311 John Greenwood, "Ottawa to wait on offshore BC," *Financial Post*, March 31, 2005. Online source. Page. www.oceanindustriesbc.ca/nr/n050331b.htm. Accessed June 18, 2005.

312 "Opening Up Oil & Gas Opportunities in British Columbia: Statistics Resource Potential 1993-2003," Online source. Page. www.em.gov.bc.ca/Publicinfo/Oil& GasStats-93-03-outside-web- version.pdf. Accessed June 18, 2005.

313 Derrick Penner, "Port's tally soared to $43 billion in '04," *Vancouver Sun*, April 27, 2005 at p D1.

314 Bruce Constantineau, "$1-billion dollar expansion expected to begin this fall," *Vancouver Sun*, April 28, 2005. Online source. Page. www.canada.com/vancouver/vancouversun/news/business/story.html?i d=9a871034-f449-4028-87ee-c5eb0b609453&page=2. Accessed June 19, 2005.

315 Don Whitely, "Prince Rupert about to become a container 'superport,'" *Vancouver Sun*, March 31, 2005 at p F4.

316 Much of the discussion in the section is from a previous book by the author, Calvin Helin, *Doing Business With Native People Makes Sense* (Victoria: Praxis Publishing Ltd., 1991).

317 Supra Note 65 at p 14.

318 Ibid. at p 15.

319 Information on this book is from a review by Mike Byfield, "Working Out a Tragedy: Despite Ottawa's Historic Stupidity, Indians are Succeeding on the Job" in *BC Report* Newsmagazine, March 18. 1991, pp 20–21. Also see Supra Note 316.

320 Supra Note 316 at p 20.

321 Ibid. at p 21.

322 Ibid. at p 21.

323 Ibid.

324 Ibid.

325 *Haida Nation v. BC and Weyerhaeuser*. Online source. Page. www.lexum.umontreal.ca/csc-scc/en/rec/html/2004scc073.wpd.html. Accessed June 23, 2005.

326 *Taku River Tlingit First Nation v. BC and Redfern Resources.* Online source. Page. www.lexum.umontreal.ca/csc- scc/en/rec/html/2004scc074.wpd.html. Accessed June 23, 2005.

327 Clark Wilson, Energy Law Newsletter, "*Haida Nation v. BC and Weyerhaeuser*: Analysis of Supreme Court of Canada Judgment," Special Edition, November 24, 2004. Online source. Page. www.cwilson.com/newsletters/energy/EL nov04.htm. Accessed June 24, 2005.

328 Ibid.

329 Ibid.

330 Stephen Hume, "Top-court judge rules for aboriginal band, halts introduction of Atlantic Salmon," *Vancouver Sun*, January 1, 2005. Online source. Page. www.dogwoodinitiative.org/news_stories/archives/000860.html. Accessed June 20, 2005.

331 Ibid.

332 Ibid.

333 Eve Edmonds, "They will have to negotiate with us," *The Richmond News*, July 25, 2005 at p 7.

334 Supra Note 327.

CHAPTER 12: BARRIERS TO ABORIGINAL ECONOMIC DEVELOPMENT
...AND THE WAY FORWARD

335 Supra Note 220 at pp 25–26.

336 Ibid. at p 44.

337 Ibid. at p 25.

338 Ibid. at p 27.

339 Don Cayo, "New Power to tax, borrow, huge for go-getter bands," *Vancouver Sun* July 5, 2005 at p D3.

340 Online source. Page. www.oipc.gov.au/ALRA_Reforms/default.asp Accessed July 1, 2005.

341 Stephen Cornell and Joseph P. Kalt, "Sovereignty and Nation-Building: The Development Challenge in Indian Country Today," Joint Occassional Papers on Native Affairs, No. 2003-03. Online source. Page. www.udallcenter.arizona.edu/publications/pubs_indigenous.htm. July 7, 2005.

342 This was a research project operated under the auspices of the Kennedy School of Government at Harvard University and the Udall Center for Studies of Public Policy at the University of Arizona.

343 Ibid. at pp 189–190.

344 Ibid. at pp 192–193.

345 Ibid. at p 188.

346 Ibid. at p 195.

347 Supra Note 339.

348 As reproduced by John f. Bryde, Supra Note 2 at p 39.

349 Supra Note III. VOLUME 3, *Gathering Strength*, Chapter 5—Education. Online source. Page. < www.ainc- inac.gc.ca/ch/rcap/sg/si42_e.html.

350 Ralph Waldo Emerson, "Experience." Online source. Page. www.rwe.org/works/Essays-2nd_Series_2_Experience.htm. Accessed July 18, 2005.

351 John Richards and Aidan Vinning, *Aboriginal Off-Reserve Education: Time for Action*, C.D. Howe Institute Publication, ISBN 0-88806-628-7 at pp 2 & 4. Online source. Page. www.policy.ca/policy- directory/Detailed/164.html. Accessed July 18, 2005.

352 Ibid. at p 7.

353 UNESCO Institute for Statistics/Organisation for Economic Co-operation and Development World Education Indicators Programme, *Financing Education—Investments and Returns: Analysis of the World Education Indicators* (2002 Edition), at p 5. Online source. Page. www.uis.unesco.org/ev.php?ID=5245_201&ID2=DO_TOPIC. Accessed July 18, 2005.

354 Ibid.

355 Ibid. at pp 6–7.

356 James Fallows, *Looking at the Sun: The Rise of the East Asian Economic and Political System* (New York: Pantheon books, 1994) at p 442.

357 Ibid. at p 443.

358 Ibid.

359 Supra Note 62 at p 4.

360 Rodolfo Stavenhagen, *Indigenous Issues: Report of the Special Rapporteur* on the situation of human rights and fundamental freedoms of indigenous people, Addendum, Mission to Canada, Commission on Human Rights, Sixty-first session, Item 15 of the provisional agenda. Online source. Page. 66.102.7.104/search?q=cache:IU7RC7g8TKYJ: www.ohchr.org/english/bodies/chr/docs/61chr/E.CN.4.2005.88.Add.3.pdf+Report+of+the+ Special+Rapporteur+on+the+situation+of+human+rights+and+fundamental+freedoms+of +indigenous+people,+Rodolfo+Stavenhagen+canada&hl=en. Accessed July 19, 2005.

361 Terry O'Neill, "The School for Scandal," *Western Standard* newsmagazine, August 8, 2005, at p 45.

362 Ibid.

363 *Maori Economic Development—Te Ohanga Whanaketanga Maori*, New Zealand Institute of Economic Research (Inc.), 2003. Online source. Page. www.nzier.org.nz/SITE_Default/SITE_Publications/x- files/883.pdf. Accessed July 21, 2005.

364 Janet Steffenhagen, "Once failing inner-city school raises expectations, then meets them" *Vancouver Sun*, October 5, 2004. Online source reproduced at. Page. www.proudtobecanadian.ca/threads/printthread.php?Board=educatio n&main=1569&type=post. Accessed July 22, 2005.

365 Margaret Wente, "It's pronounced suc-cess-ful: Once, parents couldn't wait to get their kids out of Vancouver's Grandview Elementary. Now, they're clamouring to get

them into the inner-city school," *Vancouver Sun*, November 20, 2004 Online source. Page. file:///C:/Documents%20and%20Settings/Administrator/My%20Documents/Personal/Grandview%20School/Globe%20&%20Mail.htm. Accessed July 25, 2005.

366   Ibid.

367   Presentation by Caroline Krause, Principal, Wendy Fouks, Primary Reading Specialist,Burt Frenzell, Grade 7 and Head Teacher, Sylvain DesBiens, Inner City Teacher, "Grandview/?Uuqinak'uuh Elementary School: The Long Journey to Success," National Inner City Conference, February 11, 2005.

368   Janet Steffenhagen, "Inner-city school top of the class," *Vancouver Sun*, May 13, 2006. Online source. Page. www.canada.com/vancouversun/story.html?id=127ec6a8-f42a-4089- ba31-9c5017e151bc&p=2.

369   From private correspondence with Te Taru White, January 19, 2006.

CHAPTER 14: ECONOMIC MODELS TO BUILD ON

370   *Maori Economic Development—Te Ohanga Whanaketanga Maori*, New Zealand Institute of Economic Research (Inc.), 2003. Online source. Page. www.nzier.org.nz/SITE_Default/SITE_Publications/x- files/883.pdf. Accessed July 26, 2005.

371   Ibid. at p 13.

372   Ibid. at p 12.

373   Ibid.

374   *Trends in Maori Labor Market: Outcomes 1986–2003*, New Zealand Department of Labor, at p 2. Online source. Page. www.huitaumata.maori.nz/pdf/labor.pdf. Accessed July 27, 2005.

375   Ibid. at p 23.

376   Mason Durie, *Te Tai Tini—Transformations 2005*, Academy for Maori Research and Scholarship, Massey University, presented at Hui Taumata 2005. Online source. Page. www.huitaumata.maori.nz/pdf/speeches/Keynotes_Durie.pdf. Accessed July 27, 2005.

377   Supra Note 369, From private correspondence with Te Taru White.

378   Ibid.

379   *Native Corporations:* 2003 *Annual Impact Report.* Online source. Page. www.ciri.com/about_ciri/ANCSA_Report.pdf. Accessed July 29, 2005.

380   Inside Out Documentaries: Casino Reservations with Anthony Brooks, "The Casino Where Everybody Wins," Online source. Page. www.insideout.org/documentaries/casinoreservations/everybody.asp. Accessed August 1, 2005.

381   "Choctaw Leader Describes Economic Miracle," April 3, 2003. Online source. Page. www.matr.net/article-6416.html. Accessed August 1, 2005.

382   John Porretto, Associated Press Writer, "From Rags to Riches: Mississpi Band of Choctaw Indians." Online source. Page. www.manataka.org/page47.html. Accessed August 1, 2005.

383   Supra Note 381.

384 Bernd Christmas, "Membertou Welcomes the World," Presentation at the Atlantic Economic Summit, September 29, 2004. Online source. Page. www.apec-econ.ca/bernd.pdf. Accessed August 25, 2005.

385 Jodi DeLong, "Membertou First Nation is Open for Business," The *Atlantic Co-operator*, June, 2002, Online source. Page. www.theatlanticco-operator.coop/web/article-index/regional/region-june02d.htm. Accessed August 27, 2005.

386 "Vintage entrepreneurs - Expanding vineyards and tourism in Osoyoos," online source. Page. www.ainc-inac.gc.ca/nr/ecd/bc/ven_e.html. Accessed August 29, 2005.

387 "Osoyoos Band are vintage entrepreneurs," Online source. Page. www.ainc-inac.gc.ca/nr/ecd/ssd/otm7_e.html. Accessed August 29, 2005.

388 Chief Clarence Louie, Speaking Notes, First Nations Economic Forum, November 7–9, 2005, Calgary.

389 Resource Expo 2005, Vancouver, BC October 31-November 1, 2005, organized by the Native Investment and Trade Association. Online source. Page. native-invest-trade.com/past_events.html. Accessed September 4, 2005.

390 Edited *Hansard* • Number 018, 38th Parliament, 1st Session, Friday, October 29, 2004. Online source. Page. www.parl.gc.ca/38/1/parlbus/chambus/house/debates/018_2004-10- 29/HAN018-E.htm. Accessed September 15, 2005.

391 "ATCO, Inupiat Partnership Awarded U.S. Defence Contract," Canadian Newswire Services. Online source. Page. www.newswire.ca/en/releases/archive/May2004/25/c7241.html. Accessed September 14, 2005.

392 Carolyn Walton, "Prospering in Partnership: How Rob Hunt develops successful joint ventures with aboriginal corporations," The *Far North Oil & Gas Review*, Winter 2001 at p 36.

CHAPTER 15: THE WAY FORWARD FOR URBAN ABORIGINALS

393 Stephen Hume, "Urban aboriginals will challenge new councilors," *Vancouver Sun*, November 20, 2005 at p A15.

394 Ibid.

395 2001 Census on Aboriginal People in Canada. Online source. Page. www12.statcan.ca/english/census01/products/analytic/companion/a bor/canada.cfm#4. Accessed September 27, 2005.

396 Online source. Page. www.lexum.umontreal.ca/csc-scc/en/pub/1999/vol2/html/1999scr2_0203.html. Accessed October 14, 2005.

397 Professor Tennant, Supra Note 95 at p 14.

CHAPTER 16: CONCLUSION

398 Peter Legge, *The Runway of Life* (Burnaby: Eaglet Publishing, 2005) at pp 8–9.

BIBLIOGRAPHY

ARCHIVAL MATERIAL

——. "Historical Development of the Indian Act," Government of Canada, Treaties and Historical Research Centre, P.R.E. Group, Indian and Northern Affairs, Ottawa, August 1978.

Issac, Tomas "Pre-1868 Legislation Concerning Indians: A Selected and Indexed Collection" (1993), University of Saskatchewan Native Law Centre.

——. "Report from His Majesty's Commission for Inquiring into the Administration and Practical Operation of the Poor Laws," 1834, Vol. 27.

——. "Report of the Select Committee on Aborigines," British Parliamentary Papers (House of Commons) 1837, no. 425.

COURT CASES

Corbière v. Canada (Minister of Indian and Northern Affairs) (Corbière) Online source. Page. www.lexum.umontreal.ca/csc-scc/en/pub/1999/vol2/html/1999scr2_0203.html >.

Haida Nation v. BC and Weyerhaeuser. Online source. Page. < www.lexum.umontreal.ca/csc-scc/en/rec/html/2004scc073.wpd.html >.

R. v. Powley. Online source. Pages. < www.lexum.umontreal.ca/csc-scc/en/com/2003/html/03-09-19.3.html >.

Reference Re Eskimos (1939) 2 D.L.R. 417 (S.C.C.).

Taku River Tlingit First Nation v. BC and Redfern Resources. Online source. Page. < www.lexum.umontreal.ca/csc-scc/en/rec/html/2004scc074.wpd.html >.

Twinsectra Limited v Yardley and Others. Online source. Page. < www.parliament.the-stationery-office.co.uk/pa/ld200102/ldjudgmt/jd020321/yardle-4.htm >.

LEGISLATION

Aboriginal Land Rights (Northern Territory) Act 1976 Online source. Page. < www.oipc.gov.au/ALRA_Reforms/default.asp >.

Canada Elections Act, R.S.C. 1952, C. 23.

Constitution Act, 1982.

Indian Act, 1880, C. 20.

Indian Act, S. C. 1876, C. 18.

Indian Act, R.S.C. 1927, C. 98.

Indian Act, R.S.C. 1985, C. I-5.

Land Ordinance, 1870 R.S.B.C. 1871, C. 44.

Municipal Election Act, R.S.B.C. 1948, S. 4.

Provincial Elections Act, R.S.B.C.

GOVERNMENT PUBLICATIONS

—. "Aboriginal Business Canada (Industry Canada) An Overview on Women
Entrepreneurs," March 23, 2003. Online source. Page.
< www.google.ca/search?hl=en&q=Aboriginal+Business+Canada+per
cent28Industry+Canadaper cent29+an+Overview+on+Women+Entrepreneursper
cent2C+March+23per cent2C+2003+&btnG=Search&meta= >.

—. Alaska Highway Pipeline Project pamphlet, produced by the Oil and Gas Branch,
Department of Energy, Mines and Resources, Yukon Government. Online source.
Page. < www.economicdevelopment.gov.yk.ca/documents/pipe.pdf >.

—. *Canada's Performance* 2004: *Annual Report to Parliament.* Catalogue No. BT1-10/2004.
Online source. Page. www.tbs-sct.gc.ca/report/govrev/04/cp-rc5_e.asp#22).

—. *Canada's Performance* 2004: *Aboriginal Peoples.* Page. < www.tbs-sct.gc.ca/report/gov-
rev/04/cp-rc5_e.asp >.

Edited *Hansard* • Number 018, 38TH Parliament, 1st Session, Friday, October 29, 2004. Online
source. Page. < www.parl.gc.ca/38/1/parlbus/chambus/house/debates/018_2004-10-
29/HAN018-E.htm >.

Ekos Research and Associates Inc. Fall 2003 Survey of First Nations People Living On-
reserve, Integrated Final Report, Submitted to Indian and Northern Affairs, March 30,
2004. Online source. Page. < www.ainc-inac.gc.ca/pr/pub/fns/2004/srv04_e.pdf >.

Greene, Jo-Ann E.C. Paper prepared for Indian and Northern Affairs Canada, Women's Issues &
Gender Equality Directorate, "Towards Resolving the Division of On-Reserve
Matrimonial Property Following Relationship Breakdown: A Review of Tribunal,
Ombuds and Alternate Dispute Resolution Mechanisms." Catalogue No. R2-270/2003E.
Online source. Page. < www.dsp-psd.pwgsc.gc.ca/Collection/R2-270-2003E.pdf >.

—. *Indian and Northern Affairs Canada and Canadian Circumpolar Commission, 1998-99
Estimates: A report on Plans and Priorities.* Online source. Page. < www.ainc-
inac.gc.ca/pr/est/ > or www.ainc-inac.gc.ca/pr/est/rpp98e.pdf >.

—. *Indian and Northern Affairs Canada and Canadian Polar Commission Performance Report*, For the period ending March 31, 2004. Catalogue No. BT31-4/6-2004 at p. 15. Online source. Page. < www.tbs-sct.gc.ca/rma/dpr/03-04/INAC-AINC/INAC-AINCd3401_e.asp >.

—. *Portraits of Canada*. Poll conducted by the Centre for Research and Information on Canada. Opinion Canada, Vol. 6, no 37 - 2004-11-2 (from 2 surveys conducted.) Online source. Page. < www.opinion-canada.ca/en/articles/article_125.html >.

—. Report titled "Aboriginal Entrepreneurs in 2002." Online source. Page. strategis.ic.gc.ca/epic/internet/inabc-eac.nsf/en/ab00313e.html >.

—. Report by Health Canada. *A Statistical Profile on the Health of First Nations in Canada*. Online source. Page. < www.hc-sc.gc.ca/fnihb-dgspni/fnihb/sppa/hia/publications/statistical_profile.htm#Highlights >.

—. Report of the Royal Commission on Aboriginal Peoples, *Restructuring the Relationship*. Ottawa, Ontario: Canadian Cataloguing and Publication Data, Minister of Supply and Services Canada, 1996. Part One, Volume 2. Online source. Page. < www.ainc-inac.gc.ca/ch/rcap/sg/ch1_e.pdf >.

—. Report of the Royal Commission on Aboriginal Peoples, *Gathering Strength*. Ottawa, Ontario: Canadian Cataloguing and Publication Data, Minister of Supply and Services Canada, 1996. Part One, Volume 3. Online source. Page. < www.ainc-inac.gc.ca/ch/rcap/sg/si3_e.html >.

—. Report of the Royal Commission on Aboriginal Peoples, *People to People, Nation to Nation: Highlights from Report of Royal Commission on Aboriginal Peoples*. 1976. Cat no. Z1-1991/1-6E.

—. Statistics Canada 2001 Census. Online source from Aboriginal Peoples of Canada. Page. < www12.statcan.ca/english/census01/products/analytic/companion/abor/canada.cfm >.

Stavenhagen, Rodolfo. *Indigenous Issues: Report of the Special Rapporteur on the Situation of Human Rights and Fundamental Freedoms of Indigenous People*, Addendum, Mission to Canada, Commission of Human Rights, Sixty-first session, Item 15 of the provisional agenda. Online source. Page. < 66.102.7.104/search?q=cache:IU7RC7g8TKYJ:www.ohchr.org/english/bodies/chr/docs/61chr/E.CN.4.2005.88.Add.3.pdf+Report+of+the+Special+Rapporteur+on+the+situation+of+human+rights+and+fundamental+freedoms+of+indigenous+people,+Rodolfo+Stavenhagen+canada&hl=en >.

The Indian and Northern Affairs Canada and Canadian Polar Commission Report for 2003-2004. Catalogue No.: BT31-4/6-2004. Online source. Page. < www.tbs-sct.gc.ca/rma/dpr/03-04/INAC-AINC/INAC-AINCd3401_e.asp >.

—. *The Fiscal Balance in Canada: The Facts*. March 2004. Online source. Page. < www.fin.gc.ca/facts/fbcfacts8_e.html >.

—. United States Department of Interior, Report of the Task Force on Indian Economic

Development (July 1986) Presidential Commission on Indian Reservation Economies, Report and Recommendations to the President of the United States. November 1984.

Working Group on Aboriginal Participation in Economy to Federal-Provincial/Territorial Minister Responsible for Aboriginal Affairs and National Aboriginal Leaders. *Strengthening Aboriginal Participation in the Economy*. Online source. Page. < www.google.ca/search?hl=en&q=strengthening+Aboriginal+participation&btnG= Search&meta= >.

—. Statistics Canada. *2001 Census: Analysis Series: The Changing Profile of Canada's Workforce*. Catalogue No. 96003oX1E2001009. Online posting. Page. < www12.statcan.ca/english/census01/Products/Analytic/companion/paid/pdf/96F0030 X1E2001009.pdf >.

NEWSPAPERS AND NEWSMAGAZINES

Alberts, Sheldon. "Canada set to be 'world's oil giant,'" *Vancouver Sun*, Oct. 18, 2005.

—. "ATCO, Inupiat Partnership Awarded U.S. Defence Contract," *Canadian Newswire Services*. Online source. Page. < www.newswire.ca/en/releases/archive/May2004/25/c7241.html >.

Baxter, James. "Nault signals end to Indian Act 'industry,'" *National Post* Apr. 19, 2002.

—. Bloomberg News, article titled "Oil-sands production may double," reproduced in *Vancouver Sun*, March 25, 2005.

—. "Residential construction booms in BC and Canada," *Business in Vancouver*.

Charelson, Karen (letter to the editor): "Finger Pointing and feuding hinder aboriginal advances," *Vancouver Sun*, March 25, 2000.

Cayo, Don. "New Power to tax, borrow, huge for go-getter bands," *Vancouver Sun*, July 5, 2005.

Cayo, Don. "Why are so few aboriginal being trained for jobs?" *Vancouver Sun*, March 30, 2005.

Cheney, Peter. "Where's our Money?" *Vancouver Province*, November 16, 1999.

Cheney, Peter. "How money has cursed Alberta's Samson Cree," *The Globe and Mail*, April 24, 1999.

Cheney, Peter. "The Money Pit: an Indian band's story," *The Globe and Mail*, October 24, 1998.

"China Effect Convulses Commodity Markets," *Financial Times*, November 15, 2003. Online source. Page. < chinese-school.netfirms.com/commodities-market-China.html >.

Chow, Krystle. "Seniors could outnumber children by 2-1 in 25 years," *Vancouver Sun*, December 16, 2005.

Constantineau, Bruce. "$1-billion dollar expansion expected to begin this fall," *Vancouver Sun*. Online source. Page. < www.canada.com/vancouver/vancouversun/news/business/story.html?id=9a871034-f449-4028-87ee-c5eb0b609453&page=2 >.

Crowley, Brian Lee. "Atlantic Canada's dole rots the soul," *National Post*, May 19, 2004.

Edmonds, Eve. "They will have to negotiate with us," *The Richmond News*, July 23, 2005.

—. "Expenses doubled natives' salaries," *The Globe and Mail*, Sept. 4, 1997.

Greenwood, John. "Ottawa to wait on offshore BC," *Financial Post*, March 31, 2005. Online source. Page. < www.oceanindustriesbc.ca/nr/n050331b.htm >.

Harris, Paul. "More crude set to flow BC's coast." *Business in Vancouver*. January 11, 2005.

Hume, Stephen. "Urban aboriginals will challenge new councillors," *Vancouver Sun*, Nov. 20, 2005.

Hume, Stephen. "Top-court judge rules for aboriginal band, halts introduction of Atlantic Salmon," *Vancouver Sun*, Jan. 1, 2005. Online source. Page. www.dogwoodinitiative.org/news_stories/archives/000860.html. >.

Janigan, Mary. "Can It Be Solved?: Paul Martin is determined to get better value for the $7 billion in Aboriginal spending," *Maclean's*, January 19, 2004. Online source at Macleans.ca. Page. < www.macleans.ca/switchboard/columnists/article.jsp?content=20040119_73501_73501 >.

Kane, Michael. "Greatest growth seen in Canada's North and West," *Vancouver Sun*, March 22, 2005.

Lawson, Dominic. "Buffet still enjoys making money the old-school way," *Vancouver Sun*, May 12, 2003.

Lunman, Kim. "Off-reserve natives need help, study says," *The Globe and Mail*, February 12, 2003. Online source. Page. < www.akwesasne.ca/gmfunding0212203.htm. To see full study referred to in article go to: < www.cwf.ca/abcalcwf/doc.nsf/Publications?ReadForm&Category=WC+per cent3E+Urban+Social+Fabric+per cent3E+Urban+Aboriginal+People >.

Mack, Dermot. "Assessing the Northwest," *Western Investor*, March 2005.

—. "Major projects set another record," *Business in Vancouver*, VRCA Advertising Supplement. January 11, 2005.

Makin, Kirk, "Top court appalled as natives fill Canada's jails," *The Globe and Mail*, Apr. 24, 1999. Online source. Page. < fact.on.ca/newpaper/gm990424.htm >.

MacDonald, Jim. "Alberta quietly becomes debt-free province," *Vancouver Sun*, March 31, 2005.

McLean, Candis. "Our own soap opera: Life and politics on the Sturgeon Lake Reserve amount to a struggle against futility," The *Report* newsmagazine April 30, 2001.

Mofina, Rick. "Native leader calls on chiefs for accountability," *Vancouver Sun*, Jan. 20, 2001.

Naumetz, Tim; O'Neil, Peter. "Liberals can't make boondoggle go away," *Vancouver Sun*, Dec. 5, 2001.

O'Neill, Terry, "The School for Scandal," *Western Standard* newsmagazine, Aug. 8, 2005.

Penner, Derrick. "More Major Projects for BC: About $62 billion in construction is being built or planned for BC," *Vancouver Sun*, Jan. 11, 2005.

Penner, Derrick. "$8.5 billion slated for BC's north," *Vancouver Sun*, April 27, 2005.

Penner, Derrick. "$7 billion in projects spurs Okanagan's urban development," Supra note 257 at p. CII.

Penner, Derrick. "Port's tally soared to $43 billion in '04," *Vancouver Sun*, Apr. 27, 2005.

Porretto, John, Associated Press, "From Rags to Riches: Mississippi Band of Choctaw Indians." Online source. Page < www.manataka.org/page47.html >.

—. "Reserve headed towards trusteeship," *The Globe and Mail*, Sept. 1, 1997.

Rinehart, Dianne. "Indian women say fraud, nepotism rife on reserves," *Vancouver Sun*, Apr. 13, 1999.

Stackhouse, John. 14-part series Canada's Apartheid. "First Step: End the Segregation." "A Cut of the Action." "Everyone thought we Were Stupid." "Comic Heroes of Red Niggers." *The Globe and Mail*.

Steffenhagen, Janet. "Inner-city school top of the class," *Vancouver Sun*, May 13, 2006. Online source. Page. < www.canada.com/vancouversun/story.html?id=127ec6a8-f42a-4089-ba31-9c5017e151bc&p=2 >.

Tait, Kathy. "Indian group warns of armed rebellion over band money issues," *Vancouver Sun*, Apr. 5, 2000.

Wente, Margaret. "It's pronounced suc-cess-ful: Once, parents couldn't wait to get their kids out of Vancouver's Grandview Elementary. Now, they're clamouring to get them into the inner-city school." *The Globe and Mail*, Nov. 20, 2004. Online source. Page. globecareers.workopolis.com/servlet/Content/fasttrack/20041120/COWENT20?section=Education

Whitely, Don. "Prince Rupert about to become a container 'superport,'" *Vancouver Sun*, March 31, 2005.

Viera, Paul. "Economic 'shock' if Boomers retire early," *National Post*, Oct. 21, 2005.

York, Geoffrey. "Ottawa's effort: No helping hand but a mortal blow," *The Globe and Mail*, Aug. 29, 1992. Online source. Page. < www.bcgreen.com/~samuel/lubicon/1992/BUCKLEY.txt >.

UNPUBLISHED MATERIAL

Krause, Caroline Principal (Presentation), Wendy Fouks, Primary Reading Specialist, Burt Frenzell, Grade 7 and Head Teacher, Sylvain DesBiens, Inner City Teacher. "Grandview/?Uuqinak'uuh Elementary School: The Long Journey to Success," National Inner City Conference. 2005.

Louie, Arnie (as cited by Chief Clarence Louie), Speaking Notes. First Nations Economic Forum, Nov. 7-9, 2005, Calgary, AB.

Louie, Chief Clarence. Speaking Notes, First Nations Economic Forum.

Mathias, Chief Joe and Yabsley, Gary R. "Conspiracy of Legislation: The Suppression of Indian Rights in Canada." *Conference Business Impact of Aboriginal Claims.*

Sanders, Professor Douglas, Faculty of Law, University of British Columbia. "Self-Government, Autonomy, Sovereignty."

Williams, Joe, Chief Judge or the Maori Land Court and Deputy Chair of the Waitangi Tribunal (speech).Online source. Page. < www.humanrights.gov.au/movingforward/speech_williams.html >. Accessed June 12, 2005.

ARTICLES AND BOOKS

Armitage, Andrew. *Comparing the Policy of Aboriginal Assimilation: Australia, Canada, and New Zealand.* Vancouver: UBC Press, 1995.

Bennet, Marilyn and Blackstock, Cindy. *A Literature Review and Annotated Bibliography Focussing on Aspects of Aboriginal Child Welfare in Canada*, prepared for the First Nations Research Site of the Centre for Excellence for Child Welfare. Online source. Page. < www.fncfcs.com/pubs/fncfcsPubs.html >.

Berger, Thomas. *Fragile Freedoms: Human Rights and Dissent in Canada.* Toronto: Clarke, Irwin, 1981.

Bennet, Marilyn and Blackstock, Cindy. *A Literature Review and Annotated Bibliography Focussing on Aspects of Aboriginal Child Welfare in Canada*, prepared for the First Nations Research Site of the Centre for Excellence for Child Welfare. Online source. Page. < www.fncfcs.com/pubs/fncfcsPubs.html >.

Boldt, Menno. *Surviving as Indians: the Challenge of Self-Government.* Toronto: University Press, 1993.

Bryde, John F., Ph.D., *Modern Indian Psychology.* Rev. Ed. Vermillion, South Dakota: Institute of Indian Studies, The University of South Dakota, 1971.

Buckley, Helen. *From Wooden Ploughs to Welfare: Why Indian Policy Failed in the Prairie Provinces.* Montreal: McGill-Queen's University Press, 1992.

Byfield, Mike. "Working Out a Tragedy: Despite Ottawa's historic stupidity, Indians are succeeding on the job," BC Report

Cairns, Alan C., *Citizens Plus: Aboriginal Peoples and the Canadian State.* Vancouver: UBC Press, 2000.

Cardinal, Harold. *Unjust Society.* Seattle: University of Washington Press, 1999.

Caroll, Lewis. *Alice in Wonderland & Through the Looking Glass*. New York: Signet Classic, 2000.

—. Online source of Canadian Council of Social Development. Page. "Census Shows Increasing Diversity of Canadian Society," January 21, 2003 release of data from the 2001 Census. < www.ccsd.ca/pr/2003/diversity.htm >.

Cornell, Stephen and Kalt, Joseph P. *Sovereignty and Nation Building: The Development Challenge in Indian Country Today*. Online source. Page. < www.innovations.harvard.edu/showdoc.html?id=2700 >.or

Cornell, Stephen and Kalt, Joseph P. Sovereignty and Nation-Building" *The Development Challenge in Indian Country Today*, Joint Occasional Papers on Native Affairs, No. 2003-03. Online source. Page. < www.udallcenter.arizona.edu/publications/pubs_indigenous.htm >.

Cowley, Brian Lee. "Property, Culture, and Aboriginal Self-Government." *Market Solutions for Native Poverty: Social Policy for the Third Solitude*, John Richards eds. Toronto: C.D. Howe Institute, 1995.

Dickason, Olive Patricia. *Canada's First Nations: A History of the Founding People*. Toronto: McClleland & Stewart Publishers, 1992.

Duff, Wilson. *The Indian History of British Columbia*. Victoria: British Columbia Provincial Museum, 1980.

Drucker, Philip. *Indians of the Northwest Coast*. New York: Natural History Press, 1963.

Emerson, Ralph Waldo. Essay "Experience." Online source. Page. < www.rwe.org/works/Essays-2nd_Series_2_Experience.htm >.

Emerson, Ralph Waldo. Essay "Power," *The Conduct of Life* (1860).Online source. Page < www.rwe.org/pages/conduct_of_life.htm >.

Fallows, James. *Looking at the Sun: The Rise of the East Asian Economic and Political System*. New York: Pantheon books, 1994.

Fentie, Premier Dennis. Press Release, Yukon Government, Premier Keynote Speaker at Alaska Pipeline Symposium.#04-284, Online source. Page. < www.emr.gov.yk.ca/info/archive.html >.

Foot, David K. (with Daniel Stoffman). *Boom, Bust and Echo 2000: Profiting from the Demographic Shift in the New Millennium*. Toronto: Macfarlane Walter and Ross, 1st ed. 1996.

Guest, Dennis. *The Emergence of Social Security in Canada*. Vancouver: University of British Columbia Press, 1986.

Hazen-Hammond, Susan. *Timelines of American History*. Berkley Publishing Group, 1997.

Helin, Calvin. *Doing Business With Native People Makes Sense*. Victoria: Praxis Publishing Ltd., 1991.

Hogg, *Constitutional Law in Canada* (2nd ed., 1985) at p. 553.

Jones, L. T. *Aboriginal American Indian Oratory: The Traditions of Eloquence among the Indians of the United States*. Los Angeles: Southland Press, Inc., 1965.

Laird, Gordon. "The Outlaw," *Saturday Night Magazine*.

Large, Dr. R.G. *Drums and Scalpel: From Native Healers to Physicians in the North Pacific Coast*. Vancouver: Mitchell Press. 1968.

Large, Dr. R.G. *Skeena: River of Destiny*. Sidney, British Columbia: Gray's Publishing Ltd., 1981.

Lysyk "The Rights and Freedoms of Aboriginal Peoples in Canada" in Tanopolosky and Beaudoin (eds.), *The Canadian Charter of Rights and Freedoms: Commentary 1982*.

Legge, Peter. *The Runway of Life*. Burnaby: Eaglet Publishing, 2005.

Maich, Steve. "Is America going broke?" *Maclean's* newsmagazine, March 7, 2005. Online source. Page. < www.macleans.ca/topstories/world/article.jsp?content=20050307_101541_101541 >. Accessed April 15, 2005.

—. *Maori Economic Development – Te Ohanga Whanaketanga Maori*, New Zealand Institute of Economic Research (Inc.), 2003. Online source. Page. < www.nzier.org.nz/SITE_Default/SITE_Publications/x-files/883.pdf >.

Manzer, Jenny. "Aboriginal sex abuse rates high, but under-researched," *The Medical Post*, Volume 37 Issue 40. Online source. Page. < www.medicalpost.com/mpcontent/article.jsp?content=/content/EXTRACT/RAWART/3740/02B.html >.

Meilleur, Helen. *A Pour of Rain: Stories from a West Coast Fort*. Victoria: Morris Printing Company Ltd., 1981.

Penner, Derrick. "More Major Projects for BC: About $62 billion in construction is being built or planned for BC," January 11, 2005, *Vancouver Sun*, at pp. D1 and D2.

Richards, John and Vinning, Aidan. *Aboriginal Off-Reserve Education: Time for Action*, C.D, Howe Institute Publication, ISBN 0-88806-628-7 at pp. 2 & 4.Online source. Page. < www.policy.ca/policy-directory/Detailed/164.html >.

Samyn, Paul. Online source *Winnipeg Free Press* Online Edition, Monday January 24th, 2005. Page. < www.google.ca/search?hl=en&q=Aboriginal+spendingpercent2Bwinnipeg&btnG=Search&meta= >.

Sainsbury, George (ed.). *The Works of Henry Fielding*. Online source. Page. < sailor.gutenberg.org/etext05/8jan210h.htm >.

Samuels, David. "In a Ruined Country: How Yasir Arafat Destroyed Palestine." *Atlantic Monthly*, Sept. 2005.

Sanders, "Prior Claims: Aboriginal People in the Constitution of Canada" in Beck and Bernier (eds.), Institute for Research on Public Policy: *Canada in the New Constitution of Canada* (1983), vol. 1.

Seguin, Margaret, Ed. *The Tsimshian: Images of the Past, Views of the Present.* Vancouver: University of British Columbia Press, 1994.

Seattle, Chief (attributed speech). Seattle *Sunday Star* on October 29, 1887 and The *Irish Times* on June 4th, 1976.

Shiller, Robert J. "American Casino: The promise and perils of Bush's 'ownership society'." *Atlantic Monthly*, March 2005.

Simpson, Scott. "Contractors hiring globally: Not enough tradespeople in Canada to fill BC's growing demand, industry says," *Vancouver Sun*, March 2, 2005 at p. 2005.

Stone, William L. *Life of Joseph Brant.* Albany: J. Munsell, 1864.

Tennant, Paul. *Aboriginal Peoples and Politics.* Vancouver: University of British Columbia Press, 1991.

—. "Top court rules Métis can claim hunting rights." Updated Sat. Sep. 20, 2003. Online source. Page. < www.ctv.ca/servlet/ArticleNews/story/CTVNews/1063980477665_59389677///?hub=TopStories# or www.Métisnation.ca/POWLEY/home.html >.

—. "United Nations Committee on the Rights of the Child: Non Discrimination and Diversity," First Nations Child and Family Caring Society, August 29, 2003 at p. 3. Online source. Page. < www.fncfcs.com/docs/UnitedNationsMay2004.pdf >.

UNESCO Institute for Statistics/Organisation for Economic Co-operation and Development World Education Indicators Programme, *Financing Education – Investments and Returns: Analysis of the World Education Indicators* (*2002 Edition*). Online source. Page. < www.uis.unesco.org/ev.php?ID=5245_201&ID2=DO_TOPIC >.

Vanderwerth, W.C. *Indian Oratory: Famous Speeches by Noted Indian Chieftains.* Norman, Oklahoma: Oklahoma University Press, 1971.

Walton, Carolyn. "Prospering in Partnership: How Rob Hunt develops successful joint ventures with aboriginal corporations," *The Far North Oil & Gas Review.*

Wesley-Esquimaux, Cynthia C., Ph.D and Smolewski, Magdalena, Ph.D. research paper prepared for The Aboriginal Healing Foundation Research Series, *Historic Trauma and Aboriginal Healing.* Online source. Page. www.ahf.ca/newsite/english/publications/research_series.shtml).

Woodward, Jack. *Native Law.* Scarborough: Carswell, 1994.

Yeomans, Matthew. "Crude Politics," *Atlantic Monthly*, April 2005.

ONLINE SOURCES

—. *Aboriginal Sports Strategy in Canada.* Online source. Page. < www.sasksport.sk.ca/aboriginalsport/pdf/AboriginalSportStrategy.pdf >.

—. AFN Renewal Commission. Online source. Page. < www.afn.ca/article.asp?id=120 >.

—. "Athabasca Issues Working Group Fact Sheet," June 2004. Online source. Page. < www.oilsands.cc/pdfs?Juneper cent202004per cent2OOilper cent2oSandsper cent2oFactper cent2oSheet.pdf >.

—. Backgrounder: New Zealand. Online source. Page. < www.state.gov/r/pa/ei/bgn/35852.htm >.

—. Blog Definition. Online source. Page. < www.marketingterms.com/dictionary/blog/ >.

Canadian Taxpayers Federation. *Dividing Canada: Pitfalls of Native Sovereignty* Online source. Page. < www.taxpayer.ca/pdf/Dividing_Canada_ (Centre_for_Aboriginal_Policy_Change).pdf >.

Canine, John D. Ed.D., PhD. "Bereavement Rituals." Online source. Page. < www.prayfuneral.com/max_living_rituals.html >.

—. "Canada ranked low in UN native Report," CBC radio April 11, 2005. On line source. Page. www.cbc.ca/story/canada/national/2005/04/11/UNNatives-050411.html >.

—. Child Care Federation. *Keeping Our Promises: Right from the Start*, The United Nations day of General Discussion, "Implementing Child Rights in Early Childhood." Online source. Page. < www.afn.ca/AGA-Confederacy/04-09-21per cent2oAGAper cent2oReport.pdf >.

"Choctaw Leader Describes Economic Miracle," April 3, 2003. Online source. Page. < www.matr.net/article-6416.html >.

Christmas, Bernd. *Membertou Welcomes the World*, Presentation made at the "Atlantic Economic Summit," September 29, 2004. Online source. Page < www.apec-econ.ca/bernd.pdf >.

Clark Wilson, Energy Law Newsletter, "*Haida Nation v. BC and Weyerhaeuser: Analysis of Supreme Court of Canada Judgment*," Special Edition, November 24, 2004. Online source. Page. www.cwilson.com/newsletters/energy/ELnov04.htm. >.

—. *Closing the Gap*: A Report of the British Columbia Chamber of Commerce Skills Shortage Initiative. Online source. Page. < www.bcchamber.org/criticalskills/skills_gap.html >.

CNN.com International, "Group: China timber demand threatens world's forests," March 8, 2005, Online source. Page. < edition.cnn.com/2005/TECH/science/03/08/china.logging.ap/ >.

Coffey, Charles S. *The Cost of Doing Nothing: A Call to Action*, October 23, 1997. Online source Page. < www.rbcroyalbank.com/aboriginal/r_speech.html >.

—. Correctional Service Canada website. Online source. Page. < www.csc-scc.gc.ca/text/prgrm/correctional/abissues/know/8_e.shtml >.

DeLong, Jodi. *Membertou First Nation is Open for Business*. The Atlantic Co-operator. Online source. Page < www.theatlanticco-operator.coop/web/article-index/regional/region-juneo2d.htm >.

—. Diabetes Information from Aboriginal Diabetes Initiative. *Diabetes Among Aboriginal People in Canada: The Evidence.* ISBN H35-4/6-2001E, Catalogue No. 0-662-29976-0. Online source. Page. < www.hc-sc.gc.ca/fnihb-dgspni/fnihb/cp/adi/publications/the_evidence.htm#Executivepercent20Summary >.

Durie, Mason. *Te Tai Tini – Transformations 2005*, Academy for Maori Research and Scholarship, Massey University, presented at Hui Taumata 2005. Online source. Page < www.huitaumata.maori.nz/pdf/speeches/Keynotes_Durie.pdf >.

Farrar, David. "Milton Friedman on Spending Money," 2005. Online source. www.kiwiblog.co.nz/archives/008879.html >.

Federal Government Funding to First Nations: The Facts, the Myths, and the Way Forward. Online source. Page. < www.afn.ca/Federalpercent20Governmentpercent20Funding percent20topercent20Firstpercent20Nations_web2.pdf >.

Flanders, Jefferson. "Bloggers are Busy Rewriting the Definition of 'Journalism'" Online source. Page. < www.freerepublic.com/focus/f-news/1361855/posts >.

Franklin, Ben (letter to James Parker). Philadelphia, March 20, 1750, Online posting. Page. < courses.pasleybrothers.com/texts/franklin_indians.htm >.

Handley, Premier Joe. Presentation to conference, Resource Expo 2004. Online source. Page. < www.exec.gov.nt.ca/minSpeech.asp >.

Hansard, Number 015 (Official Version). Online source. Page. < www.parl.gc.ca/38/1/parl-bus/chambus/house/debates/015_2004-10-26/han015_1900-e.htm >.

—. Inside Out Documentaries: Casino Reservations with Anthony Brooks. "The Casino Where Everybody Wins." Online source: Page. < www.insideout.org/documentaries/casinoreservations/everybody.asp >.

—. "Is there a Misery Industry?" Online source. Page. < www.aptn.ca/forums/index.php?showtopic=288 >.

—. *Journal Sentinel.* "Health care spending eases, but huge growth predicted." February 11, 2004. Online source. Page. < www.jsonline.com/bym/news/feb04/206853.asp?for-mat=print >.

Kayseas, Curtis. "The Illusion of Democracy." Online source. The Aboriginal Youth Network. Page. < www.ayn.ca/ViewNews.aspx?id=194 >.

—. Labrador Inuit Association website. Online source. Page. www.nunatsiavut.com/en/voiseysbay.php >.

Lamontagne, Francois. *The Aboriginal Workforce: What Lies Ahead.* Canadian Labour Business Centre. Online source. Page. < www.clbc.ca/files/Reports/Aboriginal_Commentary_piece.pdf >.

Lang, Honourable Archie, Minister of Energy & Resource Development. Yukon Territory, presentation made at conference Resource Expo 2004. Online source. Page. < www.emr.gov.yk.ca/info/archive.html >.

—. *Legacy of Hope: An Agenda for Change*, Volume I, Final Report from the Commission on First Nations and Métis Peoples and Justice Reform. Online source. Page. < www.justicereformcomm.sk.ca/volume1.gov >.

Mair, Victor H. (Contributions from Denis Mair and Zhang Liqing.) Online source. Page. "How a misunderstanding about Chinese characters has led many astray." < www.pinyin.info/chinese/crisis.html >. Accessed January 12, 2005.

Mendelson, Michael, *Aboriginal People in Canada's Labour Market: Work and Unemployment, Today and Tomorrow*. March 2004, Caledon Institute of Social Policy, ISBN 1-55382-090- at p. 1.8. Online source. Page "Publications by Date, April 2004." < www.caledoninst.org/ >.

Murphy, Gerald, distributed by the Cybercasting Services Division of the National Public Telecomputing Network (NPTN). Online source. Page < www.wsu.edu:8080/~dee/NAANTH/IRCONST.HTM >.

—. *Native Corporations: 2003 Annual Impact Report*. Online source. Page. < www.ciri.com/about_ciri/ANCSA_Report.pdf >.

—. "Native Protestors End-Run Government and take Protest Directly to Canadian Taxpayers," July 21, 1999. Online source. Page. < www.taxpayer.com/main/news.php?news_id=1618 >.

—. "Opening Up Oil & Gas Opportunities in British Columbia: Statistics Resource Potential 1993-2003." Online source. Page. < www.em.gov.bc.ca/Publicinfo/Oil&GasStats-93-03-outside-web-version.pdf >.

"Osoyoos Band are vintage entrepreneurs ." Online source. Page. < www.ainc-inac.gc.ca/nr/ecd/ssd/otm7_e.html >.

"Outsourcing leads to demand for resources," August 19, 2004. Online source. Page. < www.openoutsource.com/resource-dated9720-Outsourcing%20leads%20to%20demand%20for%20resources.phtml >.

Policicchio, Sett, President of ATCO Electric. Resource Expo 2005, Vancouver, BC Online source. Page. < native-invest-trade.com/past_events.html >.

—. *Prevention of Violence Against Indigenous Children: Proceedings from An International Gathering*, Online source. Page. < web.uvic.ca/iicrd/graphics/PVAIC%20Proceedings.pdf >.

—.Rain Forest Atlas Website. Online source. Page. < www.inforain.org/rainforestatlas/rainforestatlas_page3.htm >. Accessed March 12, 2005.

Rogers, Jim. "Why Raw Materials?" 2002. Online source. Page. < chineseschool.netfirms.com/raw-materials.html >.

Roslin, Alex. "Power Struggle: Native groups balk at national chief's plan to boost his power." Online source. Now Online Edition, Toronto. Online source. Page. < www.nowtoronto.com/issues/2001-04-05/news_story3.html >.

Sandberg, Don. "Hefty Personal Price Writing About Aboriginal Politics: Given the consequences, would you speak up?" Online source. Page. < www.fcpp.org/main/publication_detail.php?PubID=779 >.

Sandberg, Don. "Native Democracy Is Broken," *National Post*. Online source. Page. < www.fcpp.org/main/publication_detail.php?PubID=802 >.

Sandberg, Don. "The Tragic Death of Bill C-7: Act quickly to write an adequate replacement." Online source. Page. < www.fcpp.org/main/publication_detail.php?PubID=691 >.

Sandberg, Don. "Where does Eight Billion Dollars Go? Much Poverty Despite Spending." Online source. Page. < www.fcpp.org/main/publication_detail.php?PubID=721 >.

Santarossa, Bruna. "Diamonds: Adding Lustre to the Canadian Economy." Online source. Page. < www.statcan.ca/english/research/11-621-MIE/11-621-MIE2004008.htm >.

—. "Saudi Arabia: Brief Country Analysis." Online source. Page. < www.eia.doe.gov/emeu/cabs/saudi.html >.

Saving, Jason L. "Privatization and the Transition to the Market Economy," Economic, Fourth Quarter, 1998. Online source. Page. < www.dallasfed.org/research/er/1998/ >.

Smith, Murray, (Speaking Notes) Alberta Minister of Energy. "Competitive Markets: Unleashing the Power of Alberta's Energy Sector," October 7, 2003, World Forum on Energy Regulation, Concurrent Session 3C, Market-based Mechanisms Driving New Investment, in Infrastructure and Production Capacity in Rome, Italy Topic: Competitive Markets: Unleashing the Power of Alberta's Energy Sector. Online source. Page. < www.energy.gov.ab.ca/docs/ newsroom/pdfs/Speech2003-10-7.pdf >.

Steffenhagen, Janet. "Once failing inner-city school raises expectations, then meets them". *Vancouver Sun*, Oct. 5, 2004. Online source. Page. < www.proudtobecanadian.ca/threads/printthread.php?Board=education&main=1569&type=post >.

—. "The Future Cost of Health Care in Canada," Conference Board of Canada, 2001. Online source. Page. < www.conferenceboard.ca/press/documents/futurehealth.pdf >.

—. The Métis National Council Website. Online source. Page. < www.Métisnation.ca/ARTS/hist_who.html >.

—. *Trends in Maori Labour Market: Outcomes 1986-2003*, New Zealand Department of Labour, at p. 2. Online source. Page < www.huitaumata.maori.nz/pdf/labour.pdf >.

Truscott, Richard. "Road to Bankruptcy Paved with Tax Dollars," Canadian Taxpayers Federation. Online source. Page. < www.taxpayer.com/main/news.php?news_id=563 >.

"Vintage entrepreneurs - Expanding vineyards and tourism in Osoyoos." Online source. Page. < www.ainc-inac.gc.ca/nr/ecd/bc/ven_e.html >.

Weston, John D. "A Nisga'a Chief Takes on Third Order of Government and the Nisga'a's Treaty." Online source. Page. < www.accesslaw.ca/cmc/cmc.asp >.

INDEX

About the Author

Calvin Helin was born and raised in the small north coastal Tsimshian village of Lax Kw'alaams (Port Simpson) in British Columbia, Canada. At age twelve, he was sent on a quest by his father and grandmother, both hereditary chiefs, with the single-minded purpose of making a difference. In his late thirties, he was named one of the top forty under-forty entrepreneurs in British Columbia by the news publication *Business in Vancouver* and granted one of the top forty under-forty national awards sponsored by the *Financial Post* magazine and other major Canadian corporations. Currently he serves as a senior advisor to communities, industry, and governments on a variety of key development issues.

Mr. Helin is a lawyer, karate instructor, Aboriginal leader, and businessman. In addition, he leads international trade missions to China and New Zealand.

About the Illustrator

Bill Helin, the author's cousin and an internationally renowned artist and designer, has long pioneered the development of Northwest Coast art. Accomplished in many artistic mediums, he designed the STS-78 space shuttle patch worn by the astronauts of the Columbia Mission in July 1996; contributed to the largest totem pole ever carved (180 feet, 3 inches tall), known as the Spirit of Lekwammen (Land of the Winds); and carved the 40-foot Ravensong canoe to help preserve traditional cedar dugout canoe-building knowledge. He teaches Northwest Coast art and contributes much of his work to the preservation of animal habitats.

Forthcoming titles in the Dances series by Calvin Helin:

DANCES WITH FREEDOM: STRENGTHENING THE WILL
Paperback; 978-1-932824-09-4

Freedom, according to the ancient Greek philosopher Epicurus, is "the great-est fruit of self-sufficiency," without which one suffers from infirmities of will leading to discontent. In moving toward freedom, we fortify the will by meet-ing our physical, emotional, psychological, and spiritual needs. Relearning this principle, on which Western civilization was founded, can promote per-sonal and collective well-being.

DANCES WITH SPIRITS: ACHIEVING BALANCE
Hardcover; 978-1-932824-11-7

Scientific and technological advances have provided the means for destroying planetary life, but does humanity have the wisdom necessary to choose sur-vival? While facing impending danger, cultures worldwide can benefit by exploring tried-and-true perspectives about humankind's place in the world. One proven measure for greater balance comes through reclaiming the spirit-infused views that ensured the survival of our ancestors for millennia.

DANCES WITH LAUGHTER: LIGHTENING UP
Hardcover; 978-1-932824-10-0

While today's socioeconomic realities call for urgent change, the more gravity "change agents" display, the more emotional pathology they later exhibit. What better time can there be for humor, practical jokes, puns, witticisms, and stories from the ridiculous to the sublime. Indigenous culture teaches children always to be prepared for a laugh, especially when they are the butt of a joke. Even at such times happiness prevails, because laughter sustains emotional health.